THE BUSINESS OF BEING A LAWYER

by

Pamela Bucy Pierson

Bainbridge-Mims Professor of Law
University of Alabama School of Law

Mat #41609591

© 2014 LEG, Inc. d/b/a West Academic

    444 Cedar Street, Suite 700
    St. Paul, MN 55101
    1-877-888-1330

West, West Academic Publishing, and West Academic are trademarks of West Publishing Corporation, used under license.

Printed in the United States of America

ISBN: 978-1-62810-016-7

This book is

dedicated to

Julie, Ben and Larry

ACKNOWLEDGMENTS

This book started on the couch in my daughter's apartment in Philadelphia, Pennsylvania, and it would not exist without her. She helped me brainstorm and bring order to random thoughts, shared what she was learning in business school, and now, as a McKinsey consultant, advises me every step of the way. Thank you, Julie. This book is as much yours as mine.

I turned to several friends as I tried to visualize a course, program, and book on the business of being lawyer. Thank you, Cathy, for inspiring me. When the path has been hard, your smile and conviction has sustained me. Thank you, Jacqueline, for helping anchor my thoughts in the science of EQ. You sent me in exciting directions I did not know existed. Thank you, Wilson, for insisting that I not just create a new course, but a book to go with it. Here it is. Thank you, Bryan, for all our lunch talks at Pepito's. I am fortunate to have a great friend with wise advice.

I am profoundly grateful to the University of Alabama School of Law Dean Ken Randall, and Interim Dean Bill Brewbaker, both of whom generously shared their time and creative thoughts, and have steadfastly nurtured this book and its related projects. I am also grateful to many others at the University of Alabama School of Law: Carol Andrews and Kimberly Boone for their advice and editing expertise; Claude Arrington, Noah Funderburg, Jami Gates, Mary Ksobiech, and Candice Robbins for their help in arranging the sometimes formidable logistics surrounding the course that accompanies this book; Iain Barksdale, Blake Beals, Penny Gibson and Robert Marshall for their extraordinary help in locating sources I've used in this book; Becca Brady, Tom Ksobiech and Glory McLaughlin for their help collecting information about admissions, public interest and careers; Helen Cauthen for her terrific help in online and print media outreach for the course based on this book; Annette Largin for her help in creating the CLE that accompanies this book; Joe DeAraujo, Terry Davis, Jay Ellis, and Jeb Richter for their patience, creativity and always friendly IT help in the "BBL" course and video library.

I am fortunate to have incredibly supportive colleagues who, on quite a leap of faith, not only approved a new course, The Business of Being a Lawyer, but made it mandatory for all UA law students. My colleagues have kindly shared their ideas, sources and contacts, making this book and the course I now teach, richer and wiser.

Most of all, I appreciate and thank Erica Nicholson, who has provided amazing support and guidance on this book and the course from which it grew, from Day One. You are a good friend. Thank you.

That so many people on the faculty and staff at UA Law School enthusiastically helped make the BBL course and this book happen is a testament to the true community of our law school. UA Law is a place where people care and support each other. I am proud to be a part of it.

For me, the joy of my job is and always will be the students. For that reason, a portion of the proceeds from this book will go the Public Interest Institute at the University of Alabama School of Law.

Many students have helped "hatch" this book. The students who took the Business of Being a Lawyer in the fall, 2013, the first time I offered this course, and the first time I used a draft of this book, are a brave lot. I had expected twenty or so students to register for the class. It was an unknown elective, attendance was mandatory, no "screens" were allowed, and class was scheduled in four-hour blocks, from 2:30–6:30 p.m., on Friday afternoons, specifically, on Friday afternoons before home football games. At the University of Alabama, such scheduling is close to heresy. Yet over one hundred upper-level law students registered for the course. Throughout the semester, they came to class, sat through days that worked (and some that didn't), were attentive, and most especially, shared invaluable feedback on the course and course materials. Their input has vastly improved this book. I am indebted to them.

I am especially indebted to one student who sat in on the BBL class even though he could not register for it because of a course overload. He has proofed parts of this book, sometimes on short notice, and provided helpful and honest feedback.

Rarely do law professors get to teach their own children. You have made doing so a joy, Ben. Thank you.

There are more lawyers who have helped with this book than I could possibly thank. But one group stands out: the "BBL Faculty." These twenty-seven incredibly busy lawyers and judges traveled to Tuscaloosa, Alabama, on Friday afternoons to serve on panels and as break-out leaders during the BBL course. They selflessly shared their time, advice, and experience with me and my students. They are the best of the best: Helen Allen, Cynthia Almond, Noel Amason, Jim Barger, Bill Bostick, Michael Bownes, Jan Brakefield, Mark Drew, Mike Ermert, Prim Escalona, Brandon Falls, Ted Hosp, Anthony Joseph, Debbie Long, David Loper, Wilson Moore, Arthur Orr, Katie Pope, Dena Prince, Richard Raleigh, Philip Reich, Cooper Shattuck, Alyce Spruell, Chad Tindol, Bill Veitch, Jill Ganus Veitch, and Cathy Wright.

Eight law students have worked with me on this book, the course, or the video library we created from interviews with lawyers and judges on topics in this book. Dana Delk and Peggy Rossmanith worked graphic design magic on the course materials that preceded this book; Morgan Henry and Will Kerby worked math magic in transforming my blank spaces and "help!" notes in Chapter Two into real numbers; Michael Morris provided expert editing on Chapter One and superb research on professional responsibility issues relevant to all subjects in this book; Thomas B. Carter, Jr, Darius A. Crayton, and Nathaniel M. Cartmell IV, have created a video library of interviews with experts on BBL topics. All of these students have graciously indulged some silly ideas on my part, been of good cheer, and provided invaluable feedback. They have been the light of many of my days during the past year.

It has been a pleasure to work with Jacklyn Nagel, PhD, Psychology, The University of Alabama, 2015. As a graduate student in psychology, Jacklyn has worked with me to develop a study of stress and stress-hardiness; obtain Institutional Review Board approval (IRB # 13-OR-265) for our study, *Stress Hardiness in Law Students and Lawyers;* collect data; and co-author publications discussing our findings. I look forward to working with Jacklyn as we continue our stress-hardiness study of law students and lawyers.

This book has been a labor of love. It has also been more of a challenge than I expected. I wanted to quit a number of times as a perfect storm of unexpected professional demands and unforeseen health issues whirled around me. Two things kept me going. The first was that I wanted to give back and to help in some way the talented, smart people who are joining a profession I love. I have many debts to pay forward. I hope this book is one way to do so. The second is Larry. I can't imagine going through life with a more wonderful partner. Thank you, Larry.

INTRODUCTION

Each of us, as a lawyer, is a business, our own business. Whether we are self-employed or work for a private firm, public interest or government office, or in a non-legal position, we need to understand our own balance sheets: What are our assets and liabilities? What are our short-term and long-term business plans? How do we implement those business plans? For which contingencies do we prepare? What are our accounts receivables? What investments have we made and need to make in our business?

This book began in two places—in my office at The University of Alabama School of Law, and in a parking garage in Birmingham, Alabama. A few years ago, I realized that the conversations I was having with students who came by my office had changed. From the mid-1980s and until about five years ago, students, even 1Ls, had several choices of summer jobs and 3Ls had several offers of post-graduate jobs. Students and I would brainstorm about which job they should take or how to sequence their options.

Today, fewer 1Ls have paying job offers for the summer. They are looking for advice on how to get an externship or volunteer position. One issue that dominates these discussions is cost—whether school loans will cover summer externship tuition or how they will pay living expenses if they volunteer. The 3L students who don't have jobs lined up by graduation are seeking advice on how to find jobs and how to navigate the gap until they do. Understandably, many students today are discouraged about the challenges they face in the legal job market.

I have found it interesting that not more students are discouraged. Some students, even though they face the same, or more difficult, challenges than others, remain enthusiastic. These students consistently fare better in the job market than others, regardless of seemingly important criteria such as grades. I begin to wonder, what is it that makes these students remain upbeat and others not? Why do they have better luck in their job quests? What are they doing differently?

During this same general time period, I spent a lot of time in a parking garage in downtown Birmingham. In 2008 and 2009, while on sabbatical, I served Of Counsel to a law firm located in a thirty-two story office building. The office building sat on a multi-floor underground parking garage. It took twenty minutes, on a fast day, to get through the parking garage and up all of the elevators to my law firm office. Many law firms and a lot of lawyers are located in this office building and as I discovered, many of these lawyers are my former students. Every day as I made the trek through the parking garage, I saw former students. My twenty-minute trips from car to office often turned into an hour or more as we visited and caught up.

I had not seen many of these former students in years. I could not help but observe how well, or poorly, a number of them had aged. After a while, I began to see a pattern. Typically, those who had aged well were excited, enthusiastic and happy as they told me about their jobs, the obvious topic we discussed. Those who had not aged well seemed weary as they told me about their professional lives. Again, I wondered, what causes the difference in attitude? I knew that many of my former students had faced personal difficulties: health issues, divorce, even the loss of loved ones. Yet, this did not seem to separate those who were upbeat from those who were not. I wondered if the difference was in the type of practice, but this did not seem to be determinative either. Many of those who seemed happy were in high-stress and difficult practices; many of those who seemed despondent were in positions of wealth and prestige and experiencing what most people would consider to be dream careers.

From these interactions with students and former students, I wondered what makes some law students maintain resilience in the face of professional challenges, and what makes some lawyers enjoy what they do. I have been fortunate to be able to devote time studying these two questions. Few working adults have the luxury of shifting professional gears. I am profoundly grateful that academic freedom has allowed me to do so. For almost forty years, I have practiced, taught and published in the field of white collar crime. I have loved it, but it has been a treat to be able to pursue something new.

As I embarked on my new endeavor, the first thing I discovered is that there is impressive scholarship on the future of the legal profession. I also found that my years of practice and involvement in various professional activities have been an invaluable guide in this project. I was fortunate to begin my career with a judicial clerkship followed by a brief stint at a large law firm before serving as an Assistant United States Attorney (EDMO) for seven years. As an academic I have stayed connected to the practicing bar by serving Of Counsel to a large law firm and as an expert witness in several white collar cases. My affiliations with the attorneys at the law firms of Maynard Cooper & Gale, PC (Birmingham, Alabama), Ropes & Gray LLP (New York, New York office), Meckler, Bulger, Tilson, Marick & Pearson LLP (Chicago, Illinois office), and Ross, Dixon & Masback LLP, now Troutman Sanders LLP (Washington DC) have given me invaluable insight into today's practice of law.

I enjoy spending time with practicing attorneys and have been able to do so while in academia through the American Bar Association, the Alabama State Bar Association, and the Birmingham and Tuscaloosa Associations. I am honored to have been elected or appointed to serve the Alabama State Bar as a Bar Commissioner, Vice President, and twice, member of the Executive Committee. One of my greatest joys as a lawyer has been serving in various capacities with the Alabama State Bar's Volunteer Lawyers Program, through which lawyers volunteer their time to assist underprivileged individuals with civil legal needs. With support from The University of Alabama School of Law and the practicing bar of Alabama, I have enjoyed establishing a variety of programs that integrate the practice of law and law school curricula. In one of the great life lessons that you never know where things will lead, I undertook all of these bar activities simply because they were fun. I never dreamed I would learn so much from them, in many respects more than I have learned anywhere else.

My forays into the practice of law and my friendships with practicing lawyers have provided me what academia cannot: insight into the day-to-day life of lawyers; the sense of accomplishment one feels when doing a good job for a client; the pressures, stresses and rewards of practicing law; the unique camaraderie lawyers share; and how networking within the legal profession works. These insights have enriched my life, and this book.

Until I started this book and the various programs related to it, I had forgotten how hard it is to start something new. Over the past year, I often wondered why in the world I would leave an area of law I knew well and venture into something unknown. However, I have seen that a fresh perspective has advantages. From my agenda-less vantage point, I have seen things I did not expect. The first is that the answer to both of my questions: why some law students are resilient in the face of professional challenges, and why some lawyers enjoy what they do, lies in the field of psychology, not law.

For this reason, Chapter One begins with a discussion of emotional intelligence (EQ). It is surprising that law schools do not regularly address EQ issues. Graduate business schools have done so for years, developing rigorous, systematic courses that build EQ skills. Certainly, if there is any profession that should address EQ, it is law, and certainly the time is now, as the legal profession undergoes dramatic changes. I hope that this book helps open the door for law schools to address the important issues of EQ.

The discussion of EQ in this book is based on three assumptions: first, life always presents challenges; second, the practice of law presents unique but predictable challenges; and third, it is possible to develop and improve one's skills for successful coping with life and professional challenges. Chapter One discusses specific, measurable EQ strategies lawyers can use to increase their productivity and happiness, relieve stress, achieve balance in life, and maintain resilience in the face of hardship.

Chapter Two addresses personal financial planning basics, covering topics such as establishing and living on a budget; dealing with educational loans and repayment; financial planning for the future; monetary implications of different employment models; the financial calculus of working part time; costs of establishing one's own practice; and saving for a home purchase, children's education, and retirement.

Chapter Two arose because of another unanticipated discovery I made in this project. Because of educational debt life for most law students and many lawyers is fundamentally different than it was for me and most lawyers who have been practicing for a while. With an average educational debt of $125,000 (for 2012 law graduates from private law schools) and $75,000 (for 2012 graduates from public law schools),[1] the educational debt most law students and new lawyers carry is a game changer. I put myself through college and law school with loans and grants and spent many years repaying these loans, but my financial burdens and those of my peers I feel certain, paled in comparison to the debt current law students carry. Today's educational costs eclipse educational costs of years past. The result is that educational debt drives the career and life choices for many law students and lawyers.

Chapter Three discusses the facts and figures of the current and evolving legal market. Chapter Three is influenced by a consistent theme I saw when studying EQ issues: a key component of good EQ is a sense of control over one's life. No lawyer can maintain a sense of control without an understanding of the realities of the legal market. The legal profession has undergone major structural changes in the past few decades; the changes have accelerated in the past few years; and there are more ahead. Those who fail to understand and embrace these facts will struggle; those who do, will thrive. Chapter Three discusses trends in the legal profession, evolving business models of law firms, and the impact of these changes on lawyers' lives.

Chapter Four addresses specific steps law students and lawyers can take to navigate their careers successfully. Today the average lawyer changes jobs seven times and this average is likely to increase as the future legal market becomes more fluid. Chapter Four discusses opportunities in non-traditional practices of law; evolving employment patterns; increasing opportunities in law-related careers; and the cost-benefit analysis of working in a government or public interest office compared to private employment.

When I began my study of the legal profession my goal was to create something that would be of help to law students. I resolved to tell the truth. Not to sensationalize, and not to sugar coat. It would be tempting to do both. So, without sensationalizing and without sugar coating, here is what I have learned. First, the way we have practiced law for the past forty to fifty years is over. Anyone who fails to recognize this will not survive. Second, this is an exciting, fun and fulfilling time for lawyers who embrace the changes in our profession. There are now unparalleled opportunities to practice law in personally and professionally rewarding ways that were not available in the past.

The story of David and Goliath, as interpreted by Malcolm Gladwell in his book, *David and Goliath*, is a perfect analogy for the opportunities ahead for new lawyers. By all expectations, David, a young shepherd with no military training, was no match for Goliath, the huge, experienced warrior with a bronze helmet, full body armor, a javelin, a spear, and a sword.[2] Yet, David prevailed because, as Gladwell states, "being an underdog can change people in ways that we often fail to appreciate: it can open doors and create opportunities and educate and enlighten and make possible what might otherwise have seemed unthinkable."[3] Freed from experience, nimble thinking is a tremendous asset.

It remains true that new, inexperienced lawyers enter the legal profession in a "weaker" position than experienced attorneys. Experience matters in life, especially in something as complex and nuanced as practicing law. Experience is important in any situation undergoing dramatic upheaval, which law is. But, because new lawyers are able to navigate technology well, and because they are unencumbered by the tunnel vision of experience, new lawyers (or those who can adapt as if they were new) will prevail and thrive in the legal profession of the future.

In the chapters that follow, there are stories about four-year olds and marshmallows, grownups who eat radishes and chocolate chip cookies, hospital custodians, starfish, pyramids, diamonds, American POWs in Chinese prisons, rats, dogs and people who are electrically shocked, colonoscopy patients, monkeys with hands stuck in coconuts, Scottish orthopedic patients, and Mick Jagger. These stories provide guidance for navigating the legal profession of the future. Enjoy.

ENDNOTES

[1]   ABA   Journal,   http://www.abajournal.com/news/article/
average_debt_load_of_private_law_grads_is_125k_these_five_schools
_lead_to_m/ (Posted March 28, 2012) (last viewed on Feb. 9, 2014).

[2]   Malcom Gladwell, David and Goliath, 4 (Little, Brown and
Company, 2013).

[3]   *Id.*

TABLE OF CONTENTS

THE BUSINESS OF BEING A LAWYER

CHAPTER I

EMOTIONAL INTELLIGENCE: THE ABCS OF EQ FOR LAWYERS

1. WHY STUDY EMOTIONAL INTELLIGENCE IN A LAW SCHOOL COURSE?

For the almost three decades I have been a law professor, I have had a bird's eye view from which to observe what makes some smart people excel and others fail. I have been privileged to teach almost 6000 law students and the good fortune to become friends with many. I have followed a number of my students' careers and been included in many of their professional and personal decisions during and after law school. I have been intrigued to see who succeeds and who does not, who soars, and who crashes. I have seen that intelligence can be used wisely, or stupidly.

The difference I have seen in who succeeds and who does not, lies in EQ, not IQ. This observation was confirmed in my research for this book on economic trends in the legal profession. The development of good EQ skills dominates the articles, books, talks, and advice columns about how to be an effective lawyer. Good EQ skills are as essential to practicing law as is passage of a bar exam.

Jon Kabat-Zinn describes why EQ matters:

"Much evidence testifies that people who are emotionally adept—who know and manage their own feelings well, and who read and deal effectively with other people's feelings—are at an advantage in any domain of life, whether romance and intimate relationships or picking up the unspoken rules that govern success in organizational politics. People with well-developed emotional skills are also more likely to be content and effective in their lives, mastering the habits of mind that foster their own productivity;

1

people who cannot marshal some control over their emotional life fight inner battles that sabotage their ability for focused work and clear thought."[1]

Lawyers are trained to deal in concrete facts, logic, reasons, and measurable outcomes. We should feel comfortable with the evidence in modern psychology. While there is plenty of superficial stuff available on emotional health, there is also solid science on the importance of EQ and proven techniques for achieving greater EQ. This is the field of positive psychology, a fairly new subspecialty in the science of psychology. Its findings confirm that once we reach a certain point of intelligence (smart enough to get into law school, for example),[2] it is emotional intelligence, not cognitive intelligence, that determines whether we are successful. Daniel Gilbert, a psychology professor at Harvard University and one of the pioneers of positive psychology, estimates that "at best, IQ contributes about 20 percent to the factors that determine life success, which leaves 80 percent to other forces."[3] These "other forces" are the ability to motivate oneself and persist in the face of frustrations; control impulses and delay gratification; regulate one's moods; keep distress from swamping the ability to think; empathize, and hope.[4]

Our profession needs to tend to its EQ. A greater percentage of lawyers experience psychological distress than the general population.[5] Lawyers are in remarkably poor mental health with a higher incidence of depression, alcoholism, illegal drug use, and divorce than almost any other profession.[6] Law students who enter law school psychologically healthy show elevated psychological distress within months, with 17–40% showing symptoms of depression, anxiety, and other psychological dysfunctions.[7]

Legal employers make hiring, promotion and retention decisions based on EQ, as do corporate clients when deciding which lawyers to retain. As one legal consultant notes: "Corporations understand that emotional intelligence is a much greater predictor of success than grades, IQ or test scores. . . . Law firms could improve their selection process [of hiring attorneys] by incorporating emotional intelligence and related criteria."[8]

2. WHAT IS EMOTIONAL INTELLIGENCE AND WHY DOES IT MATTER?

Positive psychology became recognized as a specialty within the psychology field late in the twentieth century. It is defined as "the scientific study of optimal human functioning"[9] and focuses on psychological health rather than psychological illness. Tellingly, an electronic search of *Psychological Abstracts* from 1887–2000 found a 14–1 ratio of articles on psychological illness rather than psychological health. There were:

- 8,072 articles on anger
- 57,800 on anxiety
- 70,856 on depression

with:

- 851 abstracts mentioning joy,
- 2,958 on happiness
- 5,701 on life satisfaction.[10]

The field of positive psychology is changing this focus. Paul Meehl was one of the first psychologists to focus on psychological health instead of illness when in 1975, he theorized that some people are born with more "cerebral joy juice."[11] Martin E.P. Seligman of the University of Pennsylvania championed the field of positive psychology in 1998 when he served as President of the American Psychological Association. Studies conducted by Seligman and other researchers show: (1) all of us have a "set point" of happiness and contentment; (2) those who have a higher set point of happiness instinctively use specific strategies in life; (3) these strategies can be studied, identified, and taught, allowing all of us to "adjust" our individual set point of happiness. This chapter, ABCs of EQ for Lawyers, builds upon these findings.

3. THE ABCS OF EQ FOR LAWYERS

A. Be Aware

All of us are influenced by our emotions. Even the most serene among us will be hijacked by our emotions some of the time. This is the first step of good EQ: to be aware of our emotions; step back and observe our emotions accurately; own our emotions non-judgmentally. If I am short-tempered and abrupt with a law student who lingers after class with questions is it because the questions are dumb, or is it because I'm stressed about how much work I have to do? If I continually postpone projects at work, is it because I have poor time management skills, or is it because I dislike my job? If I am sick with colds all winter, is it because there are a lot of cold germs going around, or is it because my immune system is compromised from the stress I feel? If we are unaware of our emotions, we are unable to deal with them, and if we aren't controlling them, they are controlling us. As Kabat-Zinn notes, "When it comes right down to it, facing our problems is usually the only way to get past them."[12]

The second step of good EQ is to recognize that there are specific strategies for managing our emotions and to practice these strategies until they become habits. Studies show that happy, contented, lucky people engage in specific, observable, and consistent habits that unhappy, discontent, and unlucky people do not. By adopting such habits we can increase our "set points" of happiness.

The habits of happy and contented people, and perhaps not surprisingly, of lucky people, include: developing optimism (Section O), knowing and using our strengths (Section S), choosing our work in a way that fits us (Section W), exerting influence (I), handling crises (Sections B,C), stress (Section U), worry (Section X), and pessimistic thinking (Sections D, Q), "reframing" (Section R), keeping perspective (Section K), journaling (Section J), taking care of our bodies (Section T), managing endings (Section E), and adequately preparing for life's challenges (Section P).

Habits are formed when neurological pathways are created in our brains.[13] Studies in which electrical probes were inserted into rats' heads have shown that when rats learn a route through a new maze, their brains, in particular their basal ganglia, "work furiously."[14] A rat's brain "explodes with activity" as it processes new scents, sights, and sounds, finding its way through the maze. As rats travel the maze hundreds of times and learn the route, the electrical probes in their brains show that mental activity decreases. Charles Duhigg, who studies habits, explains: "It was as if the first few times a rat explored a maze, its brain had to work at full power to make sense of all of the new information. But after a few days of running the same route, the rat didn't need to scratch the walls or smell the air anymore, and so the brain activity associated with scratching and smelling ceased."[15]

Studies of people show the same process. Our repeated behaviors create neurological pathways in our basal ganglia. Like rats, we create habits by practicing behaviors until they become fixed pathways in our brains. Once they become habits, these behaviors are not hard for us. They become automatic.

Lawyers should be at an advantage in mastering this first step of EQ. We are trained to be rational when our client is emotional and to think logically about legal issues rather than letting our opinions and preferences guide us. As Duncan Blair, an experienced ERISA lawyer and renowned musician, says, "A lawyer must be able to see when the client is acting emotionally and against her own best interests. A lawyer must be the rational thinker in the room—always asking what is in the client's best interest. This technique can be used by the lawyer on himself when making important decisions."[16]

B. Buffer

Martin Seligman began his career by shocking dogs.[17] He found that administering random, painful electric shocks to dogs made them passive. The dogs gave up trying to eat and would simply lie in one place, whimpering. Eventually the shocked dogs would not help themselves to food or move around even when they were not being shocked. They had learned helplessness. In his private practice, Seligman also noticed that his depressed patients were passive, slower to learn, sad, and anxious. Seligman's patients displayed brain chemistry similar to that of the shocked dogs.[18]

However, Seligman noted, not all of the dogs became helpless after the shocks, nor did all of his patients become depressed when presented with difficulties in life. According to Seligman, "One out of three individuals never gives up, no matter what. . . . Moreover, one out of eight is helpless to begin with—it does not take any experience . . . to make them give up."[19] Seligman set out to study the question, "What is it about some people that imparts buffering strength, making them invulnerable to helplessness? What is it about other people that make them collapse at the first inkling of trouble?"[20]

Through his research, Seligman offers answers to these questions. Some people are resilient. They display "buffering traits." They "interpret their setbacks as surmountable, particular to a single problem and resulting from temporary circumstances. . . ."[21] (Sections L, O, and Q). They learn how to put their problems aside (Section X). They build psychological capital that they rely upon in difficult times.[22]

In economics, capital is defined as resources withdrawn from consumption and invested in the future for higher anticipated returns."[23] Psychological capital consists of our "buffering traits": resources that we build, store, and use during times of stress. Just as we should invest in our savings account after we have made a withdrawal, we need to rebuild our psychological capital after a time of stress. We do so by reconnecting with family and friends; returning to enjoyable activities that we let slide; taking care of our bodies and getting sleep or getting well if we have become run-down; and rebuilding our confidence by participating in things we do well.

Rebuilding Psychological Capital After Making a Withdrawal

- *Reconnect with family and friends.*
- *Return to enjoyable activities.*
- *Take care of your body.*
- *Get enough sleep.*
- *Get well if you've become run down.*
- *Rebuild your confidence by participating in things you do well.*

C. Crisis Management

Goldfish live in water that ranges in temperature from fifty to seventy degrees Fahrenheit. When hot water is slowly added to a goldfish bowl, goldfish will continue swimming around until the water exceeds seventy-five degrees and the fish die. However, if the same amount of hot water is added suddenly, goldfish jump out.

Bad situations can sneak up on us. We become habituated to deteriorating circumstances, not realizing that our situation has escalated to a crisis and requires immediate action. Like goldfish, we continue our old patterns of behavior that used to serve us fine, sometimes until it is too late.

Six Steps in Crisis Management

(1) Recognize that there is a crisis. Some crises are obvious: a car accident, the loss of a job, diagnosis of a serious disease. Other crises evolve. Family members get the flu, we get the flu, we get behind at work, we get further behind. At some point, what was difficult but do-able becomes impossible. We have reached a crisis. Recognizing that the game has changed is the first step in dealing with a crisis.

(2) Restore and maintain calm. None of us can think clearly, solve problems, or respond appropriately when we are upset. We must gain control of ourselves long enough to deal with a crisis.

(3) Assess the facts. What, exactly, is the problem we face? Are we "catastrophizing" and making things worse than they really are? What are our resources? What are our options? Is it possible to deal with one part of the crisis at a time? Who will be affected? Who are the players? What is our time line for addressing the crisis?

In assessing available resources, it is important to recognize that one of the most important resources we have is ourselves and that we must take care of ourselves during a crisis. Just as a car cannot run without gasoline, we cannot function without sleep, food, and water. When we face a crisis, it is important to assess what else we need to operate optimally: a visit with a comforting friend? Exercise? A relaxing bath? One of the instructions given to airline passengers prior to take-off is that if the plane loses oxygen, place the oxygen mask on yourself first, then on a child or others you are trying to help. This is a good analogy. None of us can take care of any situation if we do not take care of ourselves.

(4) Be grateful for the resources we have. Gratitude is one of the most consistent strategies practiced by people who cope with life effectively (Sections H, O, Q). In a crisis, take note of the fortunate aspects of the situation, however bad it may be. Think of others who are not as fortunate. Gratitude gives perspective. Perspective helps us cope.

(5) Deploy our resources. Implement the solution you have decided upon.

(6) Learn from the crisis. Studies of those who successfully navigate hardships show that they engage in an evaluative process when they encounter problems. There is an obvious incentive in doing so: we have less chance of repeating a bad situation if we learn how to avoid it. But there is an additional advantage in viewing difficulties as learning opportunities. No situation is a complete failure if we learn something from it.[24] This small sense of success can empower us.

D. Dispute Pessimistic and Catastrophic Thinking

We all get caught in loops of pessimistic thinking. One negative thought leads to another, and before we realize it, we are treating our pessimistic thoughts as though they were reality: "I didn't get a call back for a job interview. I'll never get a job. I'll be broke. I'll have to live in my parents' basement. . . ."

One of the well-documented methods for building EQ is recognizing and disputing pessimistic thoughts. The key in doing so is recognizing that sometimes our beliefs are just that: beliefs. As Seligman notes, "We tend to treat our thoughts as if they have validity because they originate with us. But our beliefs may or may not be facts. What we say to ourselves when we face a setback can be just as baseless as the ravings of a jealous rival. It is essential to stand back and distance yourself from your pessimistic explanations, at least long enough to verify their accuracy. Checking out the accuracy of our reflexive beliefs is what disputing is all about."[25]

Seligman outlines five steps for disputing pessimistic thinking: ABCDE.[26] A is recognizing adversity; B is realizing beliefs we form about the adversity; C is consequences of our beliefs; D is disputing our beliefs; and E is energy we gain by taking constructive action when we recognize that our catastrophic beliefs are not reality.[27]

Here is an example of applying ABCDE to a distraught first year law student who has just received her first semester grades:

> *Adversity:* Alice gets her first semester law school grades. Two C's, two B's. She is devastated. These are the worst grades she has received in her life. She has received only A's and three B's, ever! Now she has a 2.5 GPA. Alice graduated from college, a really hard college, with a double major and a 3.78 GPA for goodness sake. Alice admits to herself that she has looked down on people who made poor grades. Now,

she is one of them. Alice is embarrassed. What will her parents say? What will her study group say? No one will listen to her opinion anymore. Alice is also mad! Although grades are supposed to be anonymous, some of her classmates seem to know everyone's grades, and they are gloating, especially that goof-off, Harry. How could Harry, who never knew anything when he was called on, have made top grades?

Beliefs: Alice starts thinking about how she will never get a job. Everyone knows jobs are tight. Everyone knows employers want only the top students in the class. Alice thinks about the sales clerk job she will have to get. That's exactly what happened to the lawyer she read about in the paper yesterday in the article talking about the tough job market. Alice is on a roll now. Even if she got lucky and got a law job, she tells herself, it will be a terrible, low-paying job, and she'll hate it and won't be able to repay her student loans, just like the guy in the article. School loans aren't discharged in bankruptcy, and of course, she will eventually go bankrupt since she has to work as a lowly sales clerk. The loop goes round and round.

Consequences: Alice is so depressed, she doesn't want to talk to anyone. She doesn't return her mother's or her boyfriend's phone calls. She doesn't return texts from her law school friends. They're probably going to brag about their grades anyway, Alice tells herself. Alice gets a big bag of potato chips and finds a sappy movie on daytime television. She doesn't want to read the cases for tomorrow. What use would it be anyway, she thinks, she's headed for bankruptcy, embarrassment, and ridicule.

Disputation: Wait a minute, Alice says to herself by the end of the movie. I know I'm smart and hardworking, whatever those grades say. I know I would make a good lawyer, and that is what I've always wanted to be. Alice reminds herself of her professors' warnings that grades would be a shocker for lots of people—like the ninety percent who aren't in the top ten percent of the class. She thought back to what her professors had said about other ways students can distinguish themselves in law school— through trial and moot court competitions, or part time jobs. Alice recalled a posting on the Career Services board about a solo practitioner in town looking for a summer intern. And what about loan forgiveness programs, Alice reminded herself. If I take a job at a public interest office, can't I get some or all of my law school loans forgiven? All the speakers who come to class talk about how rewarding it is to work at public interest offices. Maybe things aren't so bad.

Energization: Alice returns the texts from Sam and Carol in her study group. She asks if they want to meet for pizza. Alice reminds herself that Sam has said he wants to work at the Public Defender's office. Maybe he'll know about summer internships at that office. Alice, Sam, and Carol meet for dinner. Alice finds out their grades were similar to hers. They all commiserate and feel better. Alice takes a summer internship at the PD's office. She loves it.

E. Endings

One of the habits of happy and contented people is that they focus on the positive, not the negative, in past experiences. As Martin Seligman says, we should "take particular care with endings" for their color will forever impact our memory of the events and relationships in our lives.[28]

Colonoscopies

Studies of colonoscopy patients confirm the importance of good endings. Colonoscopies are screening procedures for colon cancer that involve insertion of a colonscope in the rectum and moving it continuously until the procedure is over and the instrument is removed. Patients' unpleasant memories of medical procedures influence their decisions to return for follow-up treatment (as shown by mammogram patients, dental patients and cardiac resuscitation patients).[29] Daniel Kahneman of Princeton University and 2002 Nobel Prize recipient in Economic Sciences, speculated that altering colonoscopy procedures to make the ending of the procedure less painful would color patients' recollection of their colonoscopies and make them more likely to return for follow-up procedures.[30]

Kahneman and his colleagues randomly assigned 682 colonoscopy patients to two groups. All subjects were given a hand-held device by which they could indicate the level of pain they were experiencing at 60-second intervals.[31] The colonoscope was allowed to rest in the rectum for up to three minutes at the conclusion of the colonoscopies in the control group. There was no suction, inflation, or movement. The patients in the control group indicated with their hand-held devices that their level of pain was lower during the final part of the procedure when the colonoscope remained at rest.[32]

After the effects of anesthesia had worn off, all patients were asked to reflect on their experience.[33] The patients who received the modified procedure ranked their colonoscopies as less unpleasant and less painful than the patients who did not receive the extended-length colonoscopies.[34] In a follow-up five years later, more of the patients in the control group returned for another colonoscopy.[35] Consistent with previous studies showing that our memories are selective, Kahneman's colonoscopy study confirmed that "last impressions may be lasting impressions when people reflect on past life experiences."[36]

Schindler's List

Daniel Gilbert, a professor at Harvard University and the author of *Stumbling on Happiness*, also makes the point that the impressions we form at the end of an experience dominate our memory of the entire experience by relating an argument he had with his wife. Gilbert's wife insisted that he had liked the movie, *Schindler's List*, which they had seen years before. Gilbert insisted he had not. They rented the movie to see who was right. Gilbert realized that they were both correct. He had enjoyed the first "ninety-eight percent" of the movie, and so his wife was right. But Gilbert did not enjoy the ending of the movie (where the characters come on screen and praise Schindler), finding it to be an "intrusive, mawkish, superfluous," ending to a powerful story. Gilbert's recollection that he did not enjoy the movie was completely colored by his view of the movie's ending.[37]

The Influence of Verbal Descriptions

A "color swatch" study demonstrates the influence on our memories of our verbal description of events.[38] Volunteers were shown a color swatch, then half of the volunteers ("describers") were asked to describe the color they had been shown. The other half ("non-describers") were not asked to describe the color swatch. All volunteers were later shown an array of colors and told to choose the color they had previously been shown. Seventy-three percent of the non-describers were able to accurately identify the color, but only thirty-three percent of the describers were able to do so. Gilbert explains, "[T]he describers' verbal descriptions of their experiences 'overwrote' their memories of the experiences themselves, and they ended up remembering not what they had experienced but what they had *said* about what they experienced."[39] Like the volunteers in the color swatch experiment, we "fill in" details of the past, "weaving the tapestry" by fabricating—not by actually retrieving—the bulk of the information that we experience as a memory."[40]

The Present Influences the Past

We tend to recall our past in light of what we *now* think, do, feel, and say. When we recall emotions this tendency to "fill in the holes in our memories of the past with material from the present is especially powerful."[41] Studies show that if test subjects are in a positive mood when they reflect on past events, they recall more of their successful tasks and fewer of their failed tasks. If they are in a bad mood at the time they reflect, they recall more of their failures than successes.[42] This explains, in part, the downward spiral of pessimism. We have the ability, for better or for worse, to spin our past recollections.

Forgiveness Is Important to Healthy Endings

Sometimes forgiveness, of others and of ourselves, is essential to good endings.[43] As Seligman says, "rewriting history by forgiveness loosens the power of bad events to embitter and actually can transform bad memories into good ones."[44] If we forgive those who wrong us, we no longer allow that offender to maintain power over us. Forgiveness is a way we take control over our lives. Its value is to us, not to the offender.

Everett Worthington, who has studied and written on forgiveness, advises a five-step "REACH" process when practicing forgiveness:

- *R*ecall the wrong.

- *E*mpathize with the wrongdoer by trying to understand why she acted as she did.

- Behave *A*ltruistically by thinking of a time someone forgave you.

- *C*ommit yourself to forgive, either publicly or in writing, for example, by writing a note to the offender, making an entry in a journal, or telling a trusted friend.

- *H*old on to the forgiveness. When memories of a wrong arise, do not wallow in those thoughts. Remind yourself that you have forgiven the offense by re-reading your journal entry or talking with the friend in whom you confided your forgiveness.[45] Forgiveness can't be conditional; if so, it is not forgiveness.[46]

F. Focus on Who You Are

Dick Poehling had a reputation as one of the best trial lawyers in St. Louis. Attorneys all over town would show up to watch him in trial. As the longtime Chief Deputy of the St. Louis City Prosecutor's Office, Dick had trained many of the trial lawyers in St. Louis. He had a loyal following who recounted his amazing victories in court, piercing cross-examinations, and eloquent arguments. As a newly hired AUSA in the Eastern District of Missouri, I was excited to hear that Dick would leave his current position and join the U. S. Attorney's office in St. Louis.

I expected to meet Atticus Finch himself but when I met Dick I was sure there must be a mix-up. Maybe there were two Dick Poehlings? The man I met was slightly built with balding blond hair, thick glasses, and a mild manner. He was unassuming and a far cry from most of the trial lawyers I knew, particularly those at the U.S. Attorney's office, many of whom resembled boxers and rugby players.

Curious how this mild-mannered man could be a courtroom tiger, I dashed up from my docket one morning to the courtroom where Dick's first case as an AUSA was in trial. I sat down just as the defense attorney, Charles Shaw, began his closing argument. Charles Shaw was renowned. Tall, distinguished, with slightly graying hair, an athletic build, and a deep, resonant voice, Shaw pounced around the courtroom, thundering about the virtues of his client and the misconduct of the prosecution. Listening to Shaw's argument I thought, poor Dick, he is going to lose his first case as an AUSA. Although I knew some of the background of the case and had a new prosecutor's ardent zeal, I was ready to acquit after hearing Shaw's closing. I predicted the jury would be out minutes before returning a Not Guilty verdict.

Dick continued to sit at the counsel table for a bit after Shaw sat down. He rose slowly, walked to the podium, looked at the jurors and said, "Wow. Don't you feel like clapping?" His mild, calm voice was a welcome respite from the bombast. The jury snickered. They smiled at Dick. With Dick. In six words, he had taken control of the courtroom.

Dick continued, "I think you want to decide this case on the facts, not on showmanship. Let's look at the facts in this case." Over the next few minutes, Dick summarized, simply and succinctly, the evidence against the defendant. He spoke to the jury as though they were sitting at a kitchen table. He was as comfortable and genuine as a favorite uncle.

Dick ended with this story: "You know, Mr. Shaw's argument reminds me of the Mama Bird with a nest of baby birds. If a predator comes upon the nest, the Mama Bird flies away to a nearby tree and flaps and caws and makes all kinds of racket to distract the predator away from the nest. That's what Mr. Shaw is doing, flapping and cawing and trying to distract you from the facts of this case. But there is only one predator in this room. His client."

The jury was out minutes. They voted with their favorite uncle.

This experience was one of the best lawyering lessons one could have. As a new AUSA with no trial experience, young (I looked 12), "a girl" (there were almost no women in federal court in those days), I assumed that to be an effective trial lawyer, I would have to be like the trial lawyers I saw around me. I was worried, and with good reason. I could not have pulled it off. After I saw Dick Poehling, I realized that to be an effective trial lawyer, I just needed to be myself. Prepared, appropriate for the situation, professional, but above all, genuine.

I have seen law students and new lawyers lose touch with who they are. It is easy to do. I always ask my upper-level students what advice they have for new law students. One student said it well. His advice is good for 1Ls and for the most experienced among us who lose our bearings. He said, "Be you. You got where you were by doing something right. Stick to what works for you."[47]

G. Goals. Make Them. Live Them.

Goals focus our efforts, help us achieve satisfaction in life, and make us more efficient, productive, and successful. Industrial organizational psychologists who study task performance in the workplace identify the following ways goal setting improves performance: First, goals "direct attention and effort toward goal-relevant activities and away from goal-irrelevant activities."[48] Second, goals have an "energizing function." Difficult goals lead to more effort than easy goals.[49] Third, "goals affect persistence."[50] Fourth, goals lead to "arousal, discovery, and/or use of task-relevant knowledge and strategies."[51] Fifth, setting and achieving goals increases one's self-pride and confidence.[52]

Goal-setting gives us control in our lives,[53] which increases our happiness and contentment (Sections H,O). Goal-setting and achievement create a positive cycle. As Sheldon and Houser-Marko explain, "[Goal attainment] leads to increased well-being and even more positive motivation for the second cycle of striving, which leads to even better attainment and further increases in well-being."[54] Effective goal-setting and attainment have the following characteristics.

• **Goals should be ours, not goals we feel pressured to achieve.** As Locke & Latham have found in their studies, "[t]he goal-performance relationship is strongest when people are committed to their goals."[55] Sheldon & Houser-Marko's research is consistent: "[A] person's inability to fully accept and internalize his or her own stated goals may significantly impede that person's attempts to effect positive change in his or her life."[56] Goals cannot be our parents', our spouses', or society's expectations; they need to be ours.

• **Goals should be worthy.** Studies show a qualitative difference in the long term satisfaction we derive from achieving goals that deal with extrinsic goods, such as material possessions and social status, and the more significant, long term satisfaction we derive from achieving internal goals directed at our personal growth.

Many researchers, including Daniel Kahneman of Princeton University, have studied the relationship between wealth and happiness. Their findings from a variety of cultures worldwide and over decades are consistent. Increases in income have a "transitory effect" on life satisfaction.[57] Overall, income has a "weak effect" on subjective well-being.[58] There are two conventional explanations for this: *relative* income (how much we earn compared to others) affects well-being more than our amount of income, and we become habituated to material goods.[59] Kahneman proposes an additional explanation. He points to data that "people with greater income tend to devote relatively more of their time to . . . activities of higher tension and stress . . . work, compulsory non-work activities (such as shopping and child care) and active leisure. . . ."[60] In other words, at some point, goals such as acquiring more money, possessions, and prestige carry a cost. They require that we engage in activities that drain, not restore us. They diminish our quality of life, not enhance it.

• **Goals should be consistent with our values.** Sheldon and Houser-Marko's studies of hundreds of college students have found that students whose goals match their values are better able to attain their goals.[61] Similarly, Milgram's study of authority (Section I) demonstrate that we feel considerable stress when we obey instructions contrary to our values.[62] Studies of law students suggest that those who suffer the most psychological stress are those who accept job offers that compromise their personal values and goals."[63]

• **Know when to update goals.** Life changes. Goals that may have been appropriate, necessary, and consistent with our values at one point in our lives may not be at another point.[64] Our goals are likely to evolve through somewhat predictable stages, beginning with maintaining an active social life (teenage years and early twenties); devoting time and energy to education and skill development (twenties and thirties); having a busy and stimulating career (thirties through sixties); and working less in favor of more leisure time. It is helpful to remember as we revise our goals, "You can have it all. You just can't have it all, all the time."[65]

• **Set short-term goals and long-term goals.** Some goals are short-term: daily, weekly, monthly. We also need "five-year plans." Long-term goals focus our current activities in directions we want to go rather than where we drift. Long term goals help us defer gratifications, and maintain perspective. Keeping an eye on the endgame directs us.

• **Write goals down; express goals publicly.** Studies of Chinese prisoners of war,[66] unemployed engineers,[67] Starbucks employees,[68] and Scottish orthopedic patients,[69] show that writing things down helps focus our thoughts, anticipate and overcome hurdles in reaching our goals, and achieve what we write down (Section J). "Making a public commitment to the goal [also] enhances commitment, presumably because it makes one's actions a matter of integrity in one's own eyes and in the eyes of others."[70]

• **Keep goals specific.** Specificity makes our goals real. Outline the steps needed to reach your goals. Thinking through the steps to reach a goal helps us anticipate and overcome challenges, marshal necessary resources, and prepare ourselves logistically and emotionally. For example, if I am a law student and my goal is to work at a DA's office after law school, the steps I need to take to reach my goal include: talk with professors at my school who teach criminal law and get their advice; go to the courthouse and observe criminal trials; register for "criminal section" trial advocacy classes rather than civil; enroll in externships and clinical courses; participate in shadow opportunities in DA, PD, and AG offices; take the necessary substantive law courses like criminal procedure; do an independent study in the criminal law/procedure area.

• **Reward goal progress.** Locke & Latham's studies show that people are more likely to achieve their goals if they receive feedback on their progress by "identify[ing] and administer[ing] rewards for making goal progress, as well as punishments for failing to make progress. . . ."[71] Treat yourself after achieving a goal.

H. Happiness

"Numerous studies show that happy individuals are successful across multiple life domains, including marriage, friendship, income, work performance, and health."[72] Happier people make better decisions on important issues,[73] live longer, and are less likely to become disabled.[74] They are more productive at work and have

> *"What a wonderful life I've had! I only wish I'd realized it sooner."*
>
> **Sidonie-Gabrielle Colette**

higher income,[75] greater physical endurance,[76] and richer social lives.[77] They display resilience in the face of setbacks.[78]

Worldwide, most people are fairly happy.[79] Myers & Diener evaluated data from 916 surveys of 1.1 million people in 45 nations. On a 0–10 scale (where 0 is "very unhappy or completely dissatisfied with life," and 10 "very happy and satisfied with life"), the average response was 6.75.[80]

Attempting to achieve happiness by filling our lives with momentary pleasures, accomplishments, or material acquisitions does not work. Studies consistently show that the more people strive for extrinsic goals such as money, the more numerous their problems and the less robust their well-being.[81] Aspiring to financial success is "associated with less self-actualization, less vitality, more depression and more anxiety."[82] Psychologists conducting these studies suggest that this is because "individuals aspiring for wealth may be more likely to focus on contingent, external goals and fleeting, superficial satisfactions unrelated to inherent needs. Consequently, they may ignore or be distracted from the intrinsic actualizing and integrating tendencies that support personality growth and well-being."[83] Additionally, we quickly habituate.[84] Not only do momentary pleasures fade (the fourth bite of ice cream is not as delicious as the first bite), but our striving for momentary pleasures can have a negative impact. We develop cravings that can be satisfied only by greater amounts of the pleasure. This is how addictions begin.[85]

The life circumstance that correlates most directly with happiness is close, intact relationships with others.[86] As Frances Bacon noted in 1625, there are two benefits to having close social ties to friends and family: "It redoubleth joys, and cutteth griefs in half."[87]

Happiness does not correlate to age, gender, wealth, health, or objective life circumstance.[88] Although our personalities continue to develop and evolve through our twenties,[89] we are born with a "set point" of happiness.[90] David Lykken's study of 4,000 adult twins found that the heritability of subjective well-being is between forty and fifty percent.[91] Studies confirm the 'hard-wired' nature of happiness: "[H]appy individuals tend to show relatively greater resting activity in the left prefrontal cortex than in the right prefrontal area; conversely dysphoric individuals display relatively greater right anterior activity."[92]

Some people have a set point at the far extreme of happiness. They are cheerful most of the time. Others have a set point of melancholy most of the time. Most of us are somewhere in between. All of us can move our set point of happiness by the habits we practice.[93] As David Lykken states: "Many people drudge along well beneath their real happiness set points because of bad habits. . . . All of us . . . can learn to bounce along above our basic set points by learning some new habits, by observing some simple rules. . . ."[94] We should be realistic about happiness. Even those with high set points of happiness cannot be happy all of the time. That is not reality. As John Claypool notes:

> "To expect constant happiness . . . is to set ourselves up for failure and disappointment. Not everything that we do can provide us both present and future benefit. It is sometimes worthwhile to forgo present benefit for greater future gain, and in every life some mundane work is unavoidable. Studying for exams, saving for the future, or being an intern and working long hours is often unpleasant but can help us to attain long-term happiness. . . . Attaining lasting happiness requires that we enjoy the journey on our way to a destination we deem valuable."[95]

One of the habits of happy people is resilience. They face hardships and setbacks like everyone but have the ability to rally their emotions with their optimism. As Muhammad Ali said, "If they can make penicillin out of moldy bread, they can sure make something out of you." The specific habits that raise our "set point" of happiness are a sense of optimism (Section O), using our strengths (Section S), reframing (Sections E and R), keeping perspective (Sections D and K), increasing positive emotions and reducing negative emotions (Sections E and Q), and maintaining a sense of meaning (Section M).

The Habits of Happiness

- *Using our strengths*
- *Reframing*
- *Keeping perspective*
- *Increasing positive emotions*
- *Decreasing negative emotions*
- *A sense of meaning*

I. Influence

It is helpful, professionally and personally, to understand influence: how we influence others, and how we are influenced. Robert Cialdini of Arizona State University has conducted numerous studies on influence. He identifies seven factors that affect influence: (1) consistency and commitment, (2) reciprocation, (3) social proof, (4) liking, (5) scarcity, and (6) authority.[96]

"Consistency and Commitment"

According to Cialdini, we all have an "obsessive desire to be (and to appear to be) consistent with what we have already done."[97] Thus, once we get someone to make a commitment, however small, we influence their future behavior because they want to behave consistently with that commitment.[98] Once we make a commitment, however small, we feel compelled to behave consistently with our commitment.

There are proven strategies for obtaining commitments: start small; get a commitment in writing; and obtain commitments in front of others. Jonathan Freedman and Scott Fraser conducted a study of these strategies. Volunteers went door-to-door in a suburban community asking residents if they would permit placement in their front lawns of a public interest billboard stating, "Drive Carefully." Almost every person (83%) turned down the request. However, when the volunteers approached another set of residents in the same community and asked if they would be willing to put up in a window of their home a small, three-inch-square sign stating, "Be a Safe Driver," and returned two weeks later with the billboard request, 76% agreed to permit the billboard in their front lawn. Freedman and Fraser explained: "Agreeing to the initial small request committed the homeowners to behave consistent with their newly formed images of themselves as concerned about safe driving."[99]

Interestingly, it may be easier in today's world to get binding commitments. We all commit in writing regularly, some of us hundreds of times each day, through email, texts, and twitter. Potentially, we do so in front of others, since every email, text, and tweet can be forwarded, shared and sent to groups of people. Most of us should bear in mind Cialdini's warning: Be careful about agreeing to small requests.[100]

Reciprocation

We are programed to reciprocate. Doing so helped ensure our survival. Historically, those who banded together to share food, security, and shelter survived.[101] This "rule" of reciprocity permeates every society and every culture.[102]

Marketers deploy the rule of reciprocity when they send gifts in the mail (*i.e.*, address labels) as part of their solicitations. Our sense of reciprocation also arises when someone makes a concession to us. Cialdini gives the following example. A Boy Scout asked Cialdini if he would buy two tickets, costing $20 each, to a Saturday night Scout banquet. When Cialdini declined, the Boy Scout asked if Cialdini would like to buy two candy bars ($2 each) instead. Cialdini bought the candy bars, feeling like he had gotten a bargain. He had spent only $4, instead of $40, and didn't have to go to a Scout Banquet on a Saturday night. Later, Cialdini realized that the Scout had used a basic principle of influence by making a concession (candy instead of tickets).[103]

Social Proof

We look to other people to determine the correct behavior for situations. Demonstrating that our relevant social group engages in desired behavior influences us to engage in such behavior. This principle generally serves us well. Following social cues helps us avoid mistakes and behave appropriately.[104]

Social proof leads us awry when social evidence is inaccurate or faked, or when an error produces "snowballing social proof" that pushes us to the incorrect decision.[105] The snowballing effect is well documented when the group is large. As Cialdini observes: "[W]e seem to assume that if a lot of people are doing the same thing, they must know something we don't. Especially when we are uncertain, we are willing to place an enormous amount of trust in the collective knowledge of the crowd."[106] The snowballing effect is why dozens of people who observe a person in distress do not come to the assistance of the apparent victim.

Liking

"As a rule, we prefer to say yes to the requests of someone we know and like."[107] Studies show that we are influenced by those who are similar to us in background, interests, and dress;[108] pay us compliments ("a bewitchingly effective device");[109] are physically attractive, rather than unattractive;[110] are familiar in some way;[111] appear to be "our teammates" (the car salesman who does battle with his boss to get us a good deal; the "good cop" in the bad cop/good cop interrogation);[112] are associated with things we enjoy (luncheon meetings are more influential than other meetings because we associate the people and topics present with the pleasant experience of eating food we enjoy);[113] or are people are we admire (the beautiful actress selling face cream).[114] The "liking" principle of influence is simple Marketing 101.

Scarcity

We tend to value things more when their availability is limited. We are motivated by the prospect of losing something more than we are by the prospect of gaining something of equal value. Sales persons regularly capitalize on the scarcity principle of influence. ("This is the last one left." "This model is available at this price only until the end of the week.")[115] One reason scarcity is influential is that it limits our freedom, and we don't like having our freedom limited. When scarcity interferes with our prior access to some item, we typically react by wanting the item more than before. Similarly, things become more valuable when there is competition for them.[116] As Cialdini notes: "Especially in those cases involving direct competition, the blood comes up, the focus narrows, and emotions rise."[117]

Newly experienced scarcity is more powerful than long lasting scarcity to which we have become habituated.[118] This is why newly poor or newly disenfranchised populations are less stable and rebel, revolt, and become violent more readily than groups that have long been poor or disenfranchised.[119]

Authority

Most of us have a "deep-seated sense of duty to authority,"[120] and will obey those we perceive to be in authority. The study conducted by Stanley Milgram of Yale University in 1963 demonstrates the influence of authority.[121] Milgram recruited volunteers through newspaper advertisements and a direct mail campaign to participate in what they thought was a study of memory and learning.[122] The volunteers were from New Haven, Connecticut, and surrounding communities and from all walks of life. They ranged in education level from elementary school to doctorates and professional degrees. The study was conducted at a laboratory at Yale University.[123]

The volunteers ("subjects") were told by the researcher ("teacher") to administer electrical shocks to the "learner" if the learner failed to correctly perform the learning exercise (recalling and pairing words). The subjects were told that the learner was a volunteer just like themselves, but in fact the learner was a researcher.[124]

The subjects were placed in front of an instrument with lever switches. The switches indicated voltage, from 15 to 450 volts. These voltage ranges were also described on the instrument as increasing from *"Slight Shock"* to *"Danger: Severe Shock"* (450 volts). The instrument's panel flashed lights and emitted buzzer sounds when the switches were pressed. The instrument appeared to administer electric shocks, but was in reality simulated. It administered no shocks.[125]

The subjects were directed by the teacher to administer shocks to the learner. The learner responded as if he was receiving the level of shock allegedly administered. The learner, in an adjacent room, was fully audible and visible to the subject through a one way mirror. During the experiment, when the learner first missed questions and the subjects were directed to administer shocks, the shocks were low voltage, and the learner gave no verbal sign or protest. Later, when the 300-volt switch was pushed, the learner responded by pounding the wall next to his chair, kicking the wall, and refusing to answer more questions. When the learner resisted in this fashion, the subjects typically turned to the teacher for guidance.[126]

At this point, the teacher instructed the subjects to continue to shock the learners. Of the forty subjects, none stopped administering shocks until a voltage of 300 was reached. Once voltage 300 was reached and the learner began to hit and kick the wall and refuse to answer additional questions, fourteen of the forty subjects defied the teacher's instructions and refused to continue shocking the victim (stopping at 300, 330, 345, 360, and 375 volts).[127]

Twenty-six of the forty subjects obeyed the teacher's instructions to the end, "until they reached the most potent shock available on the shock generator."[128] As Milgram noted in describing the data, these twenty-six subjects did so even though disobeying the teacher brought them no material loss or punishment and their compliance appeared to be extremely painful to those receiving the shocks.[129]

The responses of the subjects varied. Many of the twenty-six subjects who obeyed until the end showed considerable signs of stress (sweating, trembling, stuttering, groaning, biting their lips, digging fingernails into their flesh). Three subjects experienced uncontrollable seizures (one so severe, the experiment was halted). Fourteen of the forty subjects smiled and had nervous laughing fits as they administered greater and greater shocks. Some subjects remained calm throughout and displayed minimal signs of tension.[130]

Conclusions from Milgram's Shock Experiments

• **"The Strength of Obedient Tendencies."** Milgram draws two conclusions from his electric shock experiment. The first is "the sheer strength of obedient tendencies."[131] Despite the fact that it is a "fundamental breach of moral conduct to hurt another person against his will," more than half of the subjects "abandon[ed] this tenet in following the instructions of an authority who has no special powers to enforce his commands."[132] The obedient behavior of the subjects was unexpected to Milgram and his research team. They had assumed that an "insignificant minority" would continue to follow the directions to shock until the highest voltage.[133] Researchers viewing the subjects through one-way mirrors "uttered expressions of disbelief as they watched subjects administer powerful and painful shocks to persons in distress when told to do so by a person in authority who the subject did not know, and from whom the subject would receive no reward."[134]

• **The Tension of Disregarding One's Own Values.** Milgram's second observation as the "extraordinary tension"[135] displayed by those who obeyed the teacher. For example:

> [One] mature and initially poised businessman enter[ed] the laboratory smiling and confident. Within 20 minutes he was reduced to a twitching, stuttering wreck, who was rapidly approaching a point of nervous collapse. He constantly pulled on his earlobe, and twisted his hands. At one point he pushed his fist into his forehead and muttered, 'Oh God, let's stop it.' And yet he continued to respond to every word of the experimenter, and obeyed to the end.[136]

Milgram notes that the majority of the subjects obeyed even though "they [were] acting against their own values"[137] and expressed "deep disapproval" of their actions or denounced the study as "stupid and senseless."[138] In part, Milgram attributes the extraordinary tension displayed by the subjects to disregarding one's own values.

Cialdini advises that as we consider our own tendencies to obey authority we should note that we "are often as vulnerable to the *symbols* of authority as to the *substance*."[139] (emphasis in original). These symbols include titles, clothing, prestige, automobiles, etc.[140]

Summary: Principles of Influence

- *We want to appear to be consistent with our prior decisions. Once we commit to something small, we will make more significant decisions to maintain our consistency with our initial commitment.*

- *We feel an obligation to reciprocate favors or concessions made by others even if we did not desire the favor or concession.*

- *We follow social cues of those we value.*

- *We are more easily influenced by those we like.*

- *We value things when we perceive that their availability is limited.*

- *We tend to do what those in authority ask us to.*

J. Journaling

The Chinese were particularly effective at indoctrinating their American prisoners during the Korean War. Studies of liberated Americans held as POWs in Chinese prisons showed that their beliefs had been shifted while in prison. The majority of them believed the Chinese stories that the United States had been the aggressor in starting the Korean War and that the United States had used germ warfare. They praised the Chinese for "the fine job they have done in China."[141]

One of the ways the Chinese perfected their indoctrination of prisoners was through use of journaling techniques. Prisoners were required to write down questions posed to them by their Chinese interrogators as well as the answers the interrogator wanted. The questions pertained to the role of the

United States in starting the Korean War and practices allegedly used by American troops. If a prisoner refused to write a given answer voluntarily, he was asked to copy it from notebooks.[142]

As the Chinese knew, writing down thoughts impacts our views and behavior. Studies of individuals who have experienced difficulties show that writing about problems reduces their impact. People get well faster and show strengthened immune systems when they journal. They experience "positive behavioral outcomes" with whatever hardship they are facing, such as faster re-employment after being laid off.[143]

Psychologists who study the effects of journaling suggest that it helps us handle traumas because the writing process forces us to label and structure traumatic events. This promotes "the assimilation and understanding of the event" and reduces "the associated emotional arousal."[144] Writing about struggles and hardships helps us name, catalog, and describe what has happened to us and how we feel. It increases our awareness of our emotions and provides an outlet for them. When we have no explanation for events, events "amplify and extend their emotional impact."[145] As Daniel Gilbert says, "Once we can explain an event, we can fold it up like freshly washed laundry, put it away in memory's drawer, and move on. . . ."[146]

Written declarations are effective in part because they provide physical evidence of our planning. It is harder to forget, deny, or depart from a written plan than simply saying we are going to do something.[147] Once we have a written plan, we tend to bring our self-image into line with our writing.[148]

The Value of Journaling

"Writing or talking about emotional experiences . . . has been found to be associated with significant drops in physician visits . . . beneficial influences in immune function . . . long-term improvement in mood and indicators of well-being . . . significant reductions in stress . . . improved grades . . . less absenteeism by employees. . . ."[149]

K. Keep Perspective:
The Worst Things Are Never the Last

At the end of my first year of law school, I interviewed with every large law firm that came to campus. Because my grades were high, I expected to receive a well-paying summer job at a firm.

I did not get a single offer. In fact, I did not get a single call-back for a second interview from any firm. In hindsight, I can see why. I had never met a lawyer or been in a law office in my life, and it showed. I wore the wrong clothes (a summer dress and sandals; those were my "dress clothes"). I said the wrong things to corporate law firms ("My favorite class was criminal law. My least favorite was corporate law.") I gave the wrong answers ("Yes, I might move out of state after I graduate from law school.") I was naïve and gullible and had no poker face.

When I received no offers, I was devastated, embarrassed, and worried. I scrambled, looking for other jobs. The market was tight and I could find nothing. Toward the end of the spring semester, after I had resigned myself to working at a temporary secretarial agency to pay the bills, I saw a notice on the Career Services Board that judges with the Missouri Court of Appeals would be interviewing for part-time summer clerks. The pay was minimum wage. Because it was so late in the semester, there were few applicants.

I applied and got an interview. During the interview, I hit it off with Judge Theodore McMillian and he hired me. That summer, a high profile public corruption trial was in session in the federal courthouse across the street from Judge McMillian's courthouse. The Lieutenant Governor, whom Judge McMillian had known professionally for years, was being prosecuted. As a sitting judge, Judge McMillian could not of course attend the trial, so he sent me to watch. I sat spell-bound for hours and came back at lunch and reported to Judge McMillian what had happened. I had lots of questions, and Judge McMillian answered them all. I learned from a master. Judge McMillian had been a renowned prosecutor and trial judge before becoming an appellate judge. During those lunch discussions, he taught me about evidence, trial strategies, and life.

Judge McMillian became my mentor. He advised me to do an internship at the U.S. Attorney's office (which had prosecuted the trial I had watched all summer), when I returned for my third year of law school. I took his advice even though all of my friends, and the Career Services staff, thought I was crazy. In those days, internships were looked down upon. Only the students at the bottom of the class took them. But I trusted Judge McMillian enough to follow his advice. During my internship, I worked on mail fraud cases, high-profile public corruption prosecutions, and a scandalous prostitution case involving famous entertainers. I loved it.

Judge McMillian hired me to be his law clerk after I graduated from law school. When he was named to the United States Court of Appeals for the Eighth Circuit, he took me with him even though, now as a federal judge, he could have chosen a clerk with superstar credentials. Our lunch time discussions had been a bonding experience.

After my clerkship with Judge McMillian, I went to work at one of the large law firms that did not give me a call-back interview during my first year of law school. I thought I had arrived. I was poised for lawyer success. I would be like the lawyers in the movies who wear cool clothes and dash off to court to save their clients. Instead, I sat in a library. All day. Every day. I never met a client. I never went to court. I researched esoteric issues and wrote a lot of memos.

Walking from the parking lot to my law firm drudgery, I saw Judge McMillian often. He asked how I liked my dream job. I told him I was miserable. He encouraged me to apply with the U. S. Attorney's office where I had done my internship. There was an opening, he said, for an AUSA. To my surprise, I was hired. I was twenty-five years old. I looked twelve. I had no trial experience. I did not fit the profile of a federal prosecutor. I was hired for two reasons. The first was Judge McMillan's support of me. It was key. The second was my internship experience at the U.S. Attorney's office. Because of it, the lawyers knew me and were willing to give me a chance.

I served as an AUSA for seven fun, exciting years. I loved my job. I woke up every morning excited to go to work. Serving in the U.S. Attorney's office led to the next opportunity in my career, academia. Had I not been rejected by every law firm that interviewed me as a law student, I wouldn't have met Judge McMillian. My minimum-wage, last-resort, summer internship led to a wise mentor whose advice and contacts opened doors I never knew existed and could not have entered but for him.

I offer this story for two lessons on perspective: First, we may not know what we want. Stay open to possibilities. Second, what appear to be the worst things are not. As John Claypool says, "Despair is presumptuous. We do not know how things will turn out."[150]

L. Luck

Richard Wiseman of the University of Herfordshire in Britain conducted studies of lucky and unlucky people. Over an eight-year time period, using a multi-factor system, Wiseman identified hundreds people as exceptionally lucky or exceptionally unlucky. Wiseman's study group came from all walks of life and ranged in age from eighteen to eighty-four.[151] During the study, subjects kept diaries, participated in experiments, completed psychological questionnaires, and were interviewed by with Wiseman and his research team.[152] The goal of the study was to examine the characteristics of each group. Wiseman found that external factors such as health, income, attractiveness, and frequency of hardships did not distinguish the two groups.[153] They were, however, distinguished by behavioral characteristics. These behaviors are learnable.[154] They overlap with characteristics found in studies of happy people (Section H), optimists (Section X), and those who are "stress-hardy" (Section U). The characteristics of very lucky people are:

Lucky People Create "Chance" Opportunities in Their Lives[155]

Wiseman measured the lucky and unlucky groups on five dimensions of personality: agreeableness, conscientiousness, extroversion, neuroticism, and openness.[156] He found no significant difference between the lucky and unlucky subjects on agreeableness and conscientiousness, but very different scores on extroversion, neuroticism, and openness. According to Wiseman, these differences "explain why lucky people constantly encounter chance opportunities in their lives while unlucky people do not."[157]

As extroverts, lucky people meet a larger number of people in their day-to-day activities than do their unlucky counterparts. As Wiseman explains, the more people the lucky participants meet, "the greater opportunity they have of running into someone who could have a positive effect on their lives."[158] The lucky and unlucky people also display differences in body language. Lucky subjects smile twice as much, engage in more eye contact, and display three times more "open" body language, such as pointing their bodies toward the person they are speaking to, uncrossing legs and arms, and using gestures with open palms. Evolutionarily we are programed to respond favorably to people with open palms because open palms demonstrate that the person to whom we are speaking is not carrying a weapon.[159]

Lucky people build bonds with more people they meet than do unlucky people. "Lucky people are effective at building secure and long-lasting attachments with the people they meet. They are easy to get to know and most people like them. They tend to be trusting and form close friendships with others. As a result, they often keep in touch with a much larger number of friends and colleagues than unlucky people."[160]

Lucky People Rely on Their Intuition and Gut Feelings[161]

In every category of decision making Wiseman studied: financial, career, business, and personal relationships, lucky people outscored the unlucky people in the frequency with which they followed their intuition.[162] Those in the unlucky group often had good intuition about situations but disregarded it. Wiseman suggested why. Intuition is based on experiences and lessons learned at some point in our past[163] and unlucky people do not have the confidence to follow their gut instincts. They often ignore their intuition and regret their decisions,[164] whereas lucky people take practical steps to boost their intuition, such as delaying decisions when their gut instinct sets off an alarm. Unlucky people do not use these delaying strategies.

Lucky People Expect Good Fortune[165]

According to Wiseman, "Lucky people are convinced that the sun will always shine on them whereas unlucky people expect storm clouds to gather in their personal and professional lives."[166] Lucky people dwell more on "positive" emotions and less on "negative" emotions (Section Q). According to Wiseman, "Lucky people see any bad luck in their lives as being very short lived. They simply shrug it off and don't let it affect their expectations about the future."[167] The lucky people in Wiseman's study acted upon their optimism in concrete, specific ways such as "attempting to achieve their goals, even if their chances of success seem slim, and persevering in the face of failure."[168] When lucky people encounter bad luck and negative events, they "consistently look on the bright side of each situation. . . . This makes them feel better and helps maintain the notion that they are lucky people living lucky lives."[169]

Lucky People Practice Strategies for Turning Bad Luck into Good[170]

The lucky and unlucky people in Wiseman's study encountered difficulties, hardships, and setbacks in life. When Wiseman studied how each group confronted their difficulties, he found that they approached them differently. The lucky people instinctively engaged in strategies of gratitude whenever they encountered a hardship. They imagined how things could have been worse and were grateful that the worse had not occurred.[171] They compared themselves to other people who had experienced more ill fortune, and were grateful for their situation.[172] The lucky people were able to focus on some benefit from their ill fortune. These practices of gratitude helped the lucky people gain perspective and maintain equanimity during their difficulty, which led them to more effective coping skills and greater resilience than the unlucky people. Notably, "gratitude strategies" are also one of the consistent habits of stress-hardy individuals (Section U).

The lucky and unlucky people approached their past differently. According to Wiseman, "Lucky people do not dwell on the ill fortune; they let go of the past and focus on the future."[173] Seligman, Kahneman, and Gilbert found similar behavioral strategies when studying how happy, resilient people deal with endings (Section E).

Lucky People Take Steps to Prevent More Bad Luck in the Future[174]

The lucky people in Wiseman's study viewed their failures as opportunities to learn and grow. This helped them persevere. The unlucky people, in contrast, "were reluctant to learn from their mistakes and were far more likely to repeat them in the future."[175] Learning from difficulties is also part of effective crisis management. The last of the six steps in effective crisis management is evaluating what went wrong that led to the crisis (Section C).

M. Meaning

Eyes are the first clue. Posture is the next. A smile, or lack thereof, is the clincher. These things tell me whether my former law students enjoy what they are doing, or are miserable. Having taught thousands of law students, I see my former law students everywhere, at bar functions and court houses, of course, but also at gas stations, grocery stores, ball fields, or just walking down the street. Often, it has been ten or fifteen years since I last saw my former student in the classroom. Sometimes, the changes I see are dramatic.

With few exceptions, every student I have on the first day of law school is eager and excited to be in law school, full of energy and, even if nervous, abundantly confident that he or she will be as successful in the years ahead as in the past. In the spring semester of the first year of law school, after grades come out, a lot of students wear that beat-down-how-could-this-happen-to-me look, but by their second or third year of law school, they've rallied. Almost everyone finds his or her niche, whether in a trial advocacy program, law clinic, rewarding part-time job, or just comfort with who they are. Almost everyone regains his or her confidence and finds away to soar again (Section D).

But when I see my students years after they have graduated, the differences among them can be stark. Many still have the energy, excitement, and joy they had as first year students. Their eyes are bright, their faces glow, they grasp my hand or give hugs with vigor. They smile when they tell me what they are doing.

Other former students, however, are shells of who they were when we first met. Their eyes are dull, they slouch, they have not aged well. Even though some of them have positions of prestige, their voices are weary when they tell me what they are doing.

Surprisingly, life circumstances don't seem to matter much. Many of my former students have suffered traumas such as divorce, illness, or even the death of loved ones. They bend and bow from such blows but come back. They have been hurt, but they are not broken. The difference, I think, is whether they are doing something that is meaningful to them. People who come to law school tend to have an expectation that they will make a difference in people's lives. This is a realistic expectation. By the nature of our work, lawyers make a difference in someone's life, whether by writing a will, helping someone navigate legal intricacies in the business world, or keeping a person out of jail. When the expectation of making a difference is not met, we begin to feel empty. Too many years of feeling empty will drain the life out of anyone.

Sources of meaning are different for each of us. For some, it will be our work. For others, it will be family or community involvement. Our source of meaning may change throughout our lives, but failing to find it somewhere will eat us up. Every study of resilience, stress-hardiness, happiness, and contentment confirms that a strong sense of meaning is necessary.[176] Victor Frankl said it well: "What man actually needs is not a tensionless state but rather the striving and struggling for some goal worthy of him. What he needs is not the discharge of tensions at any cost, but the call of a potential meaning waiting to be fulfilled. . . ."[177]

Studies have found that "among various personality variables . . . meaning in life is the most consistent predictor of psychological well-being at every stage of the life span, from adolescence to late adulthood."[178] Meaningful experiences are distinguishable from pleasures. Pleasures help brighten our days but are like cotton candy; they cannot sustain us. Accolades, accomplishments and material possessions may make us happy for a while but their pleasure subsides as we become habituated to them.[179] Those who hope to satisfy themselves with homes, cars, clothes, and acquisitions find that they need more, and bigger, acquisitions. Satisfaction remains elusive.[180]

Lawyers, Meaning and Pro Bono

One easy way lawyers can add meaning to our lives is by rendering pro bono legal services. There are at least six reasons why attorneys should provide some pro bono service, even if only a few hours a year.[181]

• **We, the lawyers, need it.** Work becomes meaningful when there is some service to someone at least some of the time. Pro bono cases, even a small one along the way, can give us meaning when the rest of our work does not. Pro bono cases are like salt—they savor everything else.

• **We can make a difference in someone's life, and with not that much effort on our part.** We become so accustomed to our lawyer skills that we forget that these are special skills that few people have. Our ability to think clearly allows us to navigate what is overwhelming to most folks. Whether it is saving someone's home from foreclosure, assisting someone who is being cheated by scoundrels, or just listening and offering advice about where to go next, lawyers have the ability to help people when they desperately need it.

• **Pro bono cases present ways to get practical experience.** Such experience is increasingly difficult for new lawyers to obtain as business clients refuse to pay for work by new lawyers and law firms opt for lateral hires instead of new lawyers. Directing one's own case, dealing with one's own client, negotiating with the other side, representing a client in court, winning and losing cases, satisfying a judgment are important skills that translate into every attorney's day-to-day career. Pro bono cases provide opportunities to learn these skills early in one's professional life, and often with the indulgence of judges and opposing counsel that is not always accorded new attorneys in paying cases. It is a rare opportunity to learn when your adversary and the judge are proud of what you are doing and are happy to help you along.

• **Pro bono cases are a great way to network.** As we all know, networking enriches our professional and private lives. Whether serving on bar committees, working on bar projects, or representing pro bono clients, these activities provide great ways to meet some of the best people in our profession. The most talented lawyers I have met throughout my career are those who regularly perform pro bono work. I'm not sure why this is. It may be that obtaining a pro bono case takes initiative, juggling it takes good organizational skills, and conducting it takes self-confidence, all of which are also characteristics of talented people. It may be that lawyers with these characteristics gravitate to pro bono cases. But whatever the reason, if you want to network with talented people, do pro bono.

• **Pro bono service is rewarding.** Imagine having a genuinely grateful client. For most pro bono clients, having their own lawyer is a miracle they never imagined. They appreciate their "miracle" in ways paying clients never can.

One of the privileges of my legal career has been pro bono service with the Alabama State Bar's Volunteer Lawyers Program (VLP). Most state bars have a similar program whereby attorneys volunteer a few hours of their time to assist underserved clients. One of my activities for a number of years has been to write brief articles about VLP cases. To conduct the research for each article I reviewed court files and visited with the lawyers who handled the case. I also visited clients in their homes as they told me about their case and the legal process they experienced.

I have visited clients who live on dirt roads deep in rural Alabama, large subsidized housing projects, metropolitan suburbs, and tiny homes in small, country towns. The gratitude these clients expressed for their VLP lawyers was overwhelming. You would think their attorneys were rock stars. Several had a framed picture of their attorney sitting alongside family photographs. One client, who had lived an incredibly tragic life, told me about her VLP attorney with a huge smile on her face, "The Lord's been good to me. He sent me Mr. Hutchinson."[182] Another client, 84 years old and bedridden, described her VLP attorney: "He is just beautiful."[183] A third client said, "They were hammering me down. I wouldn't have made it without Mr. Crosby" (her VLP attorney).[184]

Nothing compares to the gratitude of pro bono clients or the satisfaction of helping someone in dire need of legal assistance. As Brad Cornett, an Alabama VLP attorney, said,

> "If you're a professional, you have privileges. You should give something back. There is a satisfaction in doing good. It's different than your paying cases. It's satisfying to know you helped someone just because you could."[185]

• **Rendering pro bono service is the right thing to do.** As lawyers, we possess intelligence, determination, work ethic and social skills. We would not have made it through law school or survived in the practice of law if we did not.

Throughout our lives, we have been encouraged by people who believed in us, supported us, helped us, and picked us up when we have fallen. We have blessings in life that few have. Providing pro bono services is a way to give back.

Summary:
Why Render Pro Bono Service

- *We, the lawyers, need the meaning pro bono service gives us.*

- *We can make a difference in someone's life without much effort on our part.*

- *Especially for new lawyers, pro bono cases present terrific ways to get practical experience.*

- *Pro bono service is a great way to network.*

- *Pro bono clients are genuinely grateful, something we may not see as much in our paying clients.*

- *Pro bono service is a way of giving back.*

N. Nourish Your Willpower

Four-year olds and marshmallows put to rest any doubts about the value of willpower. Walter Mischel of Stanford University conducted a study in which four-year olds were brought into a room and given a choice of eating one marshmallow right away or two marshmallows if they waited a few minutes. Seventy percent of the children ate the marshmallow right away. The remaining thirty percent waited fifteen minutes and got to eat two marshmallows. Years later, when the four-year olds were in high school, they were contacted and reassessed. The high schoolers who had the willpower at age four to wait fifteen minutes for two marshmallows had better grades, higher SAT scores, were more popular, and did fewer drugs. The study's authors interpreted their results as follows: "The marshmallow-ignoring kids had self-regulatory skills that gave them an advantage throughout their lives."[186]

Willpower Exercised in One Area of Life Increases Our Ability to Exercise Willpower in Other Areas of Life

Two Australian scientists, Megan Oaten and Ken Cheng, studied the phenomenon of willpower.[187] They enrolled subjects in a physical exercise program that required the subjects to increase their physical training regularly throughout the program. The subjects who were able to increase their training the most also smoked fewer cigarettes, drank less alcohol, ate less junk food, did more homework, and watched less television during the study even though these activities were not part of the study's regime.[188]

To focus on whether it was increased willpower that helped the subjects reduce their unhealthy activities or a side benefit of the exercise, Oaten and Cheng set up a new study. They enrolled test subjects in a four-month financial management program. Participants established a budget and had to stick to it by denying themselves luxuries like eating out.[189] Again, the participants who succeeded the most, this time in managing their finances, were more successful than their less financially disciplined peers in the collateral behaviors of cutting back on cigarettes, alcohol, and junk food. The budget followers were also more productive at work and school.[190] Again, it appeared that the willpower exercised in one area spilled over to other areas of life.

In a third study, Oaten and Cheng enrolled students in an academic improvement program that required new study habits.[191] Once again, the participants who improved the most academically reduced their intake of cigarettes and alcohol, and exercised more and ate healthier, even though these behaviors were not part of the study.[192]

Charles Duhigg, who studies willpower, explains this "spill over" phenomenon: As our willpower muscles strengthen, good habits seem to spill over into other parts of our lives. "People get better at regulating their impulses. They learn how to distract themselves from temptations. And once you've gotten into that willpower groove, your brain is practiced at helping you focus on a goal."[193]

Like Other Muscles, Willpower Becomes Tired

Researchers conducting an experiment with radishes and cookies show how will power can become worn out. According to Mark Muraven, the research director, "Willpower isn't just a skill. It's a muscle, like the muscles in your arms or legs, and it gets tired as it works harder, so there's less power left over for other things."[194]

Muraven recruited subjects for what they thought was a study on perceptions. The subjects had been told to skip their meal prior to coming to the experiment and to come hungry. The subjects were placed one at a time in a room with a bowl of radishes and a bowl of hot chocolate chip cookies. One group of was told to eat the cookies and ignore the radishes. The other group was told to eat the radishes and ignore the cookies. According to Mulraven, the cookie-eaters "were in heaven" and the radish-eaters were "in agony."[195]

The researchers left the subjects alone with the radishes and cookies and watched them from a one-way mirror, then re-entered the room and asked the subjects to complete a puzzle.[196] Unknown to the subjects, the puzzle was impossible to solve. The researchers observed the subjects through the one-way mirror. The cookie-eaters worked on the puzzle an average of nineteen minutes before giving up. The radish-eaters worked on the puzzle an average of eight minutes before giving up. The researchers' conclusion: the radish-eaters who had already used up their willpower to resist the cookies were worn out when it came time to work the puzzle.[197] Muraven's advice: "If you want to do something that requires willpower—like going for a run after work—you have to conserve your willpower muscle during the day. If you use it up too early on tedious tasks like writing emails or filling out complicated and boring expense forms, all the strength will be gone by the time you get home."[198]

On the bright side, studies also show that willpower shows long-term improvement. The more we use it, the stronger it gets.[199]

Willpower Improves Whenever We Have a Plan, Especially if the Plan Is Written Down

A study of Scottish orthopedic patients demonstrates the value of making a plan to maintain willpower.[200] British researchers recruited sixty patients who had hip or knee replacement surgery to participate in a study on willpower.[201] Rehabilitation after hip or knee replacement surgery is crucial to achieve full post-operative recovery, but it is painful, difficult, and requires considerable self-discipline.[202] The sixty patients in the study were not good candidates for completing their post-operative rehabilitation. On average, they were elderly (sixty-eight years old), poor (most earned less than $10,000 per year), and relatively uneducated (most did not have more than a high school education).[203]

All sixty patients were given booklets with detailed descriptions of their rehabilitation schedule. Half of the patients were given thirteen additional, blank pages in their booklets to write out in detail their plan for completing each step of rehabilitation.[204] For example, one rehabilitation exercise was to walk a certain distance each day. One patient devised a plan to walk from his home to the bus stop when his wife arrived home after work, every day at 3:30 PM. In writing up his plan, the patient noted the time he would leave home to meet his wife's bus, which route he would walk, which coat he would wear if it was raining, and which pills to take with him if walking became painful.[205]

Three months later, there were striking differences in the patients who wrote out their plans for rehabilitation and those who did not. The plan writers started walking almost twice as soon as the non-writers. They got in and out of their chairs, unassisted, almost three times as fast. The plan writers were able to put on their shoes, do the laundry, and make their own meals much quicker than the non-writers.[206]

When the researchers examined the written plans, they found that the plan writers had focused on how they would handle specific moments of difficulty, such as pain. They detailed obstacles they expected to face.[207] For example, aware that rising from the couch was especially excruciating, one patient's plan was to take a step immediately upon rising from the couch so he would not be tempted to sit back down.[208] The plan writing patients anticipated specific hurdles they would face and listed specific steps for dealing with the hurdles. Comparing the plan-writers to the non-writers, the researchers concluded, "[T]he patients who didn't write out any plans were at a significant disadvantage, because they never thought ahead about how to deal with painful inflection points. They never deliberately designed willpower habits."[209]

O. Optimism

One characteristic of happy people is that they are optimists. They look on the bright side of life. Being an optimist is not being unrealistic, naive, or in denial of the true seriousness of things. As Seligman says, "Learned optimism . . . is about accuracy . . . for usually the negative beliefs that follow adversity are inaccurate."[210] Optimism is the ability to face a bad situation and still find silver linings, rays of hope, and ways to cope. Optimists encounter the same hardships and ill fortune as pessimists, but they are more resilient and bounce back.

All studies of optimists and pessimists show that optimists achieve more, enjoy life more, and have longer and healthier lives.[211] By comparison, pessimists get depressed easily, achieve less at work than they are capable, suffer more ill health, and do not find much pleasure in life.[212] "Even when things go well for the

> **A True Optimist**
>
> *"After I learned I had cancer, one of my doctors gave me some advice. 'It's important,' he said, 'to behave as if you're going to be around awhile.'*
>
> *"I was already way ahead of him. 'Doc, I just bought a new convertible and got a vasectomy. What more do you want from me?"*
>
> **Randy Pausch, The Last Lecture 120 (Hyperion 2008); (Upon being diagnosed with pancreatic cancer)**

pessimist, he is haunted by forebodings of catastrophe."[213]

Granted, there is a constructive side to pessimism. It "serves the purpose of pulling us back a bit from the risky exaggerations of our optimism, making us think twice, keeping us from making rash, foolhardy gestures."[214] We do not, however, want to become captives of pessimistic cycles or tendencies. We want to deploy pessimism only when it is useful.[215]

All of us experience both optimism and pessimism. They are habits of thought. Pessimists can learn to be optimists by learning new habits of thought, and optimists can slip into pessimism with depressing patterns of thought. Our habits of thought need not be forever. As Martin Seligman states, we "can choose the way we think."[216]

Seligman and others have spent years studying the traits of optimists and pessimists. They have found the following differences.

- **A sense of control.** Pessimists have a sense of helplessness. They believe nothing they do affects what happens to them.[217] Optimists have a sense of control over their lives.

- **Permanence.** Pessimists believe that the bad things that happen to them are permanent. They give up easily. Optimists believe bad things are temporary. They do not give up easily, but persevere through difficulties. When faced with a mistake, the pessimist thinks, "I'm all washed up." The optimist thinks, "I'm having a bad day."[218]

Conversely, pessimists believe good things are temporary while optimists believe that good things are permanent. When faced with a success, the pessimist thinks, "It was a fluke." The optimist thinks things will continue to work out.[219]

- **Pervasiveness.** Pessimists believe bad fortune permeates everything. Optimists believe bad fortune is only periodic. Seligman explains, "People who make *universal* explanations for their failures give up on everything when a failure strikes in one area. People who make *specific* explanations for a failure may become helpless in that one part of their lives yet "march stalwartly" on in the other aspects of their life."[220] When confronted with rejection, the pessimist thinks, "I'm repulsive." The optimist thinks "I'm repulsive to him."[221]

- **Personalization.** Pessimists blame themselves when faced with failures. Optimists are able to see when external events are at fault. Seligman explains: "People who blame themselves when they fail have low self-esteem as a consequence. They think they are worthless, talentless, and unlovable. People who allocate some or all blame to external events are more resilient and have more confidence in themselves."[222] When faced with rejection on a job application, the pessimist thinks, "I didn't get the job because I'm stupid." The optimist thinks, "I didn't get the job because they're looking for someone with more experience."[223]

- **Disputation.** Optimists are able to dispute negative thoughts. Disputation of pessimistic thinking is a learnable skill. Optimists distract themselves from difficulties by objectively looking at adversities, assessing their beliefs arising from the adversity, recognizing that their beliefs may not be an accurate assessment of the situation, and disputing their unfounded beliefs. This process builds the energy to address the adversity[224] (Section D).

P. Prepare[225]

Saturday, November 5, 2011, was homecoming at the University of Tennessee. The game was scheduled to start at 7:00 PM before 88,211 fans. Tennessee's starting kicker, Michael Palardy, pulled a leg muscle after practice the Thursday before the Saturday game but was expected to recover in time to play. During pre-game warm-ups on Saturday, however, it was clear that Palardy's leg had not recovered. He was benched. A few moments later, the second-string kicker, Chip Rhome, also warming up, pulled a muscle. He was benched. The third-string kicker, sophomore Derrick Brodus, was not at the stadium.[226] Brodus had checked the squad listing the day before the game. He was not listed and so did not suit up. Told that Brodus was not present, head coach Derrick Dooley said, "Get an APB out for Brodus." Dooley assumed his third-string kicker might be partying, and allegedly told his coaches, "An intoxicated Brodus is better than nobody. Get him in here and we'll do a breathalyzer."[227]

Brodus was Tennessee's third-string, walk-on, redshirted freshman kicker. He had suited up for only two University of Tennessee football games. He had never played a single down in a college football game. Brodus was sober on November 5, 2011. He was relaxing on his couch, watching football at his apartment.[228]

Brodus's cell phone rang. He did not recognize the number, so didn't answer. Seconds later, his phone rang again and Brodus answered, but the call was dropped. Brodus walked to the spot in his apartment where cell coverage was better. This time, the call came through. It was the University of Tennessee Director of Football Operations, Brad Pendergrass, who, according to Pendergrass, "made thirty-six phone calls" before reaching Brodus. Pendergrass explained the situation and told Brodus he was needed, in the stadium, suited up, by 7:00 PM. It was 6:10 PM.

One of Brodus's roommates and a friend from high school, Daniel Sullivan, asked what was up. Brodus said, "I can't believe it. They said they need a kicker and need me to get to the stadium as fast as I can." They loaded into Sullivan's car and left for the stadium. In the car, darting through traffic, Sullivan asked Brodus, "What do you need to get your mind right? Music? UT pre-game?" Brodus called his mother.[229]

Brodus and Sullivan saw an unmarked police car with blue lights flashing coming their way. Pendergrass had sent it to escort Brodus to the stadium. Brodus jumped out of Sullivan's car and into the police car which then wove from lane to lane through heavy game-day traffic, lights flashing, siren blaring. When the police car arrived at the stadium, the tailgating and foot traffic was too dense for the car to continue. Brodus jumped out and ran through the crowds to the locker room.[230]

When he arrived at the locker room, Brodus's teammates, doubled over in laughter, were waiting for him. As Brodus ran in, they started a slow clap and shouted, "Bro-dus, Bro-dus, Bro-dus." One trainer helped Brodus get his pads and uniform on while another helped him stretch and warm up. Brodus made it out on the field with the team. Kickoff was at 7:08 PM. During the game, Brodus made all three of his extra points and kicked a 21-yard field goal. Tennessee won the game, 24–0.[231]

Why Is This Story in a Law Book?

Because it offers five lessons about preparation.

• **Maintain your skills.** Derrick Brodus was a two-time, all-state, soccer player in high school as well as a three-year, high school football letterman. Although he had college athletic scholarship offers, Brodus chose to come to the University of Tennessee and "be a regular student." After his freshman year at UT, Brodus realized that playing on an intramural soccer team wasn't enough competition for him. He tried out for the University of Tennessee football team and made it. Despite being third-string with little likelihood of playing, Brodus worked hard in practices, completing the same number of practice kicks as the first and second-string players. Brodus was prepared when his challenge came.

• **Nourish your support system of family and friends.** Brodus's friend drove him to the stadium and was supportive, asking, "What do you need?" "Are you OK, man?" Brodus's friend helped him get what he needed—a ride. Brodus talked with his parents while his friend drove him to the stadium. His parents gave him encouragement, reminding him how he had handled other challenges well. Brodus's support system was there for him, in a crunch, on short notice, and when pressure hit because Brodus had been attentive to those relationships day in and day out. Brodus had built up his psychological capital (Section D).

• **Rely on professional help when you need it.** Brodus needed experts to do what he could not do himself. He needed the police, with their blue lights and siren, to get to the stadium. When you need experts, such as a therapist, psychiatrist, tutor, plumber, or whatever, seek them out.

• **Do not let fear grip you.** Although Brodus thought to himself, "What's going to happen to me if I kick this out?" he persevered. As his teammate, University of Tennessee tight end Mychal Rivera told reporters, "Coming off the couch, man. That's awesome . . . our kicker got hurt and I turned around, and Brodus is running in to save the day. I don't know if I'd have taken the call. I really don't, but he did, and he was clutch. It says a lot about him."[232]

• **Do what you love.** Derrick Brodus missed competitive sports and took steps to get it back into his life. He was willing to accept competitive sports on terms that were available to him. In high school, Brodus had been a soccer and football star. On his intramural team at the University of Tennessee, he had been a star, kicking four goals in one game. But on the University of Tennessee football team, he was third string. He was not listed on the team's depth chart. He was not asked to be at most games. Brodus's job on the football team was to support the first and second string kickers. Brodus accepted this. He did not let pride get in the way of doing what he loved.

Derrick Brodus's story reminds us what we need to do to prepare for the inevitable stormy seas that we will encounter: Maintain our skills. Nurture, and rely on, our support systems. Turn to professional help when we need it. Don't let fear get the best of us. Keep what we love in our life.

Q. Quotient—Increase Positive Emotions, Decrease Negative Emotions

Negative emotions such as fear, sadness, and anger are important to survival. Fear warns us to protect ourselves. Sadness keeps us quiet and still so we can grieve and heal from traumas. Anger protects us against those who could hurt us.[233] Negative emotions alert us that something is awry.[234] However, once negative emotions have served their constructive purpose, we need to let them go. The key is to recognize when they have served their purpose and do not allow them to intrude in our lives.

Letting go of negative emotions is easier said than done. Negative emotions are rewarding, even if in unhealthy ways. As Frederick Buechner says of anger, "Of the seven deadly sins, anger is possibly the most fun. To lick your wounds, to smack your lips over grievances long past, to roll your tongue over the prospect of bitter confrontations to come, to savor to the last toothsome morsel of both the pain you are given and the pain you are giving back—in many ways it is a feast fit for a king."[235] Guilt and remorse, other negative emotions, keep us "center stage" in our internal dramas. They give us an excuse not to venture forth into the world where we might make more mistakes, or get hurt again.

Positive emotions such as good cheer, tolerance, creativity, and joy, enhance our lives.[236] As a practical matter, increasing our ratio of positive emotions to negative emotions increases our happiness and contentment, and makes our lives easier and more successful (Sections H, L, and O). As Martin Seligman states: "[F]eeling positive emotion is important, not just because it is pleasant in its own right, but because it *causes* much better commerce with the world. Developing more positive emotion in our lives will build friendship, love, better physical health, and greater achievement."[237]

Whereas our "set point" of happiness is hard-wired (Section H), our ability to develop positive affectivity is not. As David

Watson, professor at the University of Iowa, explains, "[U]nless a person already has reached his or her maximum phenotypic value (a condition that should occur rarely, if at all), it should be possible to increase positive affectivity significantly, regardless of whether one was born 'three drinks behind' or 'three drinks ahead.' "[238]

The following are specific, learnable behaviors that increase positive emotions and decrease negative emotions.[239]

• **Positive emotions can "undo" negative emotions.**[240] Experiments conducted by Barbara Fredrickson of the University of North Carolina, Chapel Hill, demonstrate how positive emotions can override negative emotions. Fredrickson created negative emotions of fear and stress in students by showing them a terrifying movie clip of a man on the ledge of a high rise city building who loses his grip and dangles above traffic. Heart rate monitors confirmed that the students experienced fear and stress while watching this movie clip. The students were then divided into four groups and shown four different film clips: ocean waves; cute puppies; a pile of sticks; and a person crying. The film clips of relaxing waves and cute puppies brought down the heart rate of the two groups shown these clips. The film of a pile of sticks did nothing to change students' heart rate. The film of a crying woman increased the students' negative emotions and increased their already high heart rates.[241]

• **Take care of your body.** A second measurable way to increase positive affectivity is to take care of your body, specifically, by getting enough sleep and exercise.[242] Sleep deprivation cripples thinking, including the ability to marshal positive emotions (Section T). Exercise releases hormones essential to our mental health. These hormones make us happier and more energetic.[243] Watson notes that "positive affect is more related to action than to thought, so that it is easier to induce a state of high positive affect through *doing* than *thinking*."[244] Exercise is "doing," and thus, one way to increase positive affectivity (Section T).

• **Reframe.** A third strategy to increase positive affectivity is to reframe how we view past experiences. As John Claypool notes, "We do not have the power to go back and undo or redo the past, but we do have the ability to 're-perceive' the past and decide what meaning we will assign to those events for the present and future."[245] This does not mean avoiding, denying, or minimizing past hurts. We must face our past experiences honestly and accurately to grieve, and to learn from mistakes. Re-perceiving the past means we do not carry bitterness with us. We focus on the positive aspects of our past such as satisfaction, contentment, fulfillment, pride and serenity.[246] Sometimes the only positive aspect of our past is that it is past; it is over (Sections E, R).

• **Socialize.** A fourth strategy to increase positive affectivity is to socialize. As Watson notes, "high levels of positive mood are most likely when a person is focused outward and is actively engaging the environment."[247]

• **Goals.** A fifth strategy to increase positive affectivity is to make and strive after goals. As Watson notes, "[T]he process of striving after goals—rather than goal attainment per se—is crucial for happiness and positive affectivity."[248] (Sections G, M).

• **Pay Attention to Your Circadian Rhythm.** The sixth strategy to increase positive affectivity is to understand your circadian rhythm. Circadian rhythms are physical, mental, and behavioral patterns that follow a roughly 24-hour cycle. As Watson notes, "Those who attempt to perform complex tasks during their naturally occurring low points in their circadian rhythm are likely to feel frustrated and incompetent because they lack the physical and mental resources to tackle them efficiently."[249] He explains, "[B]y monitoring our moods and becoming more sensitive to our own internal rhythms, we are able to maximize feelings of efficacy and enjoyment and minimize stress and frustration."[250]

———————

R. Reframe

Just as we transform a painting by reframing it, we transform a situation by reframing the way we look at it. We do not always have a choice about the circumstances, situations, crises, or difficult individuals we encounter, but we do have a choice about how we think about them. Controlling our emotional reaction to difficulties gives us control over situations. Studies of "stress-hardy" individuals, those who handle stress well, show the importance of a sense of control. A key characteristic of stress-hardiness is a greater sense of control, including the ability to interpret and appraise situations, thereby "deactivat[ing] their jarring effects"[251] (Section U).

Disaster Strikes:
A Law Firm Dissolves

Assume you are a three-year associate at a law firm. You go to work one day to learn that your firm is dissolving. The two firm partners, who have been in conflict for years over who brings in the most business, works the longest hours, and contributes more to the equity of the firm, have decided to go their separate ways. The business manager breaks the news to you. Neither partner is currently in the office.

You are taken aback. You did not realize the seriousness of the partners' disputes. You have not been included in any transition plans. You are angry that your years of loyalty and hard work are for naught. You feel that the partners have treated you disrespectfully by not telling you personally of their plans. Just a few months ago, one of your friends confidentially inquired whether you would be interested in joining her firm. Her firm is growing and one of her partners asked her to inquire discretely about your availability. You did not pursue the matter because of *your* loyalty to your current firm. You are worried. Your friend's firm has hired a new lawyer so that firm is no longer an available option. You know of no firms hiring. Panic sets in. Now, you'll be looking for a job as a laid-off, desperate lawyer, not a sought-after catch. And the bills you have! School loans, a mortgage, car payment. You are mad, and scared.

How to Reframe?

Maybe, you tell yourself, the two partners are not just tossing you out. Just because they are not in the office this morning and have not spoken to you doesn't mean they have no plans for you. Maybe it is simply too awkward for them to be in the office when the news is announced. Maybe they're both busy dealing with the issues of dissolving their partnership—finding new office space, talking to clients, obtaining bank loans. Maybe they *both* would like you to come with them but want to leave the decision to you. Maybe they're so busy they just haven't had time, yet, this morning to talk with you. You start thinking, given the choice, what would *you* like to do? Would you like to remain with one of the partners? Would you like to go out on your own? Setting up your own practice has always been your goal, you just didn't expect to do so now. Maybe your friend's law firm still needs an additional lawyer. She did say that her firm's business was growing rapidly.

You come up with a plan. You decide that if it is an option, you would like to be in practice with Partner A. He is a kind person and has been a great mentor to you. You have worked the most with him and you like the type of cases he handles. Partner A is about twenty years older than Partner B, and you know from casual conversations with Partner A that he is hoping to scale back his practice soon. With the benefit of hindsight, you can see that Partner A's preference to cut back may be one of the sources of tension between him and Partner B, a hard-charging personality who is always seeking new clients and talking about expanding the firm. In fact, you realize, if you are in practice with Partner A, he may turn clients over to you as he winds down. You decide you will approach Partner A and tell him of your interest in going with him. You draft an email to Partner A.

By reframing the situation, this third-year associate has gotten control of his emotions. He has not let his emotions prevent him from thinking rationally about his situation. He has come up with options for dealing with the situation, evaluated his options, and come up with plan for pursuing his top choice.

S. Know Your Strengths. Use Them.

In life as in cards, we should play to our long suit. Studies show that happy people use their strengths. The Gallup Organization's study of millions of people in over one-hundred countries show that "people who have the opportunity to focus on their strengths every day are six times as likely to be engaged in their jobs and more than three times as likely to report having an excellent quality of life in general."[252]

It feels good to do something well. From his studies of happy people, Seligman concludes: "We feel elevated and inspired when we use our strengths."[253] Gallup's studies further show that once we are aware of our "lesser talents," our successes in life come more from focusing on our strengths rather than improving on our weaknesses.[254] Doing well at a task builds a positive self-image.[255]

Flow

One measure of whether we are using our strengths is whether we are "in the flow."[256] "Flow," a phenomenon studied by Mihaly Csikszentmihalyi of the University of Chicago, occurs when we "are so involved in an activity that nothing else seems to matter; the experience is so enjoyable that [we] do it . . . for the sheer sake of doing it."[257] Csikszentmihalyi studied athletes, musicians, chess players and ordinary people, looking for the common characteristics of joyful activities.[258] From these studies, he identified the following characteristics of "flow":

- **We use our skills.**[259] This is why many of us find flow in our work. According to Csikszentmihalyi, "[W]orking people achieve the flow experience—deep concentration, high and balanced challenges and skills, a sense of control and satisfaction—about four times as often on their jobs, proportionately, as they do when they are watching television."[260]

- **We concentrate on what we are doing.**[261] Csikszentmihalyi quotes a dancer: "My concentration is very complete. My mind isn't wandering. I am not thinking of something else. I am totally involved in what I am doing. My energy is flowing very smoothly. I feel relaxed, comfortable, and energetic."[262]

• **Our task has clear goals**[263] **that originate within us.**[264] For example, a tennis player knows she must return a tennis ball hit by her opponent and keep it within the lines.[265] These are clear goals. When goals are vague (*i.e.*, a new summer associates wants to "do a good job"), individuals "must develop a strong personal sense of what to do to meet the goal."[266] (Meet and visit with all lawyers and staff in the office, work hard, seek out new assignments, etc.) (Section G).

• **Our task provides immediate feedback.**[267] According to Csikszentmihalyi, "[a]lmost any kind of feedback can be enjoyable, provided it is logically related to a goal in which one has invested . . . energy."[268]

• **We stop thinking of our cares and worries of everyday life.**[269] Again, a dancer describes it best: "Dance is like therapy. If I am troubled about something, I leave it out of the door as I go in the dance studio."[270]

• **We have a sense of control over our actions.**[271] Csikszentmihalyi's studies of individuals enjoying flow experiences show that these individuals are not *actually* in control (the ballet dancer may fail to make the perfect turn, or could fall), but rather, have "the sense of *exercising* control in difficult situations."[272] A sense of control is essential to optimism (Section O), a key ingredient of happiness (Section H), essential to stress hardiness (Section U), and enjoying one's work (Section W).

• **Our sense of time is altered.** When we are in the flow, hours pass in what seem like minutes, or minutes seem to last hours.[273] A rock climber describes his state of mind when climbing: "It is as if my memory input has been cut off. All I can remember is the last thirty seconds, and all I can think ahead is the next five minutes."[274]

Summary: "Flow"

- *Requires us to use our skills.*

- *Requires us to concentrate.*

- *Focuses on clear goals that originate with us.*

- *Provides immediate feedback.*

- *Allows us to stop thinking of our everyday cares.*

- *Provides a sense of control.*

- *Sense of time stands still.*

T. Take Care of Your Body. You Have Only One.

We all know the basics. Don't overeat. Don't smoke. Don't drink to excess. Eat healthy foods. Exercise. This section focuses on two of these basics: sleep and exercise. Given the sedentary work of most lawyers and the long hours many lawyers work, these are probably the most difficult issues for many lawyers. Maladaptive ways of attempting to deal with stress create health problems; these are addressed in the section on understanding stress (Section U).

Sleep

Sleep deprivation makes our brains malfunction. As John Medina, author of *Brain Rules*, summarizes: "Sleep loss cripples thinking in just about every way you can measure thinking. Sleep loss hurts attention, executive function, immediate memory, working memory, mood, quantitative skills, logical reasoning ability, general math knowledge. Eventually, sleep loss affects manual dexterity . . . and even gross motor movements, such as the ability to walk on a treadmill.[275] Sleep deprivation also causes irritability, forgetfulness, and physical ailments like nausea and headaches.[276] Sleep deprivation is linked to mental health problems including depression, anxiety, and psychosis."[277]

Internal Clocks

Our bodies have an internal clock, the "supra chiasmatic nucleus," which is located in the hypothalamus of our brains. This nucleus contains a timing device for sleep[278] and is why some of us wake up early in the morning, are most productive in the mornings, and fade at night (larks, or "early chronotypes"). About ten percent of us are larks. Some of us wake up late in the morning, are most productive late at night, and do not tire until very late at night or in the early morning hours (owls, "late chronotypes"). About twenty percent of us are owls. Owls tend to be sleep deprived throughout life. The rest of us are "hummingbirds," and while we may gravitate to one end or the other of the spectrum, we can operate optimally with flexibility in our sleep schedules.[279]

> *"One study followed soldiers responsible for operating complex military hardware. One night's loss of sleep resulted in a 30% loss in overall cognitive skill. . . . If they lose two nights, they lose 60%.*
>
> Tal Ben-Shahar, *Happier* 99 (McGraw Hill 2007)

The circadian rhythm of our body temperature determines our chronotype. Our body temperatures fluctuate by about one-half of one degree in each direction in a twenty-four hour cycle. The low point in this cycle for most people is 5:30 AM. Larks' minimum temperature occurs around 4:30 AM, and owls' occurs around 7:00 AM.[280]

How Much Sleep Do We Need?

Different people need different amounts of sleep. Just as we do not expect everyone to wear the same size shoe, we should not expect everyone to need the same amount of sleep. Most of us need between seven and seven and one-half hours per night. A few of us need nine to ten hours. A few of us (those with "healthy insomnia") need only four or five hours per night.[281] Our sleep needs will vary with age, gender, and pregnancy.[282] Seven to seven and one-half hours of sleep per twenty-four hour cycle is about average for mammals. Horses need three hours, cows and elephants need four hours, rabbits need eight hours, and bats need nineteen hours.[283]

Naps . . . Really?

Naps, the right kind of naps, are an important part of good sleep health.[284] There is a "nap zone" for most of us. As Medina explains: There is "a period of time in the midafternoon when we experience transient sleepiness. It can be nearly impossible to get anything done during this time, and if you attempt to push through, which is what most of us do, you can spend much of your afternoon fighting a gnawing tiredness. It's a fight because the brain really wants to take a nap and doesn't care what its owner is doing."[285] Studies confirm that we get vitality from naps, particularly in cognitive performance.[286] NASA pilots, for example, improved performance by more than thirty-four percent after a 26-minute nap.[287]

Exercise

Most lawyers sit too much. Our bodies were built to move. Exercise reduces our risk for heart disease, stroke, diabetes, cancer and arthritis.[288] It improves our muscle strength, delivers oxygen to our tissues, boosts our endurance, and gives us more energy. Exercise helps us fall asleep faster and deeper, enhancing the quality of our sleep.[289]

Exercise improves our mental health. For example, "One study of female depressed students at the University of Kansas divided the women into three groups, one was left untreated, another practiced relaxation techniques and the third engaged in regular aerobic exercise. The first

> *"One simple but effective treatment for the ordinary blahs or blues is physical exercise."*
>
> **David Lykken, Happiness: The Nature and Nurture of Joy and Contentment 24 (St Martin's Griffin 2000)**

group saw no improvement, the second group showed mild improvement, the third group showed dramatic improvement."[290]

Exercise reduces stress hormones by releasing more of the three neurotransmitters most commonly associated with the maintenance of mental health: serotonin, dopamine, and norepinephrine. Studies have shown that "burning off 350 calories three times a week through sustained, sweat-inducing activity can reduce symptoms of depression about as effectively as antidepressants."[291] Exercise stimulates the growth of neurons in brain regions damaged by depression.[292] It increases production of the protein "BDNF" which helps our bodies fight the physical damage of an overabundance of stress hormones, adrenalin and cortisol.[293] Exercise is beneficial immediately and over the long term for both depression and anxiety, and is equally effective for men and women.[294] Scientists studying the impact of exercise on depression conclude that exercise is "astonishingly successful."[295]

Exercise is good for our brains. It is "cognitive candy."[296] Working out, especially between the ages of twenty-five and forty-five, increases the neuropathways in the hippocampus of our brains. These neuropathways are key to memory and learning.[297] Complicated activities, like playing tennis or taking a dance class, which engage our brain as well as our body, give the biggest brain boost.[298] Exercise has a long-term impact on cognition. Our lifetime risk for general dementia is cut in half if we participate in leisure-time physical activity, and cut the risk of Alzheimer's by more than sixty percent.[299] As John Ratey of Harvard Medical School states: "Exercise is the single best thing you can do for your brain in terms of mood, memory and learning."[300]

U. Understand Stress. Become "Stress-Hardy"

Stress is any "life event that causes changes in, and demands readjustment of a person's routine."[301] Lawyers experience a lot of stress. In part, this is due to the opportunities lawyers have. Studies show that stress increases with increasing opportunities and resources.[302] Compared to most people, lawyers have many opportunities in life and many resources. What lawyers do matters. When we impact people's lives, we feel stress. Lawyers also feel stress because of our lifestyle. Most lawyers don't have enough time for work or for personal lives. Feeling rushed most of the time creates stress.

When psychologists need a control group of stressed individuals, they often study lawyers.[303] Interestingly, they do so not just because lawyers experience stress but also because lawyers are perceived as "thriving" under stress, as remaining "clear-headed, in control, shrewd, and calm throughout it all."[304]

In every study of stress, including of lawyers, a percentage of those experiencing stress are "stress-hardy." These individuals have developed strategies and habits for dealing with stress so that they do not experience stress as intensely or unhealthily as the rest of us. These strategies and habits are identifiable and learnable.

The Body's Response to Stress

Our body's stress response is amazingly effective—if we have to run away from a lion. When we sense danger, our adrenal glands, located above our kidneys, shoot hormones, adrenaline followed by cortisol, throughout our bodies. The adrenaline increases our heart rate and blood pressure, pumping oxygen-rich blood to our large muscles so we can run faster. Our blood flow increases 300–400% when we experience a stress response. Our digestive system shuts down, diverting blood to our large muscles. Blood flows away from our skin toward our large muscles and brain, making us less sensitive to pain and causing us to bleed less if the lion claws us. Our spleen discharges more red and white blood cells, allowing our blood to transport more oxygen throughout our body. Adrenaline in our pancreas, liver, muscles, and fatty tissues inhibits our production of insulin and stimulates the synthesis of sugar and fat to give us quick energy.[305]

Adrenaline

Adrenaline causes our brains to release "neuropeptide S." This increases our alertness and anxiety (anxiety helps give us a sense of urgency to run away). We suppress activity in the areas at the front of our brain that control short-term and long-term memory, concentration, inhibitions and rational thought so to intensify our ability to react quickly to immediate stimuli.[306]

Although essential to survival in the past, our biological stress response is *not* well suited to today's world. Our bodies can tolerate only minutes of adrenaline-pumping stress before damage sets in. Today, our stresses last days, months, and years. We sit in traffic jams. We have demanding work schedules. We juggle crying toddlers, deal with rebellious teenagers, care for aging parents, and worry about inadequate retirement accounts. We don't get enough sleep. We experience chronic stress. When our stress response lasts only a few minutes, our bodies return to normal functioning by releasing tranquilizing chemicals that turn off adrenaline and cortisol. With chronic stress, this tranquilizing mechanism is not activated. Our bodies keep pumping adrenaline and cortisol.[307]

Chronic Stress

Chronic stress does "nasty" things to our bodies.[308] Prolonged rushes of adrenaline scar our blood vessels. Cortisol constricts our blood vessels. The "sticky stuff" in our blood adheres to these scars in our constricted arteries, and we get clogged arteries.[309] Cortisol in small quantities enhances our immune response, helping us heal more quickly if the lion claws us. Prolonged elevated levels of cortisol, however, suppress our immune system.[310] Individuals with chronic stress are three times more likely to get colds and suffer from autoimmune diseases like asthma and diabetes.[311] Because our digestive system shuts down during times of stress, those of us who experience chronic stress get peptic ulcers. Because blood flow is diverted from our skin, those who experience chronic stress get skin disorders.

Chronic stress makes us depressed. Here's why. Our bodies make the adrenaline we need from dopamine, which is present in our bodies. Dopamine regulates our moods and gives us feelings of happiness and pleasure. Dopamine is "cerebral joy-juice."[312] As David Watson describes, the "dopaminergic system arises from cell groups in the midbrain and plays a key role in positive affectivity."[313] An imbalance in dopamine causes depression. When we use up our dopamine to make adrenaline, which we do when under stress, we have less of the "joy juice" we need to make us happy.

Stress and Cognition

Chronic stress impairs our cognitive ability. Elevated levels of cortisol damage the hippocampus of the brain, which governs short-term and long-term memory and cognitive function. Adults with high stress levels perform fifty percent worse on cognitive tests when they are under stress.[314] Rats with raised cortisol levels are unable to find their way through mazes they easily traversed before their cortisol levels were raised. Chronic stress injures our brains in the long term. Chronically elevated cortisol levels cause our brain's hippocampus to shrink. A shrunken hippocampus correlates with the onset of Alzheimer's disease.

Stress as a Cycle

Chronic stress becomes a cycle. Our hippocampus is designed to signal our bodies to stop producing cortisol, but elevated cortisol levels present during chronic stress prevent our hippocampus from sending this shut-down signal. We become locked in a destructive cycle.

If we do not have healthy ways of releasing our stress, we develop maladapative ways of handling stress including denial, workaholism, busyness, and overindulgence in alcohol, food, and drugs.

Not Sure If You're Stressed?
Here Are the Clues:

- *"Tight neck or jaw muscles*
- *Tight shoulders or back*
- *Jutted-out chin*
- *Gritting or grinding of teeth*
- *Tight, strained voice*
- *Hunched shoulders*
- *Tightly curled toes or fingers*

- *Drumming with fingers*
- *Foot tapping, legs constantly in motion*
- *Rigid spine*
- *Tight forehead muscles, sometimes with a headache*
- *Sweating hands, feet or armpits*
- *Irritability, overreacting to small things*
- *Frowning*
- *High pulse rate, heart pounding rapidly*
- *Brusque, jerky movements with muscles tight or braced*
- *Irregular, shallow breathing or sighing*
- *Feeling of suffocation*
- *Nervous stomach, cramping or nausea*
- *Urinating frequently*
- *Smoking intensely*
- *Fluttering eyes or eyestrain."* [315]

Stress Hardiness: Dealing with Stress

Studies of those who are "stress-hardy," including studies of stress-hardy lawyers, show that these individuals have developed strategies for dealing with stress. Stress-hardy individuals are those who experience stress without adverse health effects. These individuals "have a personality structure differentiating them from persons who become sick under stress."[316]

Characteristics of "Stress-Hardy" Individuals

• **Sense of Control.** Stress hardy individuals have a sense of control over what occurs in their lives, including "decisional" control ("choosing among various courses of action")[317] and "cognitive" control ("the ability to interpret, appraise 'situations deactivating their jarring effects' ").[318]

- **Coping Skills.** Stress hardy individuals have positive coping skills,[319] including specific behaviors to resolve stressful situations (Section C). They view difficulties in life as opportunities for personal growth (Sections H, L, O, Q). Stress-hardy individuals do not use maladaptive coping strategies or engage in "regressive" coping skills, such as attempts to avoid the stressful situation.

- **Sense of Purpose.** Stress-hardy individuals have a strong sense of purpose. They believe in the importance of what they are doing."[320] Their sense of purpose provides a context in which to place the stressful events (Section G). This finding is consistent with studies that show individuals who find meaning in their lives are happier, healthier and more productive (Section M).

- **Commitment to Oneself.** Stress-hardy individuals have a commitment to oneself.[321] They have an ability to recognize their "distinctive values, goals, and priorities and an appreciation of [their] capacity to have purpose and to make decisions. . . .[322] (Section S).

- **Flexible.** Stress-hardy individuals "value a life filled with interesting experiences. They welcome change, and are 'cognitively flexible' "[323] (Section Q). This flexibility "allows them to integrate and effectively appraise the threat of new situations."[324]

As lawyers, we are fortunate that our chosen profession provides ingredients for stress-hardiness. Unlike some jobs, being a lawyer provides us opportunities for exercising decisional and cognitive control, purpose, and constant change. As noted, "increasing levels of stress tend to coincide with increasing opportunities and potential resources."[325] Lawyers have exceptional opportunities to engage in significant, meaningful, complex, and creative work. Lawyers also have significant resources to deploy, including intelligence, communication skills, training, and ambition. Psychologists have determined that life's "best moments" "occur when a person's body or mind is stretched to its limits in a voluntary effort to accomplish something difficult and worthwhile."[326] Lawyers have opportunities for many "best moments."

V. Value of Hard Knocks

"You're not bleeding."

That was about the only positive thing that could be said.

It was my second trial. I was in federal court as a new Assistant United States Attorney. As proof of the adage, "We don't know what we don't know," I thought I was prepared. I had worked for weeks preparing my case, logging hundreds of hours. I had reviewed, re-marked, and re-reviewed all of my exhibits. My witnesses were worn down from the many trial-preparation conferences I had forced upon them. I had researched every issue I could think of and consulted every lawyer in my office for tips and advice. I had left no stone unturned. Or so I thought.

It was a short trial, a simple fraud prosecution that was expected to last only days. On the second day of the trial, I was conducting the direct examination of a custodian of records. It was approaching noon, and the judge was on a tight schedule. He had set a hearing on a contentious, emergency motion involving a large commercial bankruptcy case for the noon recess in our jury trial. Shortly before noon, the courtroom filled with dozens of lawyers arriving for the hearing. I saw a few familiar faces from law school. I was proud to be trying a case, in federal court, by myself.

At the podium, with my stack of exhibits, I plodded onward, showing each document, one by one, to the witness. I was concentrating hard on asking each necessary foundation question before asking questions that tied the document to the case and, I hoped, pulled my case together. I was oblivious to the judge's impatience. Finally, the judge could stand it no longer. "Counselor!" he yelled at me. "March yourself out of my courtroom and upstairs." The U.S. Attorney's office was one floor above his courtroom. Red-faced with fury, the judge boomed at me, "Find a LAWYER who knows how to try cases. Do not come back to my courtroom until YOU do."

I tried not to cry. Mumbling, "Yes, your Honor," I slunk out of the courtroom. I couldn't look at the jury or the lawyers in the rows as I walked out. It was the longest walk of my life. I was grateful for one thing: I had not left a puddle on the floor.

One suited spectator rose and followed me out of the courtroom. I was afraid it was a former law school classmate. I was humiliated. The last person I wanted to see was a law school colleague. However, the person who walked out was my friend, Kevin, a twenty-year veteran federal prosecutor. Kevin was a Department of Justice superstar who had started his career at DOJ headquarters in Washington D.C., specializing in organized crime prosecutions. Our offices were next to each other and in the few months I had been an AUSA, Kevin had mentored and guided me. My despair was now complete. My whole office would know of my catastrophe. I had not just humiliated myself, I had humiliated everyone in my office. I hung my head. I did not belong in a U.S. Attorney's office.

"Well, *now* you can be a trial lawyer," Kevin said, cheerily. My body shaking, I could not comprehend his words.

I croaked, "I guess I better go up and resign."

"No," Kevin calmly repeated, "*Now* you can be a trial lawyer." He continued, "We all have to go through this. Being yelled at. Doing something dumb in front of God and everyone. It's the only way to become fearless. You have to be fearless to be a trial lawyer or you cannot do the job. You have to experience the worst thing possible and see that it's not the end of the world. You have to see that you can handle it. You have been yelled at by a federal judge. But that's it. You are not bleeding."

Lips trembling, I could only look at the ground.

"Hold your head up," Kevin commanded. "Go back into the courtroom this afternoon. This is your case. Try it. When the trial is over, make an appointment to see the judge, apologize, and ask his advice on how to get exhibits into evidence."

Almost forty years after that incident, I still shiver when I think about it. But Kevin was right. I had a lot to learn about being a trial lawyer, beginning with a more efficient way to handle exhibits. I went back into court that afternoon. I finished trying the case. If anything, the jury seemed to be more on my side after the judge's tirade. Over the years, several of the lawyers who were in the courtroom and observed my spectacle made a point of telling me how scary the incident had been and congratulated me on not totally losing it. I will always appreciate their kind sympathy. I hope I have passed their kindness on to others in similar need. I met with the judge after the trial. He could not have been nicer (I think he must have felt guilty). He gave me good tips on how to handle documents more efficiently. Routinely, over the next five years he would send some poor quaking lawyer he had just yelled at to me "to learn how to do documents." When I left DOJ for academia years later, the judge was one of my references.

This experience, although painful, was a "high" leverage learning opportunity (See Chapter IV (5)(A)(iv)). Here are the lessons it taught me.

• **Steep learning curve.** We are on a steep learning curve at the beginning of our careers, especially in a complicated and sophisticated career like law. We will make mistakes. It's inevitable and it's okay.

• **Learn from mistakes.** Making mistakes, and learning from them, is the only way we can become good, experienced attorneys. If we insulate ourselves from opportunities to make mistakes, we never grow professionally. Learning from our mistakes is one way to maintain resilience (Section C), and increase our happiness (Section H), luck (Section L) and optimism (Section O), and decrease our stress (Section U).

• **Don't get discouraged.** When you make horrible, terrifying mistakes, and you may, don't quit.

• **Help others.** Reach out to others when they make mistakes. They need a kind word.

• **Mentors.** Do all you can to surround yourself with friends and mentors who know more than you do and will share what they know with you (See Chapter IV (2)(A)(i); IV (3)(B); IV (5)(A)(vii)).

• **Law school isn't the real world.** Appreciate the value of real world experience. I thought I knew how to get exhibits into evidence. I did it in court exactly as I had learned in law school. I would have made an "A" if I were in an evidence class. But the real world of practicing law is light years away from law school. Do all you can while in law school to get exposure to the real world of practicing law. It will give you a leg up.

• **Don't give up.** No matter what happens, hold your head up and get back on the horse.

W. Work

Studies by industrial psychologists show that we experience meaning in our work if three conditions are met: (1) We have some control over our jobs. (2) Our job enhances a positive self-image. (3) Our work provides connection to other people.[327] If these needs are not initially met, successful workers engage in "job crafting" to meet them. They "chang[e] the cognitive, task, and/or relational boundaries to shape interactions and relationships with others at work."[328] A public defender, for example, changes the cognitive boundaries of her job by viewing it as "protecting the constitutional rights of all citizens to a fair trial," not "helping criminals avoid condemnation."[329] A chef changes the task of food preparation by valuing the "presentation" of the food he prepares.[330] Hairdressers reshape the boundaries of their work by building personal friendships with clients, not just fixing hair.[331]

"Job Crafting"

A study of hospital workers demonstrates use of "job crafting" strategies. Hospital custodians were divided into two groups, those who described their job as meaningful and those who did not. All workers had the same prescribed duties. The daily habits of the workers in each group were observed. Those who did not find their job to be meaningful did only the necessary tasks and interacted with as few people as possible.

Those who described their work as meaningful frequently interacted with others ranging from patients to vistors to nurses. They expanded their duties beyond their prescribed tasks of cleaning rooms, such as inquiring if patients or hospital visitors needed help or directions.

The workers in the first group who did not enjoy their jobs, "disliked cleaning in general, judged the skill level of the work to be low, and were less willing to step outside formal job boundaries to engage with others and alter job tasks."[332] The workers in this group "restricted the meaning of the work to being simply about cleaning and did not see themselves as anything other than room cleaners."[333]

By contrast, the workers in the group which enjoyed their jobs, "liked the job, enjoyed cleaning, felt the work was highly skilled, and engaged in many tasks that helped patients and visitors and made others' jobs in the unit go more smoothly."[334] The contented workers cognitively altered the nature of their job (viewing it not as just cleaning facilities but as valuable in healing patients)."[335] They altered the tasks of their job by including as one of their tasks, "brightening someone's day."[336] They enhanced the relational aspects of their job by interacting with patients, visitors, and staff.[337] In "crafting" their job, the contented workers "integrated themselves into patient care functions, [were] . . . able to see their work as being about healing people and to see themselves as a key part of this process, thus enhancing work meaning and creating a more positive work identity. . . ."[338]

Ways to View Work

How do you view work? Studies find that people tend to think of work in one of three ways:

- As a job, focusing on financial rewards,
- As a career, focusing on career advancement, promotions, prestige, and power, as well as more income,
- As a calling, focusing on fulfilling, socially useful work.[339]

Those who think of work as a job choose tasks and make career decisions based primarily upon pay. Those who think of work as a career make a point to interact with those who are powerful and can help them advance. Those who view their work as a calling make career decisions based upon what is meaningful to them, regardless of pay or promotion. Research suggests that workers will "craft" their work to align with their motivations for work.[340] There is no right or wrong way to view work. Our views of work may change throughout our careers. The key is to assess how you view work and make career decisions consistent with your view.

X. Put It in a Box

If you want to catch a monkey, get a coconut, drill a hole in the coconut, and put peanuts in the coconut. Place the coconut on the ground and tie a rope around it. Hide behind a tree. When a monkey comes, he will put his hand in the coconut. Pull the coconut (and monkey) towards you with the rope. When the monkey is close, grab the monkey.

At any point in the above scenario, the monkey could take his hand out of the coconut and run away, but he won't because he doesn't want to turn loose of the peanuts. We all are like the monkey when we get hold of a worry. We won't turn loose of it. We obsess. We ruminate. Our worry becomes an endless loop. We can't get it out of our minds. There is nothing constructive about needless worry. It wears us out. It keeps us from dealing with other responsibilities and enjoying pleasures. It keeps us from living in the moment. It makes it harder to deal with the source of our worry. We can't get a fresh perspective on the problem.

To "ruminate" is "to go over in the mind repeatedly. . . . To chew repeatedly for an extended period."[341] Rumination consumes our cognitive resources.[342] Studies show that test subjects are slower in completing simple cognitive exercises when they score high on rumination indices.[343] For pessimists, the endless loop of rumination becomes especially crippling because pessimists "repeatedly tell themselves how bad things are."[344] As Martin Seligman notes, "Rumination combined with pessimistic explanatory style is the recipe for severe depression."[345]

Learning to put our worries in a box and put the worry aside is one of the most important EQ skills we can develop. As Seligman describes, "Some people can put their troubles neatly into a box and go about their lives even when one important aspect of it—their job, for example, or their love life—is suffering. Others bleed all over everything. They catastrophize. When one thread of their lives snaps, the whole fabric unravels."[346] The ability to put our worries aside is a key trait of optimists (Section O), happy people (Section H), and lucky people (Section L). It helps us build resilience and deal with stress (Section U).

Y. Yes, You Can Make A's . . . If You Realize How the Test Is Scored

I have taught Criminal Law to first-year, first-semester law students for almost thirty years. Here is the question I always give on their final exam (after a few pages of facts):

QUESTION: "You are a prosecutor. You have been made aware of the above facts. What are the possible charges against whom and why, considering as part of your decision all possible defenses and evidence?"

Assume a student's complete answer is the following:

ANSWER: "I will charge Adam with burglary, assault, rape, and conspiracy with Bill. I will charge Bill with the same offenses, and also mail fraud. Both Adam and Bill have possible defenses of insanity, intoxication, and self-defense. Bill also has a possible defense of necessity."

This student will fail the exam even though she correctly identified all issues present. Why? Because of the italicized portion of the question:

QUESTION: "You are a prosecutor. You have been made aware of the above facts. What are the possible charges against whom and *why*, considering as part of your decision all possible defenses and evidence?

The student did not answer the "why" part of the question. By the time first-year law students take law school exams, they know from class discussions, reviewing prior exams, and talking to faculty and upper class students, in short by absorbing the "culture" of law school, what it means to answer the "why" part of exam questions. They understand that a complete answer will be twenty-plus pages of discussion, not three sentences. However, if a new prosecutor is asked by her supervisor this same question about a case, the appropriate answer, at least for starters, is the three sentences, exactly what would have earned the student an F on her law school exam. The new prosecutor will have wasted considerable time if she wrote her supervisor a twenty-page memo answering the question. Wasting time on unnecessary work in the practice of law is akin to making an F on the "resource allocation" test.

The Tests Continue . . .

A friend, who is in-house counsel for a large company, requested that the company's outside counsel look at a particular legal issue. Outside counsel did so and provided the answer—and more. Outside counsel had assumed, without clarifying with his client, that his client needed more issues addressed than the specific question sent to him. The client's lawyer, my friend, was surprised. She had given a narrow, defined assignment to outside counsel. He had expanded the assignment, adding issues that were, in fact, relevant to the question referred to him but unknown to him, already addressed in-house.

When my friend's company received the bill from outside counsel, the bill included time spent by multiple firm attorneys on the non-requested issues. My friend surmised that outside counsel was trying to save face within his law firm and recoup at least a portion of the large number of hours the firm had put in on the project. There were tense discussions about the bill and soon thereafter, my friend's company ended its relationship with the law firm and retained other outside counsel.

Two Lessons

• **Know what test you are taking.** The first lesson in both of the above scenarios is to know which question you are to answer. The first year law student, who would have made an F on the law school exam, and outside counsel, who lost a lucrative client, did not follow instructions. They did not accurately understand the "test" they were taking. A student who gives a bottom-line answer with no analysis on a law school exam will fail. An outside counsel who expands an assignment beyond what he has been retained to do will fail.

• **Allocate the right amount of resources.** The second lesson is that "making an A" is measured not only by the quality of what we do, but by how accurately we allocate appropriate resources to the job. In the practice of law where we are paid for our time, allocating appropriate resources to a task is crucial. The decision of how many and what type of resources are needed for a project is an important one. When we accurately assess that a project requires "C" resources and we put "C" resources into the project, we have made an "A" on the "resource allocation" test. If a project requires "C" resources and we put "A" resources into it, like outside counsel in the above scenario, we make an "F" on the resource allocation test. If a project requires "A" resources, and we put "C" effort into it, like the law student, we have made an "F" on the resource allocation test. Accurately assessing and allocating resources is one of the most important skills lawyers need to develop, not just to comply with a client's desires, but to conserve our time for work we must do and activities we want to do.

Z. Zest and Margins

The only good thing about getting a root canal is that after you get it, your tooth doesn't hurt any more. After I had my first, and I hope, only root canal, I asked my dentist how I could avoid future root canals. I expected him to tell me to add more fluoride, have my bite checked, brush differently, or some such dental answer. Instead, he said, "Margins."

My confusion was apparent.

He asked, "Do you like to read?"

"Yes," I answered.

"Would you like to read a book if it had no margins on the pages?"

"No." I was clueless.

"You're clinching your teeth. Eventually that will require more root canals. We clinch our teeth when we have too much stress. No matter how much you enjoy what you're doing, if you're too busy, back off, and put some margins in your life. Then, no more root canals."

Webster's Dictionary defines zest as "spirited enjoyment; gusto." Most lawyers and law students are Type A in some, if not all, of their life's activities. Our Type A personalities bring spirited enjoyment, gusto, and zest to our lives. There are advantages to our Type A'ness. Because of our intensity we are able to set ambitious goals and meet a lot of them. We do fun, interesting, rewarding things that many other people never get to experience. We have opportunities to make a difference in the communities in which we live. We pack a lot into our days.

But there are disadvantages to having lots of zest. When we add more and more to our schedules, when our responsibilities increase because we are good at what we do, when we fill our plates too full, we create an unhealthy amount of stress. Before we know it, we are "wound as tight as a rubber band about to break."[347] Adding margins to our lives reduces stress (Section U), promotes good physical and psychological health (Sections H and T), and avoids root canals.

Keep the zest. Add margins.

TABLE OF AUTHORITIES

Allan, Rick B. "Alcoholism, Drug Abuse and Lawyers: Are We Ready to Address the Denial?" *Creighton Law Review* 31 (1997): 265–266.

Beck, Connie J.A., Bruce D. Sales & G. Andrew H. Benjamin. "Lawyer Distress: Alcohol-Related Problems and Other Psychological Concerns Among a Sample of Practicing Lawyers." *Journal of Law and Health* 10 (1995–96): 1.

Ben-Shahar, Tal. *Happier*. New York: McGraw Hill, 2007.

Bradberry, Travis & Jean Greaves. *Emotional Intelligence 2.0*. San Diego: TalentSmart, 2009.

"Brodus, Buddies and Burgers." http://tennessee.247sports.com/Article/Tennessee-Vols-football-A-tale-of-Brodus-buddies-and-burgers-47510.

Bucy, Pamela H. "The VLP and the IRS." *Alabama Lawyer* 61 (2000): 376.

Bucy, Pamela H. "The One-Hour VLP Case." *Alabama Lawyer* 61 (2000): 308.

Bucy, Pamela H. "Pro Bono Services: No Shuckin' and Jivin.'" *Alabama Lawyer* 70 (2009): 456.

Bucy, Pamela H. "Why Do They Do It? The Motives, Mores, and Character of White Collar Criminals." *St. John's L. Rev.* 82 (2008): 401, 410–413, 435–437.

Buechner, Frederick. *Wishful Thinking, A Seekers Guide*. HarperOne, 1973, 1993.

Canter, Rachelle J. "Five Things Law Firms Can Learn From Corporations." *American Bar Journal* 38 (Oct. 15, 2012) http://www.americanbar.org.

Cialdini, Robert B. *Influence, The Psychology of Persuasion*. New York: HarperCollins, 1984.

Claypool, John. *Opening Blind Eyes*. Abington Press, 1983.

Claypool, John. *Mending The Heart*. Rowman & Littlefield, 1999.

Claypool, John. *The Hopeful Heart*. Morehouse, 2003.

Claypool, John. *The Light Within You*. Word, Inc., 1983.

Covey, Stephen. *The 7 Habits of Highly Effective People.* New York: Free Press, 1989.

Csikszentmihalyi, Mihaly. *Flow.* New York: Harper Perennial, 1990.

Csikszentmihalyi, Mihaly. *Finding Flow.* New York: Basic Books, 1997.

Duhigg, Charles. *The Power of Habit.* New York: Random House, 2012.

Eich, Eric, Dawn Macaulay & Lee Ryan. "Mood Dependent Memory for Events of the Personal Past." *J. of Experimental Psychology* 123 (1994): 201–215.

Epstein, Lawrence J. *A Good Night's Sleep.* New York: McGraw Hill, 2007.

Flanigan, Beverly. *Forgiving the Unforgivable.* New York: Wiley Publishing, Inc., 1992.

Fleming, Larry. "Emergency Kicker Spurs Vols Victory." *The Chattanoogan.com* (Nov. 5, 2011).

Frankl, Victor. *Man's Search for Meaning.* Beacon Press, 1959.

Galbenski, David J. *Unbound.* Unbound Legal, 2009.

Gilbert, Daniel. *Stumbling on Happiness.* New York: Vintage Books, 2006.

Goleman, Daniel. *Emotional Intelligence.* New York: Bantam Books, 1995.

Haidt, Jonathan. *The Happiness Hypothesis.* New York: Basic Books, 2006.

Hauri, Peter & Shirley Linde. *No More Sleepless Nights.* New York: John Wiley & Sons, 1991.

Henry, Deborah Epstein. *Law & Reorder: Legal Industry Solutions for Restructure, Retention, Promotion & Work/Life Balance.* Chicago: ABA, 2010.

Johnson, Spencer. *Who Moved My Cheese?* New York: G.P. Putnam's Sons, 1998.

Kabat-Zinn, Jon. *Full Catastrophe Living: Using the Wisdom of Your Body and Mind to Face Stress, Pain, and Illness.* New York: Dell Publishing, 1990.

Kahneman, Daniel, Alan B. Kruger, David Schkade, Norbert Schwarz & Arthur A. Stone. "Would You Be Happier If You Were Richer? A Focusing Illusion." *Science* 312 (2006): 1908.

Kasser, Tim & Richard M. Ryan. "A Dark Side of the American Dream: Correlates of Financial Success as a Central Life Aspiration." *J. of Personality & Psychology* 65 (1993): 410–422.

Katz, Deborah & Angela Haupt. "Seven Mind-Blowing Benefits of Exercise." *U.S. News & World Report: Health*, http://health. usnews.com.

Kelley, Robert E. *How To Be A Star At Work*. New York: Times Books, 1998.

Khalsa, Dharma Singh, M.D., with Cameron Stauth. *Brain Longevity*. New York: Wellness Central, 1997.

King, Laura A., Joshua A. Hicks, Jennifer L. Krull & Amber K. Del Gaiso. "Positive Affect and the Experiences of Meaning in Life." *J. of Personality and Social Psychology* 90 (2006): 179–196.

Kobasa, Suzanne. "Stressful Life Events, Personality and Health: An Inquiry into Hardiness." *J. of Personality & Social Psychology* 37 (1979): 1, 3.

Kobasa, Suzanne. "Commitment and Coping in Stress Resistance Among Lawyers." *J. of Personality & Social Psychology* 42 (1982): 707–717.

Krieger, Lawrence S. "Institutional Denial About the Dark Side of Law School." *J. Legal Educ.* 52 (2002): 112, 123.

Kushner, Harold S. *Living a Life That Matters*. New York: Anchor Books, 2001.

Locke Edwin A. & Gary P. Latham. "Building a Practically Useful Theory of Goal Setting and Task Motivation." *American Psychologist* 57 (2002): 705–717.

Lykken, David. *Happiness: The Nature and Nurture of Joy and Contentment*. New York: St. Martin's Griffin, 2000.

McCann, Lisa & David S. Holmes. "Influence of Aerobic Exercise on Depression." *J. of Personality & Social Psychology* 46 (1984): 1142–1147.

Medina, John. *Brain Rules*. Seattle: Pear Press, 2008.

Meehl, P.E. "Hedonic Capacity: Some Conjectures." *Bull. of the Menninger Clinic* 39 (1975): 295–307.

Mischell, Harriet, and Walter Mischel. "The Development of Children's Knowledge of Self-Control Strategies." *Child Development* (1983): 54.

Muraven, Mark & Roy F. Baumeister. "Self-Regulation and Depletion of Limited Resources: Does Self Control Resemble a Muscle?" *Psychological Bulletin* 126 (2000): 247, 254.

Myers, D.G. & E. Diener. "The Pursuit of Happiness." *Scientific American* (1996): 55–56.

Myers, David G. "The Funds, Friends and Faith of Happy People." *American Psychologist* 55 (2000): 56.

Niven, David. *The 100 Simple Secrets of Happy People.* New York: HarperCollins, 2000.

Orbell, Sheina & Paschal Sheeran. "Motivational and Volitional Processes in Action Initiation: A Field Study of the Role of Implementation Intentions." *J. of Applied Social Psychology* 30 (2000): 780–797.

Pausch, Randy, with Jeffrey Zaslow. *The Last Lecture.* New York: Hyperion, 2008.

Pennebaker, James W. "Writing About Emotional Experiences As A Therapeutic Process." *American Psychology Society* 8 (1997): 162–163.

Pennebaker, James W., Tracy J. Mayne, & Martha E. Francis. "Linguistic Predictors of Adaptive Bereavement." *J. of Personality & Social Psychology* 72 (1997): 863–871.

Pierson, Pamela Bucy. "Why Do Pro Bono?" *Capstone Lawyer* 8 (2012).

Ratey, John J. *A User's Guide to the Brain.* New York: Vintage Books, 2002.

Ratey, John J. *Spark: The Revolutionary New Science of Exercise and the Brain.* Little Brown & Co., 2013.

Rath, Tom. *Strengths Finder 2.0.* New York: Gallup Press, 2007.

Redelmeier, Donald A., Joel Katz & Daniel Kahneman. "Memories of Colonoscopy: A Randomized Trial." *Pain* 104 (2003): 187–197.

Rubin, Gretchen. *The Happiness Project.* New York: HarperCollins, 2009.

Scott, V.B., Jr. & W.D. McIntosh. "The Development of a Trait Measure of Ruminative Thought." *Personality and Individual Differences* 26 (1999): 1045, 1054.

Seligman, Martin, E.P. *Authentic Happiness: Using the New Positive Psychology to Realize Your Potential for Lasting Fulfillment.* New York: Simon & Schuster, 2002.

Seligman, Martin, E.P. *Learned Optimism.* New York: Vintage Books, 2006.

Sheldon, Kennon M. & Linda Houser-Marko. "Self-Concordance, Goal Attainment, and the Pursuit of Happiness: Can There Be an Upward Spiral?" *J. of Personality & Social Psychology* 80 (2001): 152–165.

Shellenbarger, Sue. "Even Lawyers Get the Blues: Opening Up About Depression." *Wall Street Journal* Dec. 13, 2007.

Snyder, Mark, Elizabeth Decker Tanke & Ellen Berscheid. "Social Perception and Interpersonal Behavior: On the Self-Fulfilling Nature of Social Stereotypes." *J. of Personality & Social Psychology* 35 (1977): 656–666.

Strack, F., M. Argyle & N. Schwarz (eds.). *Subjective Wellbeing: An Interdisciplinary Perspective.* New York: Pergamon, 1991.

Watson, David. *Positive Affectivity, Handbook of Positive Psychology.* Oxford Press, 2009.

Wegner, D.M. & J.W. Pennebaker (eds.). *Handbook of Mental Control.* Englewood Cliffs, N.J.: Prentice Hall, 1993.

Wiseman, Richard. *The Luck Factor.* New York: Miramax, 2003.

Worthington, Everett L. *A Just Forgiveness: Responsible Healing Without Excusing Injustice.* Downers Grove: InterVarsity Press, 2009.

Wrzesnieski, Amy and Jane E. Dutton. "Crafting a Job: Revisioning Employees As Active Crafters of Their Work." *Academy of Management Review* 26 (2001): 179–201.

ENDNOTES

¹ JON KABAT-ZINN, FULL CATASTROPHE LIVING 287 (Delta Books 1990).

² A relatively high IQ seems to be required for success in a number of fields of human endeavor. People with IQs lower than about 115, for example (and that includes about eight out of every ten), are unlikely to get through medical or law school. DAVID LYKKEN, HAPPINESS: THE NATURE AND NURTURE OF JOY AND CONTENTMENT, 51 (St. Martin's Griffin 2000) [hereinafter, LYKKEN, HAPPINESS].

³ DANIEL GOLEMAN, EMOTIONAL INTELLIGENCE 34 (Bantam Books 1995) [hereinafter GOLEMAN, EQ].

⁴ *Cf.* MARTIN SELIGMAN, AUTHENTIC HAPPINESS: USING THE NEW POSITIVE PSYCHOLOGY TO REALIZE YOUR POTENTIAL FOR LASTING FULFILLMENT 45–62 (Simon & Schuster 2002) [hereinafter SELIGMAN, AUTHENTIC HAPPINESS].

⁵ Connie J.A. Beck, Bruce D. Sales, G. Andrew H. Benjamin, *Lawyer Distress: Alcohol-Related Problems and Other Psychological Concerns Among a Sample of Practicing Lawyers*, 10 J. OF LAW AND HEALTH 1–3 (1995–96) [hereinafter *Lawyer Distress*].

⁶ Rick B. Allan, Alcoholism, Drug Abuse and Lawyers: Are We Ready to Address the Denial?, 31 CREIGHTON L. REV. 265–266 (1997); Lawyer Distress, supra note 5 at 3; Sue Shellenbarger, Even Lawyers Get the Blues: Opening Up About Depression, WALL ST. J. (Dec. 13, 2007).

⁷ *Lawyer Distress, supra* note 5 at 4.

⁸ Rachelle J. Canter, *Five Things Law Firms Can Learn From Corporations*, 38 AM. BAR J., Oct. 15, 2012, http://www.americanbar.org.

⁹ David G. Myers, *The Funds, Friends and Faith of Happy People*, 55 AMERICAN PSYCHOLOGIST 56 (2000) [hereinafter Myers, *Happy People*].

¹⁰ David G. Myers & Ed Diener, *The Pursuit of Happiness*, SCIENTIFIC AMERICAN 54 (May 1996).

¹¹ P.E. Meehl, *Hedonic Capacity: Some Conjectures*, 39 BULL. OF THE MENNINGER CLINIC 295–307 (1975), discussed in David

Watson, POSITIVE AFFECTIVITY, HANDBOOK OF POSITIVE PSYCHOLOGY, Oxford Press 107 (2009) [hereinafter WATSON, POSITIVE AFFECTIVITY].

[12]   *Id.* at 203.

[13]   CHARLES DUHIGG, THE POWER OF HABIT: WHY WE DO WHAT WE DO IN LIFE AND BUSINESS, xiv–xv 15, 21 (2012) [hereinafter DUHIGG, POWER OF HABIT].

[14]   *Id.* at 15.

[15]   *Id.* at 15.

[16]   Duncan Blair, Banjo Musician and Director of ERISA practice group, Burr Forman LLP, Birmingham, Alabama (Retired).

[17]   SELIGMAN, AUTHENTIC HAPPINESS, *supra* note 4 at 20.

[18]   SELIGMAN, AUTHENTIC HAPPINESS, *supra* note 4 at 22–23.

[19]   *Id.*

[20]   *Id.* at 23.

[21]   *Id.* at 24.

[22]   *Id.* at 116.

[23]   *Id.*

[24]   JOHN CLAYPOOL, THE LIGHT WITHIN YOU, 111–120 (Word Inc. 1983).

[25]   SELIGMAN, AUTHENTIC HAPPINESS, *supra* note 4 at 188.

[26]   SELIGMAN, AUTHENTIC HAPPINESS, *supra* note 4 at 93–95, 98–101.

[27]   *Id.*

[28]   SELIGMAN, AUTHENTIC HAPPINESS, *supra* note 4 at 7.

[29]   Donald A. Redelmeier, Joel Katz, Daniel Kahneman, *Memories of Colonoscopy: A Randomized Trial*, 104 PAIN 187–197 (2003).

[30]   *Id.* at 192–193.

[31]   *Id.* at 188.

[32]   *Id.* at 189.

[33]   *Id.*

[34]   *Id.* at 190.

[35]   *Id.* at 192.

[36]   *Id.*

[37]   DANIEL GILBERT, STUMBLING ON HAPPINESS (Vintage Books 2006).

[38]   *Id.* at 44.

[39]   *Id.* at 44.

[40]   *Id.* at 87 (actual quote is "reweave the tapestry").

[41]   *Id.* at 125–26.

[42]   Eric Eich, Dawn Macaulay, Lee Ryan, *Mood Dependent Memory for Events of the Personal Past*, 123 J. OF EXPERIMENTAL PSYCHOLOGY 201–215, 214 (1994).

[43]   SELIGMAN, AUTHENTIC HAPPINESS, *supra* note 4 at 70, 75–81.

[44]   SELIGMAN, AUTHENTIC HAPPINESS, *supra* note 4 at 70. The full quote is, "forgiveness loosens the power of the bad events to embitter (and actually can transform bad memories into good ones)."

[45]   EVERETT L. WORTHINGTON, A JUST FORGIVENESS: RESPONSIBLE HEALING WITHOUT EXCUSING INJUSTICE 101–104 (Intervarsity Press 2009); *Cf.* BEVERLY FLANIGAN, FORGIVING THE UNFORGIVABLE (Wiley 1992).

[46]   FREDERICK BUEHNER, WISHFUL THINKING 33 (HarperOne 1993).

[47]   Hunter Carmichael, The University of Alabama School of Law, Class of 2014.

[48]   Edwin A. Locke & Gary P. Latham, *Building a Practically Useful Theory of Goal Setting and Task Motivation,* 57 AMERICAN PSYCHOLOGIST 706 (2002) [hereinafter Locke & Latham, *Goal Setting*].

[49]   *Id.*

[50]   *Id.* at 707.

[51]   *Id.*

[52]   *Id.* at 710.

[53]   *Id.* at 714.

[54]   Kennon M. Sheldon & Linda Houser-Marko, *Self-Concordance, Goal Attainment, and the Pursuit of Happiness: Can There Be an Upward Spiral?* 80 J. OF PERSONALITY & SOCIAL PSYCHOLOGY 152–165 (2001) [hereinafter Sheldon & Houser-Marko, *Goal Attainment*].

[55]   Locke & Latham, *Goal Setting, supra* note 48 at 707.

[56]   Sheldon & Houser-Marko, *Goal Attainment, supra* note 54 at 153.

[57]   Daniel Kahneman, Alan B. Kruger, David Schkade, Norbert Schwarz & Arthur A. Stone, *Would You Be Happier If You Were Richer? A Focusing Illusion*, 312 SCIENCE pp. 1908 (2006).

[58]   *Id.* at 1909.

[59]   *Id.* at 1910.

[60]   *Id.* at 1910.

[61]   Sheldon & Houser-Marko, *Goal Attainment, supra* note 54 at 160–61.

[62]   Stanley Milgram, *Behavioral Study of Obedience,* 67 J. OF ABNORMAL & SOCIAL PSYCHOLOGY 376 (1963).

[63]   Lawrence S. Krieger, *Institutional Denial About the Dark Side of Law School*, 52 J. LEGAL EDUC. 112, 123 (2002).

[64]   Sheldon & Houser-Marko, *Goal Attainment, supra* note 54 at 162.

[65]   Camille Wright Cook, John S. Stone Professor, the University of Alabama School of Law, Keynote address, Protective Life Women's Leadership Event, March 9, 2006, The University of Alabama School of Law. Professor Cook was the first woman named to the faculty at the University of Alabama School of Law, and the first woman to hold a chair on the law faculty. Professor Cook taught at the University of Alabama School of Law from 1969–1993.

[66]   ROBERT B. CIALDINI, INFLUENCE, THE PSYCHOLOGY OF PERSUASION 57 (Harper Collins 1984) [hereinafter CIALDINI, INFLUENCE].

[67]   James W. Pennebaker, Tracy J. Mayne, & Martha E. Francis, *Linguistic Predictors of Adaptive Bereavement*, 72 J. OF PERSONALITY & SOCIAL PSYCHOLOGY 863 (1997) [hereinafter Pennebaker, *Linguistic Predictors*].

[68]   DUHIGG, THE POWER OF HABIT, *supra* note 13 at 144–149.

[69]   Sheina Orbell & Paschal Sheeran, *Motivational and Volitional Processes in Action Initiation: A Field Study of the Role of Implementation Intentions*, 30 J. OF APPLIED SOCIAL PSYCHOLOGY 780–797 (2000) [hereinafter Orbell & Sheeran, *Implementation Intentions*].

[70]   Locke & Latham, *Goal Setting, supra* note 48 at 707.

[71]   *Id.* at 712.

[72]   LYKKEN, HAPPINESS, *supra* note 2 at 1, 11, 17.

[73]   SELIGMAN, AUTHENTIC HAPPINESS, *supra* note 4 at 38.

[74]   *Id.* at 40.

[75]   *Id.*

[76]   *Id.* at 41.

[77]   *Id.* at 56.

[78]   *Id.* at 41.

[79]   D.G. Myers & E. Diener, *The Pursuit of Happiness,* SCIENTIFIC AMERICAN, 55–56 (1996).

[80]   *Id.* at 56–57.

[81]   Myers, *Happy People, supra* note 9 at 61.

[82]   Tim Kasser & Richard M. Ryan, *A Dark Side of the American Dream: Correlates of Financial Success as a Central Life Aspiration*, 65 J. OF PERSONALITY & PSYCHOLOGY, 420 (1993) [hereinafter Kasser & Ryan, *A Dark Side*].

[83]   Kasser & Ryan, *A Dark Side, supra* note 82 at 410–422.

[84]   SELIGMAN, AUTHENTIC HAPPINESS, *supra* note 4 at 103, 105.

[85]   *Id.* at 106.

[86]   Myers, *Happy People, supra* note 9 at 62.

[87]   As quoted in Myers, *Happy People, supra* note 9 at 62.

[88]   SELIGMAN, AUTHENTIC HAPPINESS, *supra* note 4 at 49; Kasser & Ryan, *A Dark Side, supra* note 82 at 420; Mark Snyder, Elizabeth Decker Tanke & Ellen Berscheid, *Social Perception and Interpersonal Behavior: On the Self-Fulfilling Nature of Social Stereotypes,* 35 J. OF PERSONALITY & SOCIAL PSYCHOLOGY, 656–666 (1977); Myers, *Happy People, supra* note 9 at 58, 60.

[89]   WATSON, POSITIVE AFFECTIVITY, *supra* note 11 at 110.

[90]   LYKKEN, HAPPINESS, *supra* note 2 at 2, 42; *Cf.* SELIGMAN, AUTHENTIC HAPPINESS, *supra* note 4 at 47.

[91]   LYKKEN, HAPPINESS, *supra* note 2 at 55–56.

[92]   WATSON, POSITIVE AFFECTIVITY, *supra* note 11 at 112.

[93]   LYKKEN, HAPPINESS, *supra* note 2 at 3, 6, 23.

[94]   LYKKEN, HAPPINESS, *supra* note 2 at 60.

[95]   JOHN CLAYPOOL, THE HOPEFUL HEART (Morehouse 2003).

[96]   CIALDINI, INFLUENCE, *supra* note 66 at 57.

[97]   *Id.*

[98]   *Id.* at 67.

[99]   *Id.* at 72–74.

[100]   *Id.* at 73.

[101]   *Id.* at 18.

[102]   *Id.*

[103]   *Id.* at 36–38.

[104]   *Id.* at 116.

[105]   *Id.* at 162.

[106]   *Id.* at 163.

[107]   *Id.* at 167 ("Few people would be surprised to learn that, as a rule, we most prefer to say yes to the requests of someone we know and like.")

[108]   *Id.* at 173–74.

[109]   *Id.* at 174.

[110]   *Id.* at 171–72.

[111]   *Id.* at 177.

[112]   *Id.* at 185–87.

[113]   *Id.* at 193.

[114]   *Id.* at 171, 199.

[115]   *Id.* at 239.

[116]   *Id.* at 262.

117   *Id.* at 266.

118   *Id.* at 257.

119   *Id.*

120   *Id.* at 213.

121   Milgram, *supra* note 62 at 376.

122   *Id.* at 372.

123   *Id.*

124   *Id.* at 373.

125   *Id.*

126   *Id.* at 374.

127   *Id.* at 375.

128   *Id.*

129   *Id.* at 375–376.

130   *Id.* at 375.

131   *Id.* at 376.

132   *Id.*

133   *Id.* at 377.

134   *Id.*

135   *Id.*

136   *Id.*

137   *Id.* at 376.

138   *Id.* at 376.

139   CIALDINI, INFLUENCE, *supra* note 66 at 220.

140   *Id.* at 221–29.

141   *Id.* at 75.

142   *Id.* at 76.

143   Pennebaker, *Linguistic Predictors, supra* note 67 at 863.

144   *Id.* at 864.

145   *Id.*

146   GILBERT, STUMBLING ON HAPPINESS, *supra* note 37 at 207.

[147]   Pennebaker, *Linguistic Predictors, supra* note 67 at 863.

[148]   *Id.*

[149]   MARTIN SELIGMAN, LEARNED OPTIMISM (Vintage Books 2006) [hereinafter LEARNED OPTIMISM].

[150]   JOHN CLAYPOOL, OPENING BLIND EYES 36 (Abington Press 1983).

[151]   RICHARD WISEMAN, THE LUCK FACTOR 13–14 (Miramax 2003) [hereinafter WISEMAN, LUCK].

[152]   *Id.*

[153]   *Id.* at 20–27.

[154]   *Id.* at xiii–xv.

[155]   *Id.* at 31.

[156]   *Id.* at 33.

[157]   *Id.* at 34.

[158]   *Id.* 34–35.

[159]   *Id.* at 37–38.

[160]   *Id.* at 38.

[161]   *Id.* at 63.

[162]   *Id.* at 67–68.

[163]   *Id.* at 70–72.

[164]   *Id.* at 73–74.

[165]   *Id.* at 89.

[166]   *Id.* at 101.

[167]   *Id.*

[168]   *Id.* at 105 ("Lucky people attempt to achieve their goals, even if their chances of success seem slim, and persevere in the face of failure.")

[169]   *Id.* at 134.

[170]   *Id.* at 128.

[171]   *Id.* at 134–135.

[172]   *Id.*

[173]   *Id.* at 139 ("Lucky people do not dwell on their ill fortune. . . . They let go of the past and focus on the future.")

[174]   *Id.* at 143.

[175]   *Id.* at 145.

[176]   SELIGMAN, AUTHENTIC HAPPINESS, *supra* note 4 at 14, 250–260.

[177]   VICTOR FRANKL, MAN'S SEARCH FOR MEANING (Beacon Press 1959).

[178]   Laura A. King, Joshua A. Hicks, Jennifer L. Krull & Amber K. Del Gaiso, *Positive Affect and the Experiences of Meaning in Life*, 90 J. OF PERSONALITY AND SOCIAL PSYCHOLOGY 179 (2006).

[179]   SELIGMAN, AUTHENTIC HAPPINESS, *supra* note 4 at 103–106, 117.

[180]   *Id.* at 106; MIHALY CSIKSZENTMIHALYI, FLOW 39–70 (Harper Perennial 1990) [hereinafter CSIKSZENTMIHALYI, FLOW].

[181]   See Pamela Bucy Pierson, *Why Do Pro Bono?*, CAPSTONE LAWYER 8 (2012).

[182]   Pamela H. Bucy, *The VLP and the IRS,* 61 ALA. LAW 376 (2000) regarding a VLP case handled by Henry H. Hutchison, Capell & Howard, P.C., Montgomery, Alabama.

[183]   Pamela H. Bucy, *The One-Hour VLP Case,* 61 ALA. Law 308 (2000) [hereinafter *One Hour VLP Case,* quoting Bradley W. Cornett, Ford, Howard & Cornell, P.C., Gadsden, Alabama.

[184]   Pamela H. Bucy, *Pro Bono Services: No Shuckin' and Jivin',* 70 ALA. LAW 456 (2009) regarding a case handled by Samuel Crosby, Stone, Granade & Crosby, P.C., Daphne, Alabama.

[185]   *One Hour VLP Case, supra* note 183 at 308.

[186]   DUHIGG, THE POWER OF HABIT, *supra* note 13 at 132–134, discussing experiments conducted by Walter Mischel of Stanford University; S*ee, e.g.,* Harriet Mischell and Walter Mischel, *The Development of Children's Knowledge of Self-Control Strategies*, CHILD DEVELOPMENT 54 (1983).

[187]   Megan Oaten & Ken Cheng, *Longitudinal Gains in Self-Regulation From Regular Physical Exercise,* 11 BRITISH J. OF HEALTH PSYCHOLOGY 717–733.

[188]   *Id.* at 724–730.

[189]   Megan Oaten & Ken Cheng, *Improvements on Self-Control from Financial Monitoring*, 28 J. OF ECONOMIC PSYCHOLOGY 487–501 (2007).

[190]   *Id.* at 495–500.

[191]   Megan Oaten & Ken Cheng, *Improved Self-Control: The Benefits of a Regular Program of Academic Study*, 28 BASIC & APPLIED SOCIAL PSYCHOLOGY 1–16 (2006).

[192]   *Id.*

[193]   DUHIGG, THE POWER OF HABIT, *supra* note 13 at 139, *quoting* Todd Heatherton, a researcher at Dartmouth.

[194]   DUHIGG, THE POWER OF HABIT, *supra* note 13 at 140–145; Mark Muraven & Roy F. Baumeister, *Self-Regulation and Depletion of Limited Resources: Does Self Control Resemble a Muscle?*, 126 PSYCHOLOGICAL BULLETIN 247, 254 (2000) [hereinafter Muraven, *Self-Regulation*].

[195]   Muraven, *Self-Regulation, supra* note 194 at 254.

[196]   *Id.*

[197]   *Id.* at 1256.

[198]   *Id. quoting* Mark Muraven; *See, e.g.,* Roy F. Baumeister, Ellen Bratslavsky, Mark Muraven & Diane M. Tice, *Ego Depletion: Is the Active Self a Limited Resource?* 74 J. OF PERSONALITY & SOCIAL PSYCHOLOGY 1252 (1998) [hereinafter *Ego Depletion*].

[199]   DUHIGG, THE POWER OF HABIT, *supra* note 13 at 140–145; Mark Muraven & Roy F. Baumeister, *Self-Regulation and Depletion of Limited Resources: Does Self Control Resemble a Muscle?*, 126 PSYCHOLOGICAL BULLETIN 247, 254 (2000).

[200]   Sheina Orbell & Paschal Sheeran, *Motivational and Volitional Processes in Action Initiation: A Field Study of the Role of Implementation Intentions*, 30 J. OF APPLIED SOCIAL PSYCHOLOGY 780–797 (2000) [hereinafter Orbell & Sheeran, *Implementation Intentions*].

[201]   *Id.* at 780.

[202]   *Id.* at 785.

[203]   *Id.* at 788.

[204]   *Id.* at 787.

[205] *Id.* at 784.

[206] *Id.* at 790–793.

[207] *Id.* at 794.

[208] *Id.* at 794.

[209] *Id.* Recognizing the importance of delivering excellent and consistent customer service to its business, Starbucks devised a system similar to that used with the Scottish orthopedic patients to help its employees. Employees write out their specific plan to address the unhappy customer, getting behind when there is a sudden rush of customers, running out of the item a grumpy customer has ordered. DUHIGG, THE POWER OF HABIT, *supra* note 13 at 145.

[210] LEARNED OPTIMISM, *supra* note 149 at 221.

[211] *Id.* at 16.

[212] *Id.* at 53.

[213] *Id.* at 207.

[214] *Id.* at 114.

[215] *Id.* at 114–15, 209.

[216] *Id.* at 8.

[217] *Id.* at 6–7, 170.

[218] *Cf. id.* at 44.

[219] *Id.* at 45.

[220] *Id.* at 46.

[221] *Id.* at 47.

[222] *Id.* at 49.

[223] *Cf. id.* at 50.

[224] *Id.* at 214–15.

[225] This section is adapted from a sermon delivered by David Meginniss, Rector, Christ Episcopal Church, Tuscaloosa, Alabama, and Class of 1980, University of Alabama School of Law. For the record, David Meginniss is a University of Alabama football fan, not a Tennessee fan.

[226] Larry Fleming, *Emergency Kicker Spurs Vols Victory*, THE CHATTANOOGAN.COM (Nov. 5, 2011).

227   *Id.*

228   *Id.*

229   *Id.*

230   *Id.*

231   *Id.*

232   *Brodus, Buddies and Burgers*, http://tennessee.247sports.
com/Article/Tennessee-Vols-football-A-tale-of-Brodus-buddies-and-
burgers-47510.

233   SELIGMAN, AUTHENTIC HAPPINESS, *supra* note 4 at 30.

234   Myers, *Happy People*, *supra* note 9 at 58.

235   FREDERICK BUECHNER, WISHFUL THINKING 2 (HarperOne
1973, 1993).

236   SELIGMAN, AUTHENTIC HAPPINESS, *supra* note 4 at 35.

237   *Id. at* 43.

238   WATSON, POSITIVE AFFECTIVITY, *supra* note 11 at 116.

239   *Id.* at 116–117.

240   SELIGMAN, AUTHENTIC HAPPINESS, *supra* note 4 at 41.

241   *Id.*

242   WATSON, POSITIVE AFFECTIVITY, *supra* note 11 at 116, 117.

243   *Id.* at 117.

244   *Id.* at 116.

245   JOHN CLAYPOOL, MENDING THE HEART xiv (Rowman &
Littlefield 1999).

246   SELIGMAN, AUTHENTIC HAPPINESS, *supra* note 4 at 151.

247   WATSON, POSITIVE AFFECTIVITY, *supra* note 11 at 116.

248   *Id.*

249   *Id.* at 116.

250   WATSON, POSITIVE AFFECTIVITY, *supra* note 11 at 116–117.

251   Suzanne Kobasa, *Stressful Life Events, Personality and
Health: An Inquiry into Hardiness*, 37 J. OF PERSONALITY & SOCIAL
PSYCHOLOGY 37 (1979) 3 [hereinafter, Kobasa, *Stressful Life Events*].

252   TOM RATH, STRENGTHS FINDER 2.0 iii (Gallup Press 2008).

[253] *Id.*

[254] TOM RATH, STRENGTHS FINDER 2.0 22 (Gallup Press 2008).

[255] SELIGMAN, AUTHENTIC HAPPINESS, *supra* note 4 at 121, 134–161.

[256] SELIGMAN, AUTHENTIC HAPPINESS, *supra* note 4 at 106; MIHALY CSIKSZENTMIHALYI, FLOW 39–70 (Harper Perennial 1990) [hereinafter CSIKSZENTMIHALYI, FLOW].

[257] *Id.* at 49.

[258] *Id.* at 48–49.

[259] *Id.*

[260] *Id.* at 83.

[261] *Id.* at 49.

[262] *Id.* at 53.

[263] *Id.* at 49.

[264] *Id.* at 209.

[265] *Id.* at 54.

[266] *Id.* at 55.

[267] *Id.* at 49.

[268] *Id.* at 57.

[269] *Id.*

[270] *Id.* at 59.

[271] *Id.* at 49.

[272] *Id.* at 60–61.

[273] *Id.*

[274] *Id.* at 58.

[275] JOHN MEDINA, BRAIN RULES 163 (Pear Press 2008) [hereinafter MEDINA, BRAIN RULES].

[276] *Id.* at 151.

[277] LAWRENCE J. EPSTEIN, A GOOD NIGHT'S SLEEP 251 (McGraw Hill 2007) [hereinafter EPSTEIN, A GOOD NIGHT'S SLEEP].

[278] MEDINA, BRAIN RULES, *supra* note 275 at 155.

279 *Id.* at 156–58.

280 EPSTEIN, A GOOD NIGHT'S SLEEP, *supra* note 277 at 31.

281 PETER HAURI & SHIRLEY LINDE, NO MORE SLEEPLESS NIGHTS, 9 (John Wiley & Sons 1991) [hereinafter HAURI & LINDE, SLEEPLESS]; EPSTEIN, A GOOD NIGHT'S SLEEP, *supra* note 277 at 29.

282 MEDINA, BRAIN RULES, *supra* note 275 at 159.

283 EPSTEIN, A GOOD NIGHT'S SLEEP, *supra* note 277 at 30.

284 *Id.* at 53.

285 MEDINA, BRAIN RULES, *supra* note 275 at 159.

286 *Id.* at 160.

287 EPSTEIN, A GOOD NIGHT'S SLEEP, *supra* note 277 at 53.

288 MEDINA, BRAIN RULES, *supra* note 275 at 9–27.

289 Exercise: Seven Benefits of Regular Physical Activity, http://www.mayoclinic.com (by Mayo Clinic staff).

290 Lisa McCann & David S. Holmes, *Influence of Aerobic Exercise on Depression,* 46 J. OF PERSONALITY & SOCIAL PSYCHOLOGY, 1142–1147 (1984).

291 Deborah Katz & Angela Haupt, *Seven Mind-Blowing Benefits of Exercise*, U.S. NEWS & WORLD REPORT: HEALTH, http://health.usnews.com.

292 *Id.*

293 MEDINA, BRAIN RULES, *supra* note 275 at 179.

294 *Id.* at 17.

295 *Id.* at 1146.

296 *Id.* at 22.

297 JOHN RATEY, SPARK: THE REVOLUTIONARY NEW SCIENCE OF EXERCISE AND THE BRAIN (Little Brown & Co. 2013).

298 *Id.* at 41–45.

299 MEDINA, BRAIN RULES, *supra* note 275 at 16.

300 RATEY, SPARK, *supra* note 297 at 223.

301 Kobasa, *Stressful Life Events*, supra note 251 at 2. [In the current studies, a life event is defined as stressful if it causes changes

in, and demands readjustment of, an *"average person's normal routine."* (emphasis in original)].

[302]   Suzanne Kobasa, *Commitment and Coping in Stress Resistance Among Lawyers,* 42 J. OF PERSONALITY & SOCIAL PSYCHOLOGY 707–717 [hereinafter Kobasa, *Commitment and Coping*].

[303]   *Id.* at 715; SELIGMAN, AUTHENTIC HAPPINESS, *supra* note 4 at 177–184.

[304]   Kobasa, *Commitment and Coping, supra* note 302 at 707.

[305]   American Psychological Assn., *Stress Weakens the Immune System,* http://www.apa.org/research/action/immune.aspx; *How Your Brain Responds to Stress,* http://www.fi.edu/learn/brain/stress.html.

[306]   *Id.*

[307]   *Id.*

[308]   MEDINA, BRAIN RULES, *supra* note 275 at 178–79.

[309]   *Id.* at 176.

[310]   *Id.*

[311]   *Id.* at 177.

[312]   WATSON, POSITIVE AFFECTIVITY, *supra* note 11 at 112.

[313]   *Id.* at 112.

[314]   MEDINA, BRAIN RULES, *supra* note 275 at 178.

[315]   HAURI & LINDE, SLEEPLESS, *supra* note 281 at 105–106.

[316]   Kobasa, *Stressful Life Events, supra* note 251 at 3.

[317]   *Id.*

[318]   *Id.*

[319]   *Id.*

[320]   *Id.* at 8.

[321]   *Id.* at 4.

[322]   *Id.* at 3.

[323]   *Id.* at 3.

[324]   *Id.*

[325]   Kobasa, *Commitment and Coping, supra* note 302 at 715.

[326] WATSON, POSITIVE AFFECTIVITY, *supra* note 11 at 116 *quoting* M. CSIKSZENTMIHALYI, FLOW: THE PSYCHOLOGY OF OPTIMAL EXPERIENCE 3 (Harper Perennial 1991).

[327] Amy Wrzesnieski and Jane E. Dutton, *Crafting a Job: Revisioning Employees As Active Crafters of Their* Work, 26 ACADEMY OF MANAGEMENT REVIEW 179–201 (2001) [hereinafter *Crafting a Job*].

[328] *Id.* at 179.

[329] *Id.* at 186.

[330] *Id.* at 193.

[331] *Id.* at 191.

[332] *Id.*

[333] *Id.*

[334] *Id.*

[335] *Id.*

[336] *Id.*

[337] *Id.*

[338] *Id.* at 183.

[339] *Id.* at 184.

[340] *Id.* at 185; SELIGMAN, AUTHENTIC HAPPINESS, *supra* note 4 at 168–69.

[341] Merriam Webster Dictionary.

[342] V.B. Scott, Jr. & W.D. McIntosh, *The Development of a Trait Measure of Ruminative Thought,* 26 PERSONALITY AND INDIVIDUAL DIFFERENCES 1045, 1054 (1999).

[343] *Id.* at 1045–1056.

[344] SELIGMAN, LEARNED OPTIMISM, *supra* note 149 at 82.

[345] SELIGMAN, LEARNED OPTIMISM, *supra* note 149 at 75; Nolen-Hoeksema, S. (1993) *Sex Differences in Control of Depression* in D.M. WEGNER & J.W. PENNEBAKER (EDS.), HANDBOOK OF MENTAL CONTROL (Prentice Hall) 306–324.

[346] SELIGMAN, LEARNED OPTIMISM, *supra* note 149 at 46.

[347] Cathy Wright, Principal, Clarus Consulting Group; Founding Partner, Maynard Cooper & Gale, P.C., Birmingham, Alabama.

CHAPTER II

FINANCIAL PLANNING

1. INTRODUCTION

Personal financial planning dictates our choices in life. It impacts our stress level, quality of life, and happiness. Yet many of us who are competent in other areas of life do a poor job tending to our finances. It is hard to do. It is difficult to stay informed and make wise decisions. Financial planning can be deathly boring. Our eyes glaze over, our heads droop, we don't absorb what we need to know. Sometimes it's hard to know where to get the financial information we need. Financial planning doesn't demand our attention like jobs, children, or broken cars. It is easy to put off.

This chapter addresses personal financial planning basics through a case hypothetical. By following the lives of two fictional law students during and after law school, this chapter focuses on many of the financial planning questions law students and lawyers face. Financial planning is important for lawyers. Financial misconduct uniformly tops the list of problems leading to loss of one's license to practice law.[1]

This chapter covers personal financial planning issues of establishing and living on a budget; educational loan repayment facts and strategies; financial implications of different employment models; the financial calculus of working part time; costs of establishing one's own practice including opportunity costs; and saving for a home purchase, children's education and retirement. There are a number of calculations in this chapter. These are averages and estimates, designed to provide models for financial planning not to give specific financial advice.

2.   BOB AND CAROL MEET

Bob thought he was leaving his apartment in plenty of time to find his way around the law school. It was the first day of orientation for 1L students. Bob had moved from the Northwest, knew not a soul at the law school, and had no idea where to go for the first orientation session. He had been at the law school once before, six months ago when he had visited as a prospective student. Today, it was raining heavily, the traffic was a mess, and finding a parking spot took forever. Soaking wet, Bob ran into the law building five minutes after the first scheduled meeting for all 1Ls.

Bob saw a bunch of students standing by tables down a hall and filtering into an adjacent lecture hall. Bob ran their direction gratified to see as he got closer that they had the awkward look of 1Ls. He must be in the right place. Bob stepped in line behind the last student and followed him into the lecture room.

Almost every seat was taken. The only seats remaining were in the middle of the front row. Still dripping wet, Bob stepped over computer bags, backpacks and purses as he moved to a vacant seat. He breathed a sigh of relief as he sat down. Despite his hectic morning, Bob was excited! This was his first day of law school. This is what he had wanted to do for as long as he could remember.

The professor began talking. It was a few minutes before Bob realized that he was in the wrong room. This was legal writing, Groups One through Six, and he was in Group Nine. The orientation schedule that he had received a few weeks before showed that orientation began in two sections, with Legal Writing Groups One through Six in one room, and Groups Seven through Twelve in another. The professor was calling the roll. Bob was horrified. How could he get out of here and find his room without causing a commotion? Grabbing his backpack, Bob started for the door. He felt a hundred pairs of eyes on him. The professor stopped talking and looked at Bob. "What is your name and where are you going?"

"Bob Hardy," Bob croaked. The room was silent.

"Which Legal Writing Group are you in?"

"Nine."

"Then you need to be in Room 187. This is Room 188."

"Yes sir." With his eyes on the professor, Bob did not see one of the backpacks in his path. He tripped on it and fell hard into the back of two chairs. The women in the chairs jumped. One squealed. The class snickered.

Bob could hear guffaws as he picked himself up and slung his backpack over his back with all the dignity he could muster. He stepped over the rest of the bags in back of seats, went to the door, opened it, and walked out. Bob found his correct room and walked in so late that the professor had already called the roll and started class. Embarrassed, Bob slunk to an empty seat. Law school was not starting off well.

Two hours later when class was over, Bob introduced himself to the professor and apologized for being late. The professor pulled out the class roll, found Bob's name, and marked him present. "Don't be late to class again," she said.

Bob had an hour to find his locker and his next classroom. Surely he could do it right this time he told himself. Bob dreaded going to his locker because he would have to pass through the dozens of students congregating by the lockers. As he maneuvered through the crowd, Bob could tell that some people recognized him. He heard wise cracks: "Good move, buddy." "Tough class, huh?" Bob was embarrassed.

Bob found his locker and was fiddling with the combination lock when a pretty brunette with a pony tail came up beside him. "Excuse me, I think that's mine," she said as she maneuvered to reach the locker next to Bob's.

"Oh sure," Bob muttered as he moved his backpack out of her way.

They worked in silence, opening their lockers. The brunette got hers open first, put some books up, and shut her locker. She turned to Bob, "Hi, I'm Carol."

"I'm Bob."

Carol smiled the nicest smile Bob had ever seen. "You're in Group Nine," she said. "I felt so sorry for you. I did the exact same thing when I started college and it felt just awful. Where are you from?" They visited for the next half hour. Bob was sure he had never met a nicer, prettier girl in his whole life.

Bob and Carol compared schedules and found that they had three courses together during the semester, starting with the next class. They walked to the classroom and sat down. Carol had attended undergraduate school at the same university and seemed to know everyone. She introduced Bob to other law students and continued to do so all day. After the last class of the day, Carol invited Bob to join her and her friends for dinner. Bob was on top of the world when he returned to his apartment that night.

Bob and Carol discovered they had a lot in common. They both liked sports and had played team sports throughout high school and college. They both had dogs. They were the oldest in their families. Bob had three younger siblings; Carol had two. Both came from financially modest backgrounds where education was highly valued. By the middle of the first semester of law school, Bob and Carol were dating.

3.   FINANCIAL INTRIGUE: WHY WORK AT TARGET?

Bob and Carol made plans for their semester break. Bob would go home to Washington State to see his family and Carol would go home, a few hours away. Bob would return a few days before spring classes and stay with Carol and her family. It was a big step. As they discussed their plans for the break, Bob was surprised to hear Carol say that she was going to work over the holidays—at Target. "Why?" he asked.

"I've worked at our local Target during the holidays almost every year of college. They need seasonal workers so they're always hiring, they know me, they're flexible with work hours, and I can earn money to pay off at least some of the interest on my school loans."

Carol explained, "I took loans out in college and I'm taking out more for law school. By the time I graduate from law school, I'll have almost $90,000 in loans. I have Stafford loans which are a great deal. I don't have to start repaying them until I get out of law school and the interest rate on them is pretty low, 6.8%, compared to 11% on a bank loan. But, the interest accrues while I'm in law school. That's because I have "unsubsidized" loans. Students who show greater financial need can get "subsidized" loans and their interest doesn't accrue until they finish school.[2] If I could work enough during college and law school to pay off the interest on my loans as it accrues, I would save a lot of money—like $30,000! I doubt I will be able to pay off the total amount of interest each year but who knows, if I got one of those high paying summer jobs, I might. I don't earn enough now to itemize my deductions, but if I did, I would also get an income tax deduction for my interest payments."

4. PAYING LOAN INTEREST WHILE IN SCHOOL

Fascinated, Bob tore a piece of paper out of his notebook and asked Carol to show him what she had just explained. Bob had $40,000 in school loans already and expected to have another $40,000 by the time he graduated from law school. "I'm a very visual learner," Bob smiled as Carol created a chart. Here's what Carol showed Bob:

Chart 1: Interest on School Loans*

	Carol	Bob
Loans in College	$50,000	$40,000
Projected Loans in Law School	$40,000	$40,000
Projected Total Loans	$90,000	$80,000
Interest Rate on School Loans	6.8%	6.8%
Projected Total Loan Balance (Principal + Interest)	$144, 671	$125,596

Projected Total Compounded Interest on Full Loan Balance—(If interest is not paid on loans while in school and thus accrues)	$54,671	$45,596
Total Interest Accruing During College and Law School	$24,117 (Paying total interest amount per year which will range from $850 in year one to $6,120 in year seven.)	$20,377 (Paying total interest amount per year which will range from $680 in year one to $5,400 in year seven.)
Total Saved Over Life of Loans by Paying Interest on Loans During School	$30,554	$25,219

* This chart was calculated using http://www.finaid.org/calculators/ scripts/interestcap.cgi (last visited on 3/14/14). While this chart reflects the impact of interest accruing on educational loans to demonstrate the point that money can be saved if one can pay interest on loans each year, the assumption for calculations in the remainder of this chapter is that Bob's and Carol's loan payments are based on their $90,000 and $80,000 loan amounts.

Carol explained that waiting to pay interest on unsubsidized loans until one has completed law school means that this interest is added to the unpaid principal of the loan. This is referred to as *capitalization* and can be a substantial amount of money.[3] The amount of capitalization is even more significant if one has multiple loans. On unsubsidized Stafford loans, interest accrues while one is in school and during the few months of "grace" period after one graduates and before loan repayments are required. This grace period typically lasts a few months.

5.   EDUCATION LOANS

"How do you know all of this stuff?" Bob asked.

"I worked in the Student Aid office in college," Carol replied.

"Can you explain more to me?" Bob asked.

Carol did. "As you know, debt is a significant issue for many law students. The average debt for 2012 law grads was nearly $125,000 (private school graduates) and $75,000 (public school graduates).[4] Loans from federal programs are the best if you need to take out loans for school because they have better loan terms. There are three kinds of federal loans: Stafford, Perkins, and Grad-Plus."

Carol continued, "*Stafford* loans offer several repayment options, generally lend money at lower interest rates than private loans, and are the largest source of loans for college students.[5] *Perkins* loans are the best because there is no origination fee on the loan, the interest rate is only 5%, and the interest is deferred while you're in school. Perkins loans also have better loan forgiveness terms if you work at a government or public interest office after graduation. But, you have to show a lot of financial need to qualify for Perkins loans. Eligibility is based on an "Expected Family Contribution" (EFC) calculation."[6]

Bob's head was spinning. How did Carol know so much?

Carol was on a roll, apparently giving Bob the spiel she must have given hundreds of times when she worked at the undergrad Student Financial Aid office. Carol continued, "The third kind of federal education loan is "*Grad Plus*, which are loans that graduate students enrolled at least half-time at eligible schools may receive. *Grad Plus* loans have a 4% origination fee, an interest rate of 7.9%, and interest may be deferred until repayment."

"Of course," Carol added, "there are also *grants*, which you don't have to repay, and *work-study*, which is a part time job during school. Neither grants nor work study require repayment but both are difficult to get; generally, they're either merit-based or based on financial hardship."[7] Carol outlined her points about the loans for Bob.

Overview of Educational Loans, Grants and Work Study[8]

- **Stafford Loans**
  - o 2013–2014 interest rate: 5.41%.
  - o Subsidized for students demonstrating financial need through the EFC calculation; interest does not accrue until repayment of the loan begins.
  - o Unsubsidized for anyone; interest accrues from the date the loan is issued; borrowers can choose whether to pay interest while in school or opt for capitalized.
  - o Repayment begins 6 months after graduation.

- **Perkins Loans**
  - o 2013–2014 interest rate: 5%.
  - o Administered directly from the participating school's financial aid department.
  - o To qualify must have extreme financial need, shown by very low EFCs.
  - o No charge or fee for Perkins Loan, unlike Stafford or Grad PLUS.
  - o Nine month grace period post-graduation to start loan repayment.

- **Grad PLUS Loans**
  - o 2013–2014 interest rate: 6.41%.
  - o Enters repayment once loan is fully dispersed; graduate students may be placed into deferment while enrolled in school.
  - o If a loan is deferred, interest will accrue during the deferment period. Borrowers may choose to pay the interest as it is accrued or capitalize the payment once the deferment period ends.

- **Consolidation Loans**
  - Provides a method for borrowers to consolidate their various student loans into one loan with one repayment plan.
  - Oftentimes the interest rate is lower than the individual loans.
  - Rate is fixed for the life of the loan and will not exceed 8.25%.
- **Federal Work-Study Program**
  - A campus-based financial aid program.
  - Allows graduate students with financial need to earn money to cover educational expenses through jobs that pay at least minimum wage.
  - Jobs can be either on or off campus, depending on the employer participating in the program.

Bob called Target when he got home for the holidays and found that they were hiring seasonal workers. He applied for a job and was hired for three weeks during the holidays. Carol was right, the work shifts were flexible. Bob was able to get shifts that let him ski on some days, stay out late with his friends other days, and sleep in a few days. He earned almost enough to pay a semester's worth of interest on his school loans.

6.   THE 1L SUMMER

In mid-January, grades came out. Although warned by upper-class students and professors that getting their first law school grades could be traumatic, it was still a blow to Carol and Bob. Both had made excellent grades throughout high school and college. Now, after studying harder than ever both were in the middle of the class.

Besides demoralizing, there were immediate practical consequences of their class rankings. Few summer jobs were available for 1Ls, and class rank basically determined who would get those. The jobs paid well, about $1,000 per week, but the firms offering these salaries usually hired only the top 10% of the class, if that. Bob and Carol, like most of their debt-ridden classmates, were disappointed that they would not be candidates for these lucrative positions.[9] The few remaining summer jobs available to 1Ls generally paid little more than minimum wage, if anything, and the word was that a lot of these jobs were terribly tedious.

Dejected, Bob and Carol consoled each other. Their professors and several upper-class friends suggested various summer options and stressed the importance of obtaining experience that would demonstrate to future employers "life skills" such as initiative, willingness to work hard, common sense, good judgment, and maturity. They also stressed the importance of using summers during law school to find out what they liked and didn't like. As one professor said, "You may be practicing law for the next fifty years. Find something you enjoy."

Bob and Carol applied for summer positions with dozens of law firms. They had no luck. Most firms were not hiring 1Ls. The few that were, hired someone else. Bob and Carol cheered each other up. Ultimately, they both landed positions they were excited about. Bob was accepted into a summer externship program with the Public Defender's Office for the first half of the summer. He would have to pay tuition for the externship but he would also get five hours course credit. The course credit would allow him to take fewer courses during the school year and work to help with expenses, or by picking up another few more hours of credit each semester, he could graduate a semester early and save tuition.

Carol was interested in the summer externship program but couldn't get additional loans for the tuition. However, she was able to obtain a volunteer position at the Juvenile Court for the first six weeks of the summer. Both Bob and Carol applied to work at their go-to place, Target, for the last part of the summer. Target anticipated its usual before-school-starts frenzy and hired them both to work full time at the end of the summer.

Bob and Carol calculated their summer budgets. They decided to set aside $20 per week to use for a trip to the beach at the end of the summer. One of their friend's family owned a beach condo. Their friend invited several law school classmates to come down for several days in August. All they had to pay for was gas and food.

Halfway through the summer, a surprising development arose for Carol. The brother of the juvenile judge with whom Carol was working during the first half of the summer was a partner at a large law firm in town and had decided to open his own firm. He needed a law clerk. The juvenile judge had been extremely impressed with Carol and recommended Carol to her brother as a summer law clerk. Things were often tense and emotional for the parties appearing in juvenile court and the judge had seen Carol handle awkward, difficult situations well. The judge thought Carol was mature, hardworking, and pleasant to be around. The timing of the position was perfect for Carol who finished her commitment with the judge and started at the law firm the next week. Carol was thrilled with her unexpected opportunity. The pay was better than Target ($15.00 per hour versus $8.25 per hour) and working at the firm would be great experience.

Carol and Bob prepared their 1L summer budgets:

Chart 2: Carol's 1L Summer Budget
(Three Months)

Revenue	
Stafford Loan	$3,440
Law Firm (estimated 40 hours/week; 4 weeks; $15/hour) (no taxes withheld)	$2,400
Total Revenue	$5,840
Expenses	
Rent and Utilities	$2,250 ($600 rent, $150 utilities/month)

Phone	$300
Gas and Car Expenses	$400
Food	$1,200
Emergencies	$500
Beach Trip	$240
Loan Interest[10]	$650
Gifts, Entertainment	$300
Total Expenses	$5,840

Chart 3: Bob's 1L Summer Budget

Revenue	
Stafford Loan	$9,785
Target (estimated 35 hours/week; 4 weeks; $8.25/hour) (no taxes withheld)	$1,155
Total Revenue	$10,940
Expenses	
Tuition for Summer Externship	$5,000
Work Clothes (khakis, shirts)	$100
Rent and Utilities	$2,250
Phone	$300

Gas and Car Expenses	$400
Food	$1,200
Emergencies	$500
Beach Trip	$240
Loan Interest[7]	$650
Gifts, Entertainment	$300
Total Expenses	**$10,940**

Working at the firm turned out to be even more enjoyable than Carol imagined. The three founding attorneys of the firm were nice, grounded people who had left their large firm so they could have a better balance in life. A number of their former clients followed them to their new firm so there was plenty to do. The firm primarily handled business and commercial law, areas of law Carol thought she would hate but which she found that she enjoyed tremendously. Carol realized that basically, commercial lawyers help people achieve their dreams. Carol liked doing that. The firm's clients were interesting people and many were good friends with the attorneys. The firm had a team feel. Carol loved it. The lawyers at the firm were as impressed with Carol as had been the juvenile judge. At the end of the summer, they asked Carol if she would work part time at the firm after school started. Delighted, Carol said yes.

7. WEDDING BELLS (AND BUCKS)

The second year of law school flew by. Carol and Bob became closer and began to talk of long-term plans together. They agreed they wanted to marry and picked the date (the Saturday after graduation, one year away).

During the summer after their second year of law school, Carol worked full time at the law firm, which was thriving. The Public Defender's office where Bob had worked as an intern the prior summer obtained grant funding and was able to pay him to work with the office all summer. Carol and Bob began discussing wedding plans, and costs. Given their educational debts, they opted for a small wedding, family only, at a ranch in New Mexico, halfway between their family homes. The ranch had been a working cattle ranch; now it was a vacation site that specialized in weddings and family reunions. It was rustic, and relatively inexpensive. Bob and Carol thought a destination wedding in a location in between both families, would be a fun way to get their families together. Here is the wedding budget Bob and Carol prepared.

Chart 4: Wedding Budget (for 25 Guests)

Venue and accommodations	$3,500
Food, cake, and drinks	$2,500
Wedding dress/jewelry/tux rental	$1,800
Wedding rings	$1,000
Extra days at ranch for honeymoon	$1,000
Transportation costs (just Bob and Carol)	$800
Decorations	$750
Ceremony officiant	$200
Miscellaneous	$800
Total	$12,350

8. LAW SCHOOL GRADUATION AND JOBS!

The third year of law school flew by for Bob and Carol. Carol was offered an associate position at the law firm after graduation and Bob was offered a position as an Assistant Public Defender. Carol's starting salary of $75,000 was one of the larger salaries offered by small firms to new graduates in her class. Carol's firm also offered a 401(k) plan. Carol's firm would match Carol's contribution, up to 3% of her gross salary per year ($2250) if she contributed 5%. The percentage of her salary which the firm would match would be negotiated each year along with Carol's salary. Carol planned to contribute at least 5% per year since by doing so she was getting at least $2250 per year without doing any extra work.

Bob's starting salary of $46,200 was less than Carol's, obviously, but it carried great benefits. As a government employee, Bob was eligible for the state retirement program, which is a "defined benefit" plan. A "defined benefit" plan means that employees pay a percentage of their salary into the system while working and, after becoming vested (for example, after ten years), receive a set percentage of their final salary, per month, for the rest of their lives. Thus Bob, unlike Carol, who will accrue only what she and her firm contribute to her 401(K) account while she is working, is contractually guaranteed a specific payout based on his years worked and salary, even if it exceeds what he paid in.[11]

Here is how Bob's and Carol's employment situations compare:

Chart 5: Carol's Salary Package
as a Law Firm Associate

Annual Salary*	$75,000.00
Less:	
Federal Withholding	$6,851.00[12]
Social Security Tax (6.2%)	$4,650.00
Medicare Tax (1.45%)	$1,087.50
Health Insurance ($130/month for individual)	$1,560.00
Dental Insurance ($16/month for individual)	$192.00

State Withholding (AL)	$2,977.45[13]
401(k) (5% of gross salary)	$3,750.00
Total Deductions (%) (28.1%)	$21,067.95
Net Salary for the Year	$53,932.05

* Plus a bonus if firm does well and 30% of billings from clients Carol brings to the firm.

Chart 6: Bob's Salary Package
as an Assistant Public Defender

Annual Salary	$46,200.00[14]
Less:	
Federal Withholding	$2,629.00[10]
Social Security Tax	$2,864.40
Medicare Tax	$670.00
Health Insurance ($60/month for individual)	$720.00
Dental Insurance ($25/month for individual)	$300.00
State Withholding (AL)	$1,748.55[11]
Retirement Contribution (5% of gross salary)	$2,310.00
Total Deductions (%) (24.3%)	$11,241.95
Net Salary for the Year	$34,958.05

9. HOUSEHOLD BUDGET

Bob and Carol prepared a post-marriage, post-graduation household budget. It was the first time they would not be students and would have real jobs with real salaries. They were excited! Before preparing their budget, Carol and Bob reviewed their expenses for the past year. This was fairly easy to do since they both had used a single debit/credit card for most of their purchases.

They made some interesting discoveries when reviewing their respective expenses. Carol, who prided herself on her frugality and had always thought she was saving money by buying clothes at discount stores or on sale, realized that she had spent a lot of money on clothes that she didn't wear. As she looked over the items she had been so thrilled to buy but had not worn, Carol faced the fact that she was a bit of an impulse clothes buyer. It was a painful but helpful observation. Bob was shocked to see that he had spent almost $200 each month ($2400 over the past year!) eating lunch out with his law school buddies. Once he looked at the numbers, they added up: $7 or $8 for each lunch, five or six days a week. Bob vowed to start bringing sandwiches for lunch.

Household Expenses

Bob and Carol calculated their monthly household expenses first, then added in their school loan repayments, which would start within months after graduation.

Bob and Carol viewed their expenses as "fixed," "variable," or "discretionary." Doing so helped them understand the flow of their money. "Fixed" expenses, like rent or mortgage payments, do not change or if they do, change very little. "Variable" expenses, like food, utilities, and transportation expenses, fluctuate from month to month. "Discretionary" expenses, such as vacations, eating out and entertainment, are luxuries, which can be eliminated if necessary.

One budgeting decision Bob and Carol made was to allot a certain amount of money, like $50 cash, per week, to "trivial" items. For instance, in Bob's case, he decided to withdraw $30 cash from the checking account on Monday, and not spend more than that on weekly lunches out.

Here are Bob and Carol's household expenses, *exclusive* of insurance and other expenses (discussed *infra*):

Chart 7: Bob and Carol's Monthly Household Expenses[15]

Expenses	
Rent Payment	$1,200
Utilities (water, power, cable/internet, trash, gas)	$350
Food	$500
Work Clothes (khakis, shirts)	$200
Phone	$200
Gas	$250
Emergencies	$200
"Trivial Money"	$400
Gifts, Entertainment	$100
Total Monthly Expenses	$3,400

School Loan Repayment

One decision Carol and Bob had to make was how to manage their loan repayments. Together they had $170,000 in school debt (Carol had $90,000 and Bob had $80,000). The decision regarding repayment of Bob's loans was easy. His Stafford loans qualified for income-based loan repayment because he was working at a government office,[16] thus his monthly loan repayments were capped at 15% of discretionary income.[17] At Bob's salary of $46,200, this meant that his monthly loan amounts were $241.31.[18] If Bob remained with the Public Defender's office for ten years and if he made at least 120 on-time payments, the balance of his loan would be forgiven at the end of the ten years.[19] Bob realized this was a great deal! If for any reason Bob decided not to remain at the Public Defender office for ten years, he could continue in the loan forgiveness program even if he left the PD's office if he went to another qualifying government or public interest position.[20]

Carol wanted to repay her loans within ten years, and faster if possible. The terms of Carol's school loans, all Stafford loans, allowed her the following options for loan repayment. Carol decided to pursue Option 1, one of the faster repayment options. She felt like she could afford the higher monthly repayments of Option 1, and a quicker repayment would decrease the interest on her loan. As Carol realized, anyone who can afford to pay higher monthly repayments on school loans (and is not working in public service with the likelihood of loan forgiveness), should repay their loans as fast as possible to minimize accruing interest.

Chart 8: Carol's School Loan Repayment Plan (Stafford Loans Without Loan Forgiveness)[21]

	Term of Repayment	Characteristics of Option	Considerations
Option One— "Standard Repayment"	10 years or less	• Minimum $50 monthly payment • Level monthly payment	• Less interest will accrue because of the shorter repayment period • Monthly payment will be higher
Option Two— "Graduated Repayment"	10–30 years	• Minimum $25 monthly payment • Low payments will increase gradually over 2 years	• Accrues more interest than standard repayment plan • Monthly payment will initially be lower than standard repayment

Option Three—"Income Sensitive Repayment"	10 years or less	• Monthly payments based on fixed percentage of income	• Accrues more interest than standard repayment plan • Lower monthly payment than standard repayment plan

Insurance Issues

Bob and Carol looked at their insurance needs. They both had cars because there was no public transportation where they lived. Bob had a fourteen-year-old Honda Civic with 250,000 miles. Carol had an eight-year-old Toyota Corolla with 140,000 miles. Throughout college and law school, Bob and Carol had been carried on their parents' car insurance policies. Now they would pay for their own auto insurance. But they had no experience with auto insurance, nor did they know what other types of insurance they needed. All they knew was that life insurance companies pestered law students all the time.

Carol's mother, an accountant for an insurance broker, was a great resource. She was able to advise them about all types of insurance, not just vehicle. "There are several basic rules," Carol's mom said. "Shop around. Compare quotes. Keep your premiums low by getting policies with the highest deductible you can afford."[22] She explained the following:

- **Auto insurance.**[23] Automobile insurance is required in all fifty states, but the requirements vary state to state. There is coverage for injury to a car, bodily injury to a person, and liability for injury to another person's car or person.

  o *Bodily Injury Liability* is coverage for bodily injury or property damage in a collision to someone other than the policy-holder.

  o *Personal-injury protection* is coverage for bodily injury the policy holder sustains in an automobile accident or for lost wages caused from injury.

- o *Collision* coverage protects the policy holder's car from damage from collision with another car or object.

- o *Comprehensive* coverage protects the policy holder's car from events aside from collisions such as theft, falling objects, weather, or fire.

- o *Gap* insurance applies when leasing a car or if the policy holder maintains a car loan that exceeds the value of a vehicle that has been damaged.

Automobile insurance may be purchased with various limits per person, per accident, or per vehicle. Most states require liability coverage, at the very least, so as to ensure that every driver is able to compensate others for damage the driver may cause.

Carol and Bob had looked forward to trading in their old cars for new ones once they got out of law school but as Carol's mom explained, there was an insurance advantage to keeping their old cars as long as they could: "Since you each have fairly old cars your auto insurance premiums will be much less than if you had expensive or new cars. Many of the premiums are based on the market value of your car and the cost to repair damage to that car."

- **Life insurance.**[24] Carol and Bob knew that life insurance replaces lost income for one's dependents upon death of the insured, pay final expenses, create an inheritance for heirs, pay federal and state "death" taxes, make significant charitable contributions, or accrue savings.[25] But they did not know what their life insurance needs were.

Carol's mom explained that there are two types of life insurance: *term* and *permanent*. *"Term"* life insurance is coverage for a specified period of time such as one year, five years, twenty years, whatever. Term life insurance is commonly referred to as "pure life insurance" because of its time-specific coverage, zero cash value, and because it offers a death benefit only when the insured dies. *"Permanent"* insurance is either "cash" or "non-cash" value. The most common type of permanent policy is "whole life," which provides beneficiaries a death benefit and cash value accumulation. Permanent insurance policies are commonly used later in life for estate planning purposes.

Carol's mom advised that adults with no financial dependents and no large debts that survive death (generally, younger adults), don't need much life insurance and may be better off purchasing minimal "term" life insurance. Carol's mom suggested that at this point in their lives Bob and Carol did not need life insurance beyond the "term" insurance both of their employers provided. However, she did advise that they purchase term policies that could be converted to permanent policies later to ensure that they did not lose their preferable underwriting category. "Generally," she explained, "the younger and healthier a person is, the cheaper life insurance is to purchase, so it is a good idea to purchase "term" insurance that can be converted into "permanent" insurance to lock in the lower premiums."

- **Home insurance.**[26] Carol's mom explained that since Bob and Carol were renting an apartment and not buying a home, they didn't need home insurance. Their landlord would obtain insurance for the apartment building they lived in but his insurance would cover only damage to the structure (other than flood or earthquake) and protect him from liability for injury to others occurring on the property. (Typically flood and earthquake protection are additional policies.)

While Bob and Carol would need homeowners insurance when they bought a home, Carol's mom advised them to get rental insurance. "Just think," she said, "if there was a fire and all of your things were destroyed how much it would cost to replace your computers, clothing, furniture, and household goods. Plus, rental insurance is relatively inexpensive." Carol's mom cautioned them to, "be sure to get a policy that covers replacement value." Bob and Carol found a rental insurance providing $50,000 in replacement coverage for annual premium of only $100.

- **Disability insurance.**[27] Carol's mom was adamant about disability insurance. "This is insurance most young people don't think about but should," she said. "Imagine if one of you was in a terrible car accident and suffered serious injuries. You may need surgery, maybe multiple surgeries, and face months of recovery. You may be unable to work for a long time. Neither your auto nor health insurance would cover your lost salary. Disability insurance is the only insurance that pays during a time of physical or mental disability. Plus," she added, "the premiums are relatively inexpensive for people your age."

  Carol's mom advised that generally the easiest way to get disability insurance once one is working is to opt in to an employer's plan, and then, if needed to ensure a higher level of income, purchase supplemental coverage with an additional disability policy plan. Carol's mom explained that by purchasing disability insurance while they were young and healthy, Bob and Carol would lock in low premiums.

- **Health insurance.**[28] Carol's mom advised that in today's rapidly changing health insurance market, health insurance offerings are difficult to sort out and compare. Luckily Carol and Bob were able to obtain good health insurance through their employers. When looking at their employers' health insurance rates, they discovered that it was cheaper, at this point when it was just the two of them, for each of them to obtain individual coverage rather than obtaining family coverage through one of their employers.

Savings

The last issue Bob and Carol discussed when preparing their household budget was how much to save. Given what they had already calculated, their net take home pay would be $7,407.50 per month. With household expenses totaling approximately $3400 per month plus loan repayments and insurance premiums, their remaining income would be about $ 1,207.50 per month.

After living on student budgets for so long, Bob and Carol looked forward to having money to go out to eat dinner, go on vacations and other extras. Carol was excited about clothes shopping. She had looked forward to buying a "work" wardrobe for a long time. She was tired of jeans and tee-shirts and was excited about buying suits and professional dresses, slacks, coat, and shoes. She had been "dream shopping" for work clothes for years. Bob was looking forward to buying a new mountain bike. There were great trails close by but his old bike, which he had had since high school, was not up to them. He had a bike picked out and was looking forward to buying it.

During their discussions about savings Bob and Carol realized they had somewhat different views about money. Bob was more risk-averse than Carol. Bob's family had struggled financially while he was growing up. At one point when his family had little savings, Bob's dad had been laid off. It was time of considerable stress for Bob's family. Bob's parents still struggled financially. Bob was determined never to live with the kind of financial insecurity his family experienced. Bob thought he and Carol should save at least 10% of their paychecks, and deposit their savings directly into a savings account where it would be safe. Carol wanted to save less so they could buy the things they had been looking forward to. She also thought they should put their savings into stocks. They reached a compromise: during the first six months of earning salaries, they would save $370 per month, 5% of their combined net salary, and each of them could spend $1500 on their longed-for items. Thereafter, they would save $740 per month, 10% of their combined income.

Here is Bob's and Carol's savings plan.

Chart 9: Bob's and Carol's Savings Plan
First Six Months of Working
(September–February)

Bob's Net Salary per month	$2,913.17
Carol's Net Salary per month	$4,494.34
Combined Net Salary Per Month	$7,407.50
Combined Estimated Loan Repayment per month	$1,800.00
Insurance (Auto, Disability, Life, Rental)	$1,000.00
Joint Household Expenses per month	$3,400.00
Savings per month	$370.00
Total Monthly Expenses	$6,570.00
Amount Remaining for Discretionary Spending and Unforeseen Expenses	$837.50

Now that they would have savings, Bob and Carol had to decide what to do with it. Although their savings would be small at first, it was fun to think about growing their nest egg. Bob and Carol divided up research duties and set a deadline to report back—just like when they were 1Ls in a study group. Their "deadline" was a candlelight dinner. At dinner, they discussed what they had learned. "Compounding interest is really neat," Bob said, going to his first assigned topic. "For example, if we start now at age 25, save $100 per month, and get 8% interest, we will have $326,353 when we are 65 years old. And we have contributed only $48,000 of that whole amount. The rest, $276,353, comes from interest! Here is the chart Bob made to show Carol how compounding interest makes money:

Chart 10: Compounding Interest
(Starting at Age 25)

Saving $100 per month, beginning at age 25 yields the following at age 65:

Amount saved per year beginning at age 25	Adds up to total contributions of (after 40 years)	At the following % rate of return	Yields the following amount at age 65
$1,200	$48,000	1%	$50,595
$1,200	$48,000	4%	$116,966
$1,200	$48,000	8%	$326,353
$1,200	$48,000	10%	$563,985

As Bob showed Carol in the next chart, waiting longer to start saving, like age 45, meant their savings would have less time to grow and less time to benefit from compounding interest. For example, the $326,353 they would have if they started saving at age 25 would only be $57,732 if they waited until age 45 to start.

Chart 11: Compounding Interest
(Starting at Age 45)

Saving $100 per month, beginning at age 45 yields the following at age 65:

Amount saved per year beginning at age 45	Adds up to total contributions of (after 20 years)	At the following % rate of return	Yields the following amount at age 65
$1,200	$24,000	1%	$26,688

$1,200	$24,000	4%	$36,722
$1,200	$24,000	8%	$57,732
$1,200	$24,000	10%	$73,071

Carol's topic to research was where to put their savings. "There are four major types of *savings options*," she explained: "savings accounts, certificates of deposit, money market accounts, and bonds." Here is what Carol summarized for Bob about savings options.[29]

Overview: Savings Options

- **Savings Accounts**
  - o Definition: Accounts at a bank, savings association, or credit union.
  - o Risk: Low risk because the federal government guarantees your money up to $100,000.
  - o Return: The interest rate on most savings accounts tends to be relatively low.
  - o Liquidity: High liquidity—you can withdraw your money at any time.
  - o Time Frame: Good for shorter time periods—3 years or less.

- **Certificates of Deposit**
  - o Definition: CDs are notes issues by banks that guarantee payment of a fixed interest rate until a future date (the maturity date).
  - o Risk: Low risk because CDs of $100,000 or less are insured by the federal government.
  - o Return: Interest rates are generally higher than the rates for savings accounts but lower than the rates for longer term or riskier investments.
  - o Liquidity: Relatively low—if you withdraw the money before the maturity date, you may pay a financial penalty.

- o Time Frame: Good for medium time frames—anywhere from 6 months to 5 years.

- **Money Market Accounts/Money Market Mutual Funds:**

  - o Definition: Money market accounts are savings accounts offered by banks requiring a high minimum balance. Money market mutual funds are available from brokers, many banks, and directly by mail. The money that you deposit in these funds is invested in a wide variety of savings instruments.

  - o Risk: Bank money market accounts have no risk on the first $100,000 because the government insures up to this amount. Money market mutual funds are not guaranteed by the government.

  - o Return: The interest rate for bank money market accounts is generally somewhat higher than for regular savings accounts. Rates on money market mutual funds are often somewhat higher than for bank money market accounts.

  - o Liquidity: High liquidity—you may withdraw your funds at any time. However, money market mutual funds do not have to send you a check for up to 3 days.

  - o Time Frame: Best for short-term savings goals, but many people keep a portion of their total college savings in these types of accounts because of their high liquidity and safety.

- **U.S. Savings Bonds:**

  - o Definition: U.S (EE) savings bonds are promises by the U.S. Treasury to repay the owner with interest when the bond is redeemed. Bonds earn interest for as long as 30 years. Bonds earn market-based rates right from the start. They can be purchased from banks and through employer payroll deduction plans in amounts as little as $50.

o   Risk: Savings bonds are completely risk-free since they are federal government obligations.

o   Return: The interest rate on a savings bond is usually higher than rates on savings accounts or money market mutual funds. However, if the bonds are cashed in (redeemed) before 5 years, they may pay a lower rate of interest.

o   Liquidity: Savings bonds are highly liquid and can be cashed in at any bank in the U.S. not just the bank where you bought funds. However, if the bonds are chased in before 5 years, they may pay a lower rate of interest.

o   Time Frame: Good for medium and longer term savings. Although they can be cashed in at any time, the maximum interest is obtained by holding them longer.

"In addition to these savings options, which are low or no-risk but generally, do not provide a high return," Carol explained, "there are *investment options* that are higher risk and generally provide a higher potential return. There are dozens, if not hundreds, of investment options but I researched four basic options: mutual funds, bonds, U.S. Treasury securities, and IRAs." Here is what Carol summarized for Bob about investment options:

Overview: Investment Options

- **Mutual Funds:**

    o   Definition: These funds can be invested in U.S. government securities or in stocks and bonds. You can purchase a mutual fund through an investment firm, brokerage house, many banks, or directly from the mutual fund by mail.

    o   Risk: Risk varies widely depending on the objectives and policies of the fund. Funds are not federally insured but your money is generally safer in a mutual fund than in a few individual common stocks because a mutual fund invests in many different stocks and bonds and thus spreads the risk over many different investments

- o Return: The return on a mutual fund depends on how the market performs and on whether the fund makes good investments.

- o Liquidity: Very liquid—you can sell the fund at any time. However, the amount of money you can get for the fund depends on the value, and the value changes regularly depending on the conditions in the stock and bond markets.

- o Time Frame: Good for longer term investing such as 5 years or more.

- **Individual Corporate Bonds or Stocks:**

- o Definition: A bond is a promise by the corporation to repay the face value of the bond, plus a fixed rate of interest, at a specific future date. Stock represents part ownership of a company. You make money on stocks either through the dividends you earn or by selling the stock at a price higher than the price for which you bought it. The prices of most stocks—and many bonds—are listed in major newspapers. Over longer periods, the price of the stock may increase or decrease. Stocks and bonds can be purchased from brokerage houses and through some banks.

- o Risk: The stocks and bonds of good companies can be quite safe over longer time periods. However, these investments are not guaranteed by the Federal Government or anyone else.

- o Return: Interest rates on bonds vary depending on the type of bond and its rating. Generally, returns are higher than on savings accounts, CDs, and U.S. Savings Bonds. The return on individual stocks can be very high depending on the dividends the company pays and the increase in the price of stock.

o Liquidity: Most types of corporate and all types of government bonds are highly liquid. Most individual stocks can be sold almost any day.

o Time Frame: Short-term bonds are good for time periods of 1–3 years. All other bonds and common stocks should be considered as longer term investments, good for periods of 5–18 years.

- **U.S. Treasury Securities:**

  o Definition: The Treasury Department and Federal agencies issue different types of fixed-income investments such as short-term bills (13-, 26-, and 52-week bills), medium-term notes (2–10 years), and long-term bonds (over 10 years). These securities can be purchased directly from regional Federal Reserve banks, through regular banks, and through brokers. Because there are relatively large minimum purchase amounts, some people prefer to invest instead in mutual funds that invest only in U.S. Government securities.

  o Risk: These securities have no risk since they are backed by the Federal Government.

  o Return: Interest rates on government securities vary with the maturity of the issue. As with other fixed-income investments, short-term issues generally have lower interest rates than longer term issues. All government securities have interest rates that are lower than corporate securities with the same maturity because the government securities are considered safer.

  o Liquidity: Government securities are highly liquid and can be sold through brokers on any day the financial markets are open.

- o Time Frame: Government securities have a wide variety of maturities and can, therefore, be tailored to any time frame needed by families saving for college.

- **Education IRAs:**

  - o Definition: A special type of IRA account that can only be used for higher education expenses. Parents, grandparents, or others can contribute up to $500 a year to any type of IRA-qualified savings or investment account. The account must be registered in the child's name. Only the child can use the money to pay for his or her higher education costs, or those of a sibling.

  - o Risk: These accounts have a wide range of risks since they can be invested in many kinds of savings and investment vehicles. These include CDs, money market funds, savings bonds, mutual funds, and individual stocks and bonds.

  - o Return: Returns (as well as risks) will usually vary depending on how the account is invested. Savings instruments that pay interest will usually have the lowest returns and the lowest risk. Individual stocks and bonds or mutual funds often have higher risks and returns that reflect the relative success of the businesses or portfolio of investments.

  - o Liquidity: Most of the investments that are eligible for an education IRA account are fairly liquid because they can be cashed in at a bank or sold through brokers on any day the financial markets are open.

  - o Time Frame: The different types of investments used for Education IRAs can generally be held for any time period. However, it is usually appropriate to hold savings-type accounts for shorter periods and to invest in stocks, bonds, or mutual funds for the longer term.

Savings for Retirement . . . Already?

Although it seemed odd to think about at age 25, Bob and Carol knew they should start saving for retirement. Bob's family's experience influenced them both in this regard. Bob's parents were older when they met, married, and had children. Currently, Bob's dad was 73 years old and his mother was 65. They had virtually no retirement savings. Bob's mother had not worked outside the home during their marriage, so she had no retirement employment accounts, nor would she receive Social Security retirement payments since only those who earn wages receive Social Security payments. As a teacher in rural areas, Bob's father had worked at a relatively low salary throughout his life and so the amount of Social Security retirement, which is calibrated to one's salary when working, would not be sufficient for him and Bob's mother to live on after he retired. The longer Bob's dad could work full time, the more he and Bob's mom could save to supplement the Social Security payments Bob's father would receive. For this reason, Bob's father continued to work full time despite his age and increasingly poor health. Both Bob and Carol wanted an easier life than Bob's parents.

Like many of their friends, Bob and Carol were also worried about Social Security. They knew that the Social Security program would have to undergo some changes or their generation would suffer. By the year 2041, for example, unless structural changes are made to the program, the U.S. Social Security program will be able to pay only 75% in scheduled benefit payments. Given this uncertainty and the fact that even with full payments, Social Security is rarely enough to live on,[30] Bob and Carol were determined to save adequately for retirement.

Through his state employment at the PD's office, Bob was able to participate in the state retirement program. Bob would be eligible to retire after thirty years of full-time employment and thereafter receive forty percent of his full salary for the rest of his life. If Carol contributed an amount equal to 5% of her gross salary from the firm, Carol's firm would contribute an amount equal to at least 3% of her gross salary (See Chapter II (8) *supra*). Carol's firm's contribution was subject to negotiation as part of her total compensation package, but for planning purposes, Carol decided to assume a three percent match on her current annual salary of $75,000, for forty years. Based on these calculating assumptions and an average of 10 % return, Carol will accumulate $1,800,000 by age 65.

Carol and Bob researched the types of retirement accounts available. There were lots of options. Some, like a "SEP" ("Simplified Employee Pension"), generally is used by self-employed individuals and thus was not relevant to Bob and Carol at this point, although if Bob ultimately followed his dream and opened his own law firm, a "SEP" retirement account could be to his tax advantage.[31] The retirement account most relevant to Bob and Carol at this point was the ROTH-IRA, which is only available to individuals earning up to certain limits. As their salaries grew in the years ahead, they would no longer be eligible for ROTH-IRA accounts and knew they should take advantage of qualifying for such accounts now. ROTH-IRAs are "a breed unto themselves."[32] For young people saving over many years the ROTH-IRA is a great deal. Once money is in a ROTH-IRA, it is never taxed again, even when one retires and takes money out of it. One can contribute to a ROTH-IRA even if participating in a retirement plan through an employer as long as annual contribution limits are not exceeded. For example, in 2014, the maximum contribution an individual can make to a ROTH-IRA is $5,500.[33] Since both Bob and Carol were contributing less than this to their retirement accounts (Bob at $2,310 and Carol at $3,750), they decided that they would re-visit their budget in a few months and determine if they could increase their retirement contributions to $5,500 per year and open ROTH-IRAs.

10. CREDIT SCORES[34]

One day, Carol saw a story in the news about credit scores, "Bob, listen to this!"

Carol read the following to Bob:

"Credit scores are important. For example, consider a couple planning to buy their first house. On a 30-year mortgage with a FICO credit score of 720, they qualify for 5.5 percent interest rate on their mortgage. But if their credit score is 580, they are likely to get no better than 8.5 percent. On a $100,000 mortgage loan, the three-point difference will cost them $2,400 dollars a year, adding up to $72,000 dollars over the loan's 30-year lifetime."

Bob and Carol decided they needed to learn more about credit scores so they could get theirs as high as possible before they bought new cars or a house.

Credit bureaus keep track of public information on individuals such as bankruptcies, judgments, liens, and use of credit cards and loans. Credit reporting agencies calculate a score based upon this information. Credit agencies' scores vary somewhat based on the information they collect and the calculations they use. Fair Isaac Corporation, a private company, created a statistical model that generates a "FICO score" and is based upon each credit agency's information. A FICO score is intended to predict how likely it is that an individual will repay his or her debts. Creditors check FICO scores in deciding whether to loan individuals money and on what terms.

FICO scores range from 300–850. Higher FICO scores are better. A good FICO score is 700 or above. A score of 600 or below may cause lenders to charge higher rates, turn down applications for loans or leases, and slow credit approvals. FICO scores are calculated from five types of data: payment history (35% of a FICO score); how much is owed (30% of a FICO score); length of credit history (15% of FICO score); types of credit in use (10% of a FICO score); and types of credit used (10% of a FICO score). [35]

Anyone may obtain a free credit report each year from www.annualcreditreport.com/index.action, a site established by Congress to help consumers access their credit information. FICO scores may also be obtained from www.myfico.com, established by The Fair Isaac Corporation (FICO), for a cost of $19.95 for one FICO score and $54.85 for three FICO scores from the three major credit reporting agencies. Credit reports generally are free when applying for a mortgage or other significant loan. When Bob and Carol checked their credit score they were glad to see that it was 749. They wanted to keep their score as high as possible.

11. BUYING A CAR[36]

Two years after Bob and Carol graduated from law school, the inevitable happened. One of their cars (Bob's Honda Civic) died. The transmission went out and the $2,200[37] it would cost to repair it was more than the approximate $2,000 value of his 14-year-old car that now had 275,000 miles (according to Kelley Bluebook (www.kbb.com)). As much as they dreaded the expense of replacing Bob's car, they knew it was time. They talked to friends and family and did research on car purchases. Here is what they learned.

Key Points to Consider When Purchasing a Car

- Try to drive your vehicles for at least ten years or 100,000 miles. Most well made cars should last at least this long.

- A car purchase generally is the largest single purchase in a family after the purchase of a home.

- Insurance, taxes, and registration fees are cheaper for used and less expensive cars.

- Assess how much space you need and driving conditions you are likely to encounter such as ice, snow, or steep climbs, which may necessitate all-wheel drive.

- Compare safety, mileage, reliability and cost of new and used vehicles. Good sources for this information are Consumer Reports and J.D. Power. You can purchase the annual Consumer Report issue on automobiles or look at it in your public library. J.D. Power is available online at http://autos.jdpower.com/ratings/. Information about the safety of various vehicles may be found at www.safercar.gov, a site operated by the National Highway Transportation and Safety Administration.

- Check the availability and pricing for new and used vehicles in your zip code at www.edmunds.com and Kelley Bluebook, www.kbb.com.

- Shop around, and be willing to walk away.

- Car purchasers can get better deals at the end of the month and at the end of the year when dealerships are trying to meet sales quotas.

Bob and Carol shopped around and narrowed their decision to two cars. The first choice was a used, two-year-old, all-wheel-drive, Jeep Grand Cherokee Laredo. Bob loved it. He could just imagine taking it out on dirt roads with his mountain bike loaded in the back. The other option was a three-year-old Toyota Corolla S. which they thought would be reliable and comfortable. Here is the Chart Bob and Carol created comparing the two cars.

Chart 12: Which Car to Buy?

	Used Jeep Grand Cherokee	Used Toyota Corolla
Cost (kbb.com)	$23,000	$15,000
Down Payment	$5,000	$5,000
Amount Financed	$18,000	$10,000
Interest Rate	2.5%	2.5%
Loan Term	36 months	36 months
Interest Paid over Life of Loan[38]	$702.18	$390.10
Total Car Cost (cost + interest − $500 rebate)	$23,202.18	$14,890.10
Mileage	23,000	30,000
Safety Rating	4/5 (NHTSA)	3/5 (NHTSA)
Annual Insurance Premium[39]	$1,300	$1,100

Bob and Carol decided on the Toyota. Although they knew it was better financially to purchase a vehicle outright rather than finance it through a car loan, they did not have enough saved to do so. They researched automobile financing and learned the following:

Automobile Financing Considerations

- Save up and pay outright for a car if you can. This will save you interest and may help you negotiate a cheaper price on the car.

- Put as much down as you can.

- Get as short of a loan as you can afford. Do not get a loan for longer than four years.

- Negotiate on the price of the car first, and then negotiate on the terms of the financing.

- Credit unions generally offer lower interest rates than banks.

- If the dealer offers a rebate for 0% interest, calculate whether you are better off with the rebate or the lower interest rate available.

- Know your FICO score (See Chapter II(10) *supra*).

- It is generally better to buy than lease. Calculations to compare the two options can be found at www.kiplinger.com, www.bankrate.com, or www.federalreserve.gov/pubs/leasing.

As demonstrated in Chart 12, Bob and Carol were able to put $5,000 down, obtain a three-year loan at 2.5% interest and get a $500 rebate. Opting for the Corolla instead of the Jeep saved Bob and Carol $8,312.08 ($8,000 cost of car plus $312 in interest over the life of the loan) plus $200 every year on lower car insurance premiums.

12. A GROWING FAMILY

The next few years were fun and exciting. Bob and Carol had ups and downs, of course, but enjoyed each other, their jobs, and married life. They spent time with family and friends. They stuck to their financial plans. They talked about having a family and decided the time was right. They were fortunate, and Carol soon became pregnant. They read baby books and went to Lamaze classes. They bought term life insurance.[40] Bob's and Carol's daughter, Alexandra, was born strong and healthy. Bob and Carol adored her. Like most first-time parents, Bob and Carol were stunned at how expensive babies are. They calculated the costs of having Alexandra, beginning with the prenatal expenses.

Chart 13: Prenatal Child Care Expenses[41]

Prenatal medical care	$2,000–4,500 (without insurance) $400–900 (with insurance, 20% co-pay)
Vitamins ($20/month)	$180
Maternity clothes	$600
Childbirth classes (five classes at $60/class)	$300
Baby books and toys	$100
Total	**$1,580–$5,680**

Chart 14: Child Expenses Birth to Twelve Months[42]

Out of pocket expenses for delivery (assumes co-pay is 20% of total average cost of $18,329 vaginal delivery[43] plus $1,000 deductible)	$4,665
Out of pocket medical expense for "well baby" health care for first 12 months of life[44]	$668 (without insurance) $70–$210 (with insurance)
Diapers	$600
Supplemental formula and food	$1,800
Car seat	$150 ($90–$350)
Stroller	$200
Baby bed, bassinet, other furniture	$350
Misc. other equipment (jumping chair, table booster, bottles, etc.)	$500
Baby clothes	$800
Daycare	$6,750
Total	**$15,825–$16,683**

As expensive as it was to have a baby, Bob and Carol knew they were fortunate. They had friends who had had difficulty conceiving and sought fertility treatments, which cost $12,000–14,000.[45] Sometimes fertility treatments are covered, at least partially, by health insurance, but not always. As of 2014, fifteen states require health insurers cover at least some fertility treatment.[46] Bob and Carol also had friends who had adopted a child, which is also expensive. Adoption costs range from $20,000–$40,000, depending on the adoption agency service and birth country of the child.[47]

13. BUYING A HOUSE

After Alexandra arrived, the apartment that had seemed so large when they moved in now seemed impossibly cramped. There were baby supplies and equipment everywhere. Bob and Carol discussed whether they could afford to buy a house. They did their research. They compared the cost of continuing to rent to purchasing a home, taking into account the tax advantage of deducting mortgage interest on their income taxes. Bob and Carol also included in their analysis likely incidental expenses of purchasing a home, such as inspection, appraisal, down payment, mortgage fees, title insurance, and moving costs. They found the website, bankrate.com, to be of great help in these calculations.

Bob and Carol found to their surprise that with the income tax deduction for mortgage interest, the annual cost of renting their current apartment was $21,660, compared to an annual housing cost of $14,534 if they purchased a $250,000 home with 20% down. Granted, the annual cost of owning a home would increase each year because the tax advantage of home ownership would decrease (as the relative percentage of interest versus principal decreased over the life of a home loan) but they were pleased with their finding. They were ready to buy a house!

Chart 15: Renting an Apartment vs. Buying a Home

Rental Cost (per month)	
Monthly Rent	$850
Utilities	$200
Maintenance Fee	$25
Rental Insurance	$10
Total Cost	$1085
Total Annual Cost	$21,660

Buying a Home (first year)*	
Closing Costs	$3,507
Mortgage Payments	$13,200
Home Insurance	$1,056
Property Taxes	$2,111
Home Repairs	$1,800
Yard Maintenance	$1,200
Total Annual Cost	$22,874
Less annual tax advantage of owning a home	$8,340
Net Total Cost	$14,534
*Calculated based on a $250,000 house with 20% down; 30-year fixed mortgage at 4.172% interest.	

Bob and Carol began looking at houses. They found several they liked and compared the estimated costs of each.

Chart 16: Choosing Which House to Buy

House #1	
Total Cost of House	$249,900
Less Tax Advantage (per year)	$8,340
Net Cost	$240,660
House Maintenance (per year)	$3,000
Yard Maintenance (per year)	$300
Commuting Cost (per year)	$400

House #2	
Total Cost of House	$240,000
Less Tax Advantage (per year)	$8,004
Net Cost	$231,996
House Maintenance (per year)	$5,000
Yard Maintenance (per year)	$800
Commuting Cost (per year)	$1,000

House #3	
Total Cost of House	$222,000
Less Tax Advantage (per year)	$7,404
Net Cost	$214,596
House Maintenance (per year)	$2,500
Yard Maintenance (per year)	$300
Commuting Cost (per year)	0

Bob and Carol opted for House # 3. They loved the house in House # 2 option, in part because several of their friends had purchased houses close by. However, House # 2 was not only a more expensive house but also carried higher "collateral" costs of home and yard maintenance, commuting costs, and the private school tuition which the location would necessitate.

Bob and Carol compared the financing options on a mortgage of $177,600, which is what they would need if they put 20% down on House # 3. They found that their good credit score of 749 was crucial in obtaining favorable financing. Here are the financing options Bob and Carol considered:

Chart 17: Home Financing Options[48]

30-Year Mortgage	
• Mortgage amount	$177,600
• Fixed interest rate	6.5%
• Monthly payments	$1,251.25
• Interest over the life of the mortgage	$208,385.91
15-Year Mortgage	
• Mortgage amount	$177,600
• Fixed interest rate	6%
• Monthly payments	$1,600
• Interest over the life of the mortgage	$85,075.48
Adjustable-Rate Mortgage (ARM): 30-Year	
• Mortgage amount	$177,600
• Possible interest rate	4%–12%
• Possible monthly payment	$787.74
• Possible interest over the life of the mortgage	$181,000

Bob and Carol decided against an adjustable-rate mortgage because of the unpredictability of interest rates. Reluctantly, they also decided against the 15-year mortgage. They knew that the 15-year mortgage was the best option because it would save them thousands of dollars in interest payments but they did not feel they could afford the $350 higher monthly payment. Bob and Carol made sure, however, that the thirty-year mortgage they obtained permitted early payoff of principal and interest if they found they could afford paying more per month.

14. GOING PART TIME

Bob and Carol couldn't believe how fun it was being parents—and how exhausting! Carol took two months off from work when Alexandra was born. Carol loved her job and looked forward to returning to her practice after maternity leave. However, once she was back at work Carol found that juggling care of a newborn and the demands of her job was harder than she expected. Carol traveled a lot with her job and had long, erratic hours given her clients' needs. Although Carol and Bob shared nighttime duties for Alexandra, Bob seemed to handle juggling work and parenthood without becoming as exhausted, probably because he did not travel for his job and because his work schedule was more predictable than Carol's. In addition, Bob was only a few years shy of his tenth anniversary at the PD office when the balance of his school loans, approximately $38,000, would be forgiven. Since her job in private practice did not qualify for loan forgiveness, Carol did not have loan forgiveness as an incentive to continue working full time.

Exhausted, Carol started thinking about whether she should stop work for a few years or perhaps go to part time. She had seen friends from law school do both. Carol and Bob discussed what to do, and talked with a number of their friends—those who had started families and continued to work, and those who had stopped working. They read books and articles on the topic. Carol decided that she did not want to stop working altogether. They needed her income and she enjoyed practicing law too much to leave completely. The issue was whether she should seek to work part-time at her firm or struggle through working full time. Here are Carol's thoughts about whether to pursue a part-time option at her firm.

Pros and Cons of Changing from Full-Time to Part-Time Employment

Pros:

- Not as exhausted.
- Not as stressed.
- Get to spend more time with Alexandra.
- Get to spend more time with Bob.

- Time to explore hobbies and get more involved in the community.

- Possibly save on child care costs. Carol realized that they may not save much on child care if she went part time. They may still need to pay for full-time care since Carol would need flexibility to work some long days when demanding work projects arose.

- Part-time employment may save on commuting, eating out at lunch, and other work-related expenses.

Cons:

- Loss of income.

- Possible loss of career advancement.

- Unable to work on some of the exciting, high-stakes, fast-paced projects at work.

- Possible feeling of resentment toward Bob who will get to go to work when Carol stays behind with dirty diapers.

- Bob's possible feeling of resentment toward Carol who gets to stay home, play with Alexandra, and enjoy leisure time and activities, when he has to go to work.

Bob and Carol discussed the options. Carol decided that ideally she would work like to work three or four days a week with some flexibility as to which days and what times of day she worked. She had been at the firm since its beginning and knew that the lawyers' schedules were driven largely by their clients' needs. As she thought of how to broach a part-time option, Carol tried to think of the ways a part-time arrangement would work well for the firm as well as for her. Carol came up with a proposal tailored to her firm's compensation system. She would propose working for the firm 25 hours per week (about half of her usual weekly billable hours) for 3/8 of her prior year's salary, retaining all employee benefits (which she knew were worth about 30% of her annual salary), foregoing bonuses (typically about 30% of billings) but retaining the customary 30% of any new business she brought to the firm.

Carol scheduled a meeting with John, the founding partner of the firm, to present her proposal. Carol texted Bob as soon as she and John had finished talking: "John agreed!!!"

With Carol's reduced salary, the increased expenses of owning a home, and the cost of a new baby, Bob and Carol were glad they had not bought the more expensive house they had considered a few years before. They watched as some of their friends who were locked into high mortgage payments and private school tuition for children struggled financially.

15. LOAN FORGIVENESS: IS THE TEN-YEAR ANNIVERSARY WORTH IT?

One day, shortly after Carol switched to part-time, Bob came home with surprising news. A friend with a firm in town had called and offered Bob a position with the firm. Bob was tempted by the offer. He knew and liked the attorneys in the firm, the firm had an excellent reputation, and Bob thought he would enjoy the work even though it would involve learning new areas of law.

Bob had been at the PD's office for eight years. He still enjoyed the office but would also enjoy doing something new. One key issue was whether it would be financially wise for Bob to leave the PD's office for private practice before the balance of his school loans was forgiven. If he remained at the PD's office for another two years or went to another qualifying government or public interest law office to reach the requirement of consecutive 120 monthly loan repayments, the balance of Bob's Stafford loans (about $38,000) would be forgiven.

Here are Bob's calculations on forfeiting forgiveness of his school loans if he left government service prior to his ten year anniversary:

Chart 18: Cost in Forgoing Full Loan Forgiveness If Bob Leaves the PD Office for Private Practice

Total amount of Bob's educational loans upon graduation from law school	$80,000
Total amount of Bob's educational loans plus interest if repaid loans in 10 years (principal + interest)	$125,596
Amount Bob has paid while working at the PD's office for eight years (repayment capped at 15% of Bob's discretionary income)	$24,765.80
Balance that will be forgiven if Bob remains at the PD's office or works at another qualifying employer for two more years	$100,830
Net increase in Bob's compensation if Bob leaves the PD's office for private practice[49] (increase in salary less deductions)	$64,800 ($32,400 per year)
Amount Bob would save by taking advantage of loan forgiveness (and forgoing increased salary at law firm)	$36,030

Bob decided to remain at the PD's office until at least his tenth-year anniversary. He wanted to get his loans forgiven and he felt confident he would also have excellent options in private practice later. In two years, Bob reached his tenth-year anniversary at the Public Defender's office, and the balance of his loans was forgiven.

Anticipating loan forgiveness, Bob had already researched the tax consequences of loan forgiveness. Loan forgiveness may constitute a taxable event, with the total amount forgiven counted as ordinary income during the year of the discharge.

However, there are some forgiveness programs that allow the balance that is forgiven not to be treated as "income" and taxed accordingly. Luckily for Bob, the Public Service Loan Forgiveness program through which he had obtained his Stafford loans was such a plan. This is because of Internal Revenue Code section 108(f)(1), which states:

> "[G]ross income does not include any amount which . . . would be includible in gross income by reason of the discharge (in whole or in part) of any student loan if such discharge was pursuant to a provision of such loan under which all or part of the indebtedness of the individual would be discharged if the individual worked for a certain period of time in certain professions for any of a broad class of employers.

According to this provision, because Bob had been employed by a governmental unit (a "qualifying employer") for ten years ("a certain period of time"), his loan forgiveness program was exempt from the loan forgiveness being income.[50] Bob learned that the following loans *will not* be treated as taxable income upon forgiveness:

- Public Service Loan Forgiveness
- Teacher Loan Forgiveness,

and that the following loans *will* be treated as taxable income upon forgiveness:

- Death and Disability Discharge
- Closed School, False Certification and Unpaid Refund Discharge
- Closed School Discharge
- Income-Contingent Repayment
- Income-Based Repayment

Bob learned that although Income-Contingent Repayment (ICR) and Income-Based Repayment (IBR) programs (which is what Bob had since his monthly loan repayments were capped at a percentage of his discretionary income) do not normally qualify for a non-taxable forgiveness, individuals who use these programs while working at a qualifying public service employer will qualify for non-taxable forgiveness. The PD office where Bob had worked was a "qualifying public service employer" within section 108(f)(1).When ICR or IBR is combined with Public Service Loan Forgiveness and loans are paid back within a certain period of time while working in public service, 108(f)(1) is satisfied and the forgiveness is non-taxable.[51]

16. BOB OPENS HIS OWN FIRM

Two years flew by, Bob reached his ten year anniversary at the P.D.'s office and repaid his school loans. Bob had always wanted to have his own firm, and now that he had ten years of great experience as a trial lawyer and no more loan debt, his dream was a possibility. Bob talked with friends who had established their own practices and did a lot of research. He found the following sources very helpful: ABA Solo/Small Firm Resource Center; local state bar websites; *Law Practice Today*; myshingle.com; and a myriad of blogs and articles specifically dedicated to the solo practitioner.[52]

From his research, Bob knew that it made financial sense to share office space, overhead, and a staff person with other solo practitioners. Such opportunities were widely available. Bob found another attorney in town who was willing to rent Bob an office in return for Bob sharing utilities and the cost of a secretary. In addition to office overhead, Bob had to pay for malpractice insurance, bar memberships, and a variety of other fixed and variable expenses. Here is a list of the types of expenses Bob incurred in starting his own law firm.

Costs Associated with Starting a Law Firm[53]

- Office space (including utilities)
- Staff
- Office supplies and furniture
- Technology (computer, scanner/printer/copier, information backup, phone, website, email)
- Malpractice insurance
- Legal research
- Bar membership and CLEs

- Accounting software
- Word processing software
- Case management software
- Marketing
- Savings for living expenses
- Taxes
- Process servers/postage
- Miscellaneous

Bob and Carol were aware that there was risk in giving up Bob's secure and stable income at the PD's office to open his own practice. However, Bob felt sure he had what it took to start his own firm, and he decided to take the plunge.

Bob and Carol wanted to have a second child. They also knew that having a second child would likely solidify Carol's part-time employment choice, at least for the next five or ten years. Bob and Carol were overjoyed to greet their second child, David, three years after Alexandra was born.

Bob opened his own law firm soon after David's birth. For the first three years of practice, Bob netted less than what he had made as a Public Defender once he paid all of his expenses. By the fourth year, however, Bob was making enough for their family to live comfortably and even to move to their dream home.

17. FUNDING CHILDREN'S COLLEGE EDUCATIONS

Life was busy with two children and two careers. Bob's firm grew. He added two lawyers. Carol continued to work on a reduced schedule at her firm. She paid off all of her school loans by the time David was two years old, increasing their monthly income. By the time Alexandra was in elementary school, Carol and Bob started thinking about college expenses for their children. Bob and Carol listed likely college costs including tuition and fees related to tuition; books, supplies, and computer; housing; food; clothing; transportation; entertainment and social activities; clubs, sororities and fraternities. They found that in current dollars average tuition and fees at:

- An in-state, four-year public institution were $8,893;

- An out-of-state, four-year public institution were $22,203; and

- A private, four-year institution were $30,094.[54]

Bob and Carol researched the options for funding college including education income tax credits. They learned that *Qualified Tuition Programs* (also known as 529 Plans) are tax-advantaged savings plans designed to encourage saving for future college expenses. If money is withdrawn from a "529 plan" for qualified educational expenses, it is not subject to federal tax and oftentimes is also excluded from state tax. There are two types of Qualified Tuition Plans: Prepaid Tuition Plans and College Savings Plans. Carol made a chart comparing the two types of Qualified Tuition Plans:

Chart 19: Comparing Prepaid Tuition Plan vs. College Savings Plan[55]

Prepaid Tuition Plan	College Savings Plan
Locks in tuition prices at eligible public and private colleges and universities.	No lock on college costs.
All plans cover tuition and mandatory fees only. Some plans allow you to purchase a room & board option or use excess tuition credits for other qualified expenses.	Covers all "qualified higher education expenses," including: • Tuition • Room & board • Mandatory fees • Books, computers (if required)

Most plans set lump sum and installment payments prior to purchase based on age of beneficiary and number of years of college tuition purchased.	Many plans have contribution limits in excess of $200,000.
Many state plans guaranteed or backed by state.	No state guarantee. Most investment options are subject to market risk. Your investment may make no profit or even decline in value.
Most plans have age/grade limit for beneficiary.	No age limits. Open to adults and children.
Most state plans require either owner or beneficiary of plan to be a state resident.	No residency requirement. However, nonresidents may only be able to purchase some plans through financial advisers or brokers.
Most plans have limited enrollment period.	Enrollment open all year.

Bob and Carol considered other options to 529 plans to finance their children's educations. They learned about the following:

- **Coverdell Education Savings Accounts:** Total contributions for the beneficiary cannot exceed $2,000 in any year. The owner has the right to direct the distribution of the funds. The distributions from this savings account are tax-free if applied to a qualified educational expense.

- **Roth IRA:** There is a $5,000 limit on contributions to Roth IRAs. Early distributions from Roth IRAs are typically taxed an additional 10% on the year of distribution; however, this tax will not be applied to if the qualified educational expense is more than the distribution.

- **The American Opportunity Tax Credit:** The AOTC makes the Hope Credit available to a broader range of taxpayers, including many with higher incomes and those who owe no tax. It also adds required course materials to the list of qualifying expenses and allows the credit to be claimed for four post-secondary education years instead of two. Many of those eligible will qualify for the maximum annual credit of $2,500 per student. The full credit is available to individuals whose modified adjusted gross income is $80,000 or less, or $160,000 or less for married couples filing a joint return. The credit is phased out for taxpayers with incomes above these levels.

- **The Lifetime Learning Credit:** This tax credit applies to tuition and enrollment fees for undergraduate or graduate degree programs that help students acquire skills that will improve their job skills. The maximum credit per family is $2,000 per year.

- **Series EE Bonds:** The savings bond education tax exclusion permits qualified taxpayers to exclude from their gross income all or part of the interest paid upon the redemption of eligible Series EE and I Bonds issued after 1989, when the bond owner pays qualified higher education expenses at an eligible institution.

- **Uniform Gift to Minors Act:** This trust allows a donor to place securities and cash in a custodial account for the benefit of the minor. The account is considered assets of the child, and this can reduce the eligibility for certain need-based financial aid.

- **Uniform Transfers to Minors Act:** The UTMA is similar to UGMA (above), but this custodial account can hold real property as well as cash and securities for the benefit of the child.

- **Employer's Educational Assistance Program:** Some employers offer an educational assistance program. Under such a program, the employer can pay for up to $5,250 of employee's tuition, books, supplies, equipment, room and board, and transportation expenses. This amount may be excluded from the employee's income.

18. RETIREMENT

The years flew by. Carol returned to work full time when David started college. Alexandra and David grew up, married, and had children of their own. By the time Bob and Carol were sixty-five years old, their finances were in good shape and they were able to retire comfortably, forty years after they graduated from law school. They traveled on wonderful bicycle trips all over the world.

19. CONCLUSION

I know, we may all hate Bob and Carol because they were so *good* at handling their finances. But, live by three rules regarding money and you will be fine. First, pay yourself. No matter how small your paycheck or how great your expenses, put some of every paycheck into savings, and leave it there. As Albert Einstein said, "Compound interest is the eighth wonder of the world. He who understands it, earns it . . . he who doesn't . . . pays it." Compounding interest is magic—it transforms little amounts of money into bigger amounts of money. Think of your savings as "freedom" money. It will give you the freedom to leave a job you may not like, change directions, or follow your dream.

Second, live below your means. Doing so will give you flexibility to respond to life's uncertainties. We never know when our lives will be complicated by illness, special needs of a child, divorce, bad investment, or law firm dissolution. These challenges are difficult enough without adding financial stress.

Third, don't let your standard of living become a prison. Don't commit to a high mortgage payment, private schools, or living on credit card debt with the expectation that you will make up the shortfall with the next raise or doing well with investments.

TABLE OF AUTHORITIES

Cole, Martin A. "55 Ways to Lose Your License." *Bench and Bar of Minnesota* Aug. 2009.

Jarvis, Heather. "Getting a Grip on Your Student Debt." 41 *ABA Student Lawyer* 41 (2012): 3.

Blumenthal, Karen. *The Wall Street Journal Guide to Starting Your Financial Life.* Dow Jones & Co., 2012).

Kobliner, Beth. *Get a Financial Life: Personal Financial Planning in Your Twenties and Thirties.* Fireside, 2009.

Siegel, Cary. *Why Didn't They Teach Me This in School?* Simple Strategic Solutions, 2013.

Malkiel, Burton G. *A Random Walk Down Wall Street.* W.W. Norton & Co., Inc., 2012.

For more specific information on loan forgiveness programs including what jobs and offices qualify, how to structure one's loans while in school, and how to structure loan repayments so as to maximize loan forgiveness see:

http://equaljusticeworks.org/ed-debt/students/public-service-loan-forgiveness

http://askheatherjarvis.com/tools

In addition, UA Law Assistant Dean for Public Interest Law, Glory McLaughlin, gmclaughlin@law.ua.edu, or 205-348-8302, can provide loan forgiveness information and counseling.

ENDNOTES

1   *See, e.g.,* Martin A. Cole, *55 Ways to Lose Your License,* BENCH AND BAR OF MINNESOTA Aug. 2009.

2   Jarvis, Heather. "Getting a Grip on Your Student Debt." 41 ABA STUDENT LAWYER 3 (2012).

3   http://www.direct.ed.gov/inschool.html (last visited Mar. 13, 2014).

4   ABA   Journal,   http://www.abajournal.com/news/article/ average_debt_load_of_private_law_grads_is_125k_these_five_schools _lead_to_m/ (Posted March 28, 2012) (last visited Feb. 9, 2014).

5   KAREN BLUMENTHAL, THE WALL STREET JOURNAL GUIDE TO STARTING YOUR FINANCIAL LIFE 116 (Dow Jones & Co 2012) [hereinafter BLUMENTHAL, GUIDE TO STARTING YOUR FINANCIAL LIFE].

6   More information on eligibility for Federal Perkins Loans can be found at http://studentaid.ed.gov. (last visited Mar. 13, 2014).

7   BLUMENTHAL, GUIDE TO STARTING YOUR FINANCIAL LIFE, *supra* note 5 at 114–118.

8   BETH KOBLINER, GET A FINANCIAL LIFE: PERSONAL FINANCIAL PLANNING IN YOUR TWENTIES AND THIRTIES 50–58 (Fireside, 2009) [hereinafter KOBLINER, GET A FINANCIAL LIFE].

9   http://www.usnews.com/education/blogs/student-loan-ranger /2012/02/01/law-school-student-debt-is-just-tip-of-the-iceberg;   http:// www.nytimes.com/2013/01/31/education/law-schools-applications-fall- as-costs-rise-and-jobs-are-cut.html?_r=0 (Last accessed Feb. 28, 2014)

10   Based   on   the   calculator   at   http://www.finaid.org/ calculators/scripts/loanpayments.cgi using the following parameters: $40,000 loan balance; 6.8% interest rate; 0% loan fees; 10 year loan term; $50 minimum payment; "still in school" enrollment status. Interest is the approximate total from months 10, 11, and 12 in the Payment Schedule, which would correspond to May, June, and July of the year following loan disbursement in August, or the summer after 1L year.

11   http://www.rsa-al.gov/ (Last visited Feb. 20, 2014). Currently many state pension plans are experiencing major financial instability, due to investment losses, falling tax revenues, and the declining ratio of current workers to retirees. http://money.cnn.com/ 2013/02/11/retirement/state-workers-pension-benefits/;   http://www. alabamapolicy.org/wp-content/uploads/API-Research-Retirement-

System-2012.pdf page 3 (Last accessed Feb. 20, 2014). The future of government pension is therefore somewhat uncertain.

[12] Based on the calculator at http://www.irs.gov/Individuals/ IRS-Withholding-Calculator using the following parameters: joint filing status; one job; no eligible children, child care expenses, child tax credit, or dependent care credit; $75,000 salary; no adjustments to income or additional withholding; zero dependents; neither spouse blind; $3,000 plan contribution; and standard deduction.

[13] Based on the chart in "Withholding Tax Tables and Instructions for Employers and Withholding Agents" located at http://www.revenue.alabama.gov/withholding/whbooklet_0112.pdf, page 7, using the following parameters for Carol: $75,000 gross income; "Married Filing Jointly (M) exemption; $6,851 federal withholding; $3,000 personal exemption; no dependents; and $61,149 taxable amount. The following numbers were used for Bob: $46,200 gross income; "Married Filing Jointly (M) exemption; $2,629 federal withholding; $3,000 personal exemption; no dependents; and $36,571 taxable amount.

[14] http://publicdefendersalary.com/ (Last accessed Feb. 21, 2014)

[15] CARY SIEGEL, WHY DIDN'T THEY TEACH ME THIS IN SCHOOL? 120–121 (Simple Strategic Solutions, 2013) [hereinafter SIEGEL, WHY DIDN'T THEY TEACH].

[16] *See, e.g.,* www.askheatherjarvis.com; www.equaljustice works.org.

[17] http://studentaid.ed.gov/repay-loans/understand/plans/ income-based.

[18] http://www.finaid.org/calculators/scripts/ibr.cgi (Last accessed Feb. 27, 2014). Numbers used to calculate payment: Table Year—2012 (most recent year available); Family Size—2; Discount Rate—5.8%; CPI—3%; State of Residence—Continental US; Income Growth Rate—2.5%; Poverty Level Change Rate—3%; Years of Forgiveness—10 Years; Tax Filing Status—Single; AGI—42000; Expected Income Jump—0; Unsubsidized Loan Amount—80,000; Interest Rate—6.8%; Loan Term—25 years; Minimum Payment— 10.00; Interest Rate Reduction—0%.

[19] http://studentaid.ed.gov/repay-loans/understand/plans/ income-based (Last accessed Feb. 27, 2014)

[20] *Id.*

21 http://www.staffordloan.com/repayment/ (last visited Mar. 13, 2014).

22 KOBLINER,GET A FINANCIAL LIFE *supra* note 8 at 208–217.

23 BLUMENTHAL, GUIDE TO STARTING YOUR FINANCIAL LIFE, *supra* note 5 at 139–142; SIEGEL, WHY DIDN'T THEY TEACH, *supra* note 13 at 140; KOBLINER,GET A FINANCIAL LIFE *supra* note 8 at 230–236.

24 BLUMENTHAL, GUIDE TO STARTING YOUR FINANCIAL LIFE, *supra* note 5 at 262–265; KOBLINER, GET A FINANCIAL LIFE, *supra* note 8 at 249–254.

25 http://www.iii.org/articles/why-should-i-buy-life-insurance.html

26 BLUMENTHAL, GUIDE TO STARTING YOUR FINANCIAL LIFE, *supra* note 5 at 158–160, 170–171; SIEGEL, WHY DIDN'T THEY TEACH, *supra* note 15 at 142–143; KOBLINER, GET A FINANCIAL LIFE, *supra* note 8 at 242–248.

27 BLUMENTHAL, GUIDE TO STARTING YOUR FINANCIAL LIFE, *supra* note 5 at 100–102; KOBLINER, GET A FINANCIAL LIFE, *supra* note 8 at 237–242.

28 BLUMENTHAL, GUIDE TO STARTING YOUR FINANCIAL LIFE, *supra* note 5 at 78–89; SIEGEL, WHY DIDN'T THEY TEACH, *supra* note 15 at 144; KOBLINER, GET A FINANCIAL LIFE, *supra* note 8 at 217–230.

29 BURTON G. MALKIEL, A RANDOM WALK DOWN WALL STREET 44 (W.W. Norton & Co., Inc., 2012); BLUMENTHAL, GUIDE TO STARTING YOUR FINANCIAL LIFE, *supra* note 5 at 219–254; SIEGEL, WHY DIDN'T THEY TEACH, *supra* note 15 at 51–116; KOBLINER, GET A FINANCIAL LIFE, *supra* note 8 at 101–133; http://www.ed.gov/pubs/Prepare/chart10.html (last visited Mar. 13, 2014).

30 http://www.ssa.gov/newsletter/Statement%20Insert%2025+.pdf (last visited on 2/25/14).

31 KOBLINGER, GET A FINANCIAL LIFE, *supra* note 8 at 164–165.

32 *Id.* at 146.

33 http://www.irs.gov/Retirement-Plans.

34 http://consumerfed.org/elements/www.consumerfed.org/file/finance/yourcreditscore.pdf; http://www.mbda.gov; BLUMENTHAL, GUIDE TO STARTING YOUR FINANCIAL LIFE, *supra* note 5 at 47–52; KOBLINER, FINANCIAL LIFE, *supra* note 5 at 70–78.

[35]   http://www.myfico.com/ (Last accessed Feb. 27, 2014).

[36]   BLUMENTHAL, GUIDE TO STARTING YOUR FINANCIAL LIFE, *supra* note 5 at 129–142; KOBLINER, GET A FINANCIAL LIFE, *supra* note 8 at 59–66.

[37]   Information found at http://www.autowyse.com/honda_civic _service/cost_to_replace_civic_transmission.html. Price based on parameters of Labor—Auto service center and Part Quality— Common aftermarket. (Last visited Feb. 21, 2014).

[38]   http://www.bankrate.com/calculators/auto/auto-loan-calculator.aspx;   http://www.bankrate.com/calculators/auto/loan-interest-calculator.aspx

[39]   http://money.msn.com/auto-insurance/auto-insurance-quotes.aspx (last visited Mar. 13, 2014).

[40]   SIEGEL, WHY DIDN'T THEY TEACH, *supra* note 15 at 145; KOBLINER, GET A FINANCIAL LIFE, *supra* note 8 at 249–254.

[41]   http://www.webmd.com/baby/features/cost-of-having-a-baby; http://www.myobgynorlando.com/how-much-do-prenatal-care-visits-cost/ (Last visited Feb. 22, 2014)

[42]   http://www.whattoexpect.com/preconception/preparing-for-baby/work-and-finance/what-babies-really-cost.aspx (Last visited Feb. 22, 2014).

[43]   http://www.cnn.com/2013/07/09/opinion/declercq-childbirth-costs/ (last visited Mar. 13, 2014).

[44]   http://children.costhelper.com/well-baby-doctor-visit.html.

[45]   http://www.resolve.org/family-building-options/insurance_ coverage/the-costs-of-infertility-treatment.html (Last visited Mar. 2, 2014).

[46]   http://kff.org/womens-health-policy/state-indicator/infertility -coverage/; http://www.resolve.org/family-building-options/insurance_ coverage/state-coverage.html (Last visited Feb. 22, 2014).

[47]   http://www.adoptionhelp.org/qa/how-much-does-adoption-cost; http://costs.adoption.com/ (Last visited Mar. 2, 2014).

[48]   BLUMENTHAL, GUIDE TO STARTING YOUR FINANCIAL LIFE, *supra* note 5 at 148–157; SIEGEL, WHY DIDN'T THEY TEACH, *supra* note 15 at 131–137; KOBLINER, GET A FINANCIAL LIFE, *supra* note 8 at 66–68, 177–178, 183–204.

[49]   Based on anticipated law firm annual gross salary of $90,000, with 28% taken out for deductions for a net take home salary of $64,800. Benefits ($27,000) are 30% of $90,000 gross salary. PD numbers based on anticipated annual gross salary of $55,000, with 28% taken out for deductions for a net take home salary of $42,900. Benefits ($16,500) are 30% of gross salary of $55,000. $91,800 (total compensation from firm)—$59,400 (total compensation from PD's office) = $32,400 per year difference.

[50]   http://www.finaid.org/loans/forgivenesstaxability.phtml; http://www.irs.gov/publications/p970/ch05.html (Last visited Feb. 28, 2014)

[51]   *Id.*

[52]   http://www.americanbar.org/portals/solo_home.html; http://www.americanbar.org/publications/law_practice_today_home/law_practice_today_archive/april12/50-web-resources-for-the-suddenly-solo-lawyer.html (Last visited Mar. 2, 2014)

[53]   http://lawyerist.com/how-much-it-really-costs-to-start-a-law-firm/; http://www.italoconsulting.com/articles/solo.htm; http://www.texasbarcle.com/materials/special/lawpractice.pdf (Last visited Mar. 2, 2014)

[54]   http://trends.collegeboard.org/sites/default/files/college-pricing-2013-full-report.pdf. (Last visited Mar. 13, 2014).

[55]   *Smart Saving for College*, FINRA (http://www.sec.gov/investor/pubs/intro529.htm) (Last visited Mar. 13, 2014).

CHAPTER III

CHANGES IN THE LEGAL MARKET

1. INTRODUCTION

According to news headlines, there is gloom and doom in the legal profession.[1] It is true that the legal profession is in a period of transformation, that law schools need to do a better job preparing students for today's practice of law, and that a legal education is an expensive investment. To conclude from these realities that the legal profession is in a crisis, however, is hyperbole.[2]

The legal profession is experiencing needed corrections. There are too many law schools that poorly prepare their students for practice while saddling them with crushing debt, too many law firms that have made poor business management decisions, and too many practicing attorneys who have not adjusted to new ways of delivering legal services. Corrections to these problems, while disruptive for some, will leave the legal profession healthy and thriving.[3]

It is important to maintain perspective about the legal profession's future. Although undergoing fundamental changes, the legal market is robust and poised to remain so for those who are positioned to take advantage of the changes underway. The legal profession is projected to experience stable growth. Lawyers will remain among the best paid professionals in the United States.

The demand for legal services has been growing steadily. In 1977, the first year such data was calculated, legal services accounted for .9% of GDP in the United States. In 2012, with $294 billion going to legal services per year,[4] legal services accounted for 1.4% of GDP.[5] The United States Department of Labor projects a growth rate of 15.1% for the legal profession between 2008 and 2018, faster than the 10.1% average projected for all occupations.[6]

The need for legal services will continue to grow as the world becomes more interconnected and complex, and as new legislation and regulation require implementation.[7] The United States is emerging as a "hot market."[8] Cellphone infrastructure, advances in 3-D printing and use of robotics in factories are transforming the United States to a place of destination for businesses. A decade ago, nine out of ten companies were thinking of building their next plant in China. Today, five out of ten want to build in the United States.[9] Labor costs have risen in China 15% annually while those in the United States have remained stable. The United States is on track to become a natural gas exporter by 2018. The stock market has regained its 2008 losses and reached new highs. Business development in the United States means more work for lawyers.

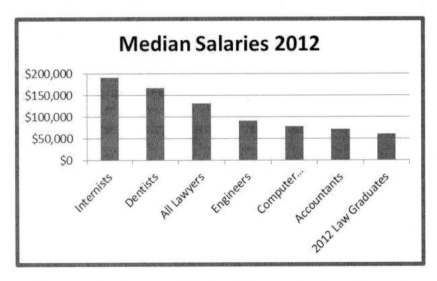

Lawyers make a good living. The national median salary for 2012 law school graduates was $61,245.[10] The mean salary in 2012 for all lawyers was $130,880. This compares to $71,040 for accountants, $78,260 for computer programmers, $90,960 for engineers, $166,910 for dentists, $191,520 for internists, and $45,790 for all occupations in the United States.[11]

Although employment rates for new law graduates were down in 2012, they were still good: 84.7% of 2012 law graduates were employed within nine months after graduation.[12] Full employment of law school graduates is not 100%. At its peak in 2007, employment by law school graduates was only 91.9%.[13] Moreover, employment for most law graduates is higher than national statistics reflect. Graduates from a handful of law schools have dismal employment statistics (at five schools, only 17% to 30% were employed nine months after graduation).[14] The unfortunate job prospects for these graduates distort national statistics.

Demographics favor those entering the legal profession today. The current bar is dominated by baby boomers who are gray, aging and likely to retire over the next decade. These retirees will need to be replaced by new lawyers. In 2010, the 45–64 age group constituted 26.4% of the United States population and the 65–older age group constituted 13.0%, for a combined total of 39.4% of the United States population.[15] This means that over the next ten to twenty years, 40% of Americans will be retiring. In the legal profession, the 45–65 and older age group dominates the top of the profession, making up 70% of law firm partners.[16] As these lawyers retire, there will more positions to fill than people to fill them. There are 76 million Baby Boomers (those born between 1946 and 1964), and only 46 million GenY-ers (those born between 1985 and 2000).

Longitudinal studies of practicing attorneys show that despite the general portrayal in the press of new lawyers as "overworked to the point of exhaustion," such an image is "greatly exaggerated, even for large firm lawyers."[17] In 2004, the National Association for Law Placement (NALP) and American Bar Association (ABA) conducted a ten-year longitudinal study of 5,000 lawyers throughout the United States to assess satisfaction with their careers.[18] It found that 80% of respondents were "moderately" or "extremely" satisfied with their decision to become a lawyer.[19]

In summary, while the legal profession is experiencing dynamic changes, these are needed corrections that will leave the profession stronger. A lot of money is going and will continue to go into the legal services profession. Lawyers make a good living and will remain among the highest paid professionals in the United States. Most lawyers are satisfied or very satisfied with their choice of profession. Large numbers of attorneys will be retiring in the next two decades, leaving a vacuum to be filled by new lawyers.

2.   EVOLUTION OF LAW PRACTICE

I recently heard the United States mail system described as follows: "It's like you write an email, print it out instead of click and send it, put it in an envelope, email your friend and ask your friend for his mailing address, write your friend's mailing address on the envelope, go to the store, buy a stamp for $.49, put the stamp on the envelope, walk to your mailbox, and put the envelope in the mailbox. The envelope travels by at least two trucks and one plane and is sorted by at least ten to twelve people into stacks with other envelopes. In several days your envelope arrives at your friend's mailbox. Your friend walks to his mailbox, gets the envelope, opens it, and reads the email."

Many aspects of the practice of law are as anachronistic as "snail mail." Lawyers who do not adjust to the changes in the legal profession will become irrelevant. Those who do adjust will thrive.[20] As Richard Susskind states, "The future of lawyers could be prosperous or disastrous."[21]

Only a few decades ago, there weren't many lawyers around, law firms could not find enough attorneys to hire, and law schools were growing to meet the unfilled need. There was no advertising by lawyers and no social media. There were the yellow pages of telephone books. An individual with a legal problem looked in the yellow pages or called friends who knew a lawyer. The individual obtained an appointment to see a lawyer, drove to the lawyer's office, and met with him (there weren't many hers). The lawyer took notes on a legal pad.

A lawyer would walk or drive to a law library with lots of books, probably at the county courthouse. It was too expensive for most firms to have their own law libraries. A lawyer would begin his research in big books called digests or in annotated statutory codes. These books list cases on a topic or on relevant statutory provisions. After making notes of the cases listed, a lawyer would go to case books. To read a case, a lawyer pulled a book off the shelf and went to the page number where the case opinion began. Sometimes the book was missing because someone else had it. Then a lawyer had to put his name on a list to get the book when it was returned.

When a lawyer prepared a letter or memo, he would write it out in longhand on a legal pad, or dictate it into a recorder. His secretary would type the letter or memo from the handwritten pages or dictation and return the draft to the lawyer for review. The lawyer would make changes. The lawyer and his secretary would repeat this process multiple times for some projects. When typing, the secretary would use carbon paper (thin, purple paper set between clean sheets of white paper) to produce a copy of the letter or memo.

The secretary or another firm employee would go to the court house, file documents with the clerk of the court, and obtain a file stamp on copies for the lawyer and client. Copies of all documents would be placed in tall, metal file cabinets in the lawyer's office. The secretary would place the client's copy in the mail. In a few days, the client would receive his copy from the attorney.

In this practice of law, even the simplest legal issue handled expeditiously, would take days, if not weeks. The infrastructure needed to support such a law practice was extensive, and expensive. The lawyer and secretary needed offices, desks, dictating equipment, typewriters, and file cabinets. The lawyer needed access to a law library with many books.

Today, an attorney-client relationship may begin with a visit by an individual to an attorney's webpage, an online post, a branded network, an online matchmaking service that connects clients with lawyers,[22] or a Facebook description of the problem or question. There may be almost instantaneous "bidding" by lawyers connected to the network explaining what they charge to handle an issue along with a description of their expertise and prior experience. There may be an interview between prospective client and counsel by Skype. An attorney needs no books or library to do research, only access to a computer. Attorneys are able to email or consult blogs for assistance, customize online forms, transmit documents digitally to the client, edit and make all necessary changes or amendments remotely, converse with consultants electronically, obtain signatures electronically, and file documents with the court electronically. Almost every aspect of a case can be done remotely. The infrastructure needed by a lawyer to render these services is a computer and a telephone.

There are challenges ahead in this new world of practicing law. Complying with rules of professional conduct is one. [23] Quality control is another. The lawyer found on Facebook, who met a client only on Skype, and did all research online may be incompetent, inexperienced, impaired or fraudulent. But the same is true of the lawyer on Main Street, whose competence may also have been compromised by his limited research access. Today, new challenges arise because remote lawyering makes it easier to disguise defective services. Bar associations, among others, are struggling to monitor and maintain high standards for the legal profession in light of technological changes.

The above scenario demonstrates the dramatic, structural shifts in the delivery of legal services. Technology is part of the reason for these changes. Evolving needs of clients is another. Some law firms have responded by moving to new business models of practice. Others need to. This Chapter discusses the changing needs of business and individual clients and how these evolving needs impact law firms and the lawyers who work in them. Chapter Four addresses the impact of these changes on government, public interest and law related careers.

3. THE DEMAND FOR LEGAL SERVICES

Lawyers exist because of clients. Clients define what lawyers do by the problems they bring and the solutions they desire. Clients are businesses and individuals, and for lawyers at public interest and government offices, the public. When clients' legal needs and expectations change, as they have in recent years, the legal profession has no choice but to change.

It is not a foregone conclusion that the legal profession will survive if it does not adjust. As Richard Susskind, one of the more prescient observers of the legal profession, states, "Law is not there to provide a livelihood for lawyers any more than illness prevails in order to offer a living for doctors."[24] Susskind cautions that if the legal profession does not embrace change it could "fade from society as other craftsmen have done over the centuries."[25]

A. Business Clients

Three independent trends have created a new world for businesses that seek legal services.

- **Expansion on in-house legal departments.** Businesses have expanded their in-house counsel departments and filled them with seasoned, experienced lawyers who provide legal services in-house and are savvy in their selection and use of outside counsel.

- **Comparison of law firms is more feasible.** Information about law firm fees and expenses has become widely and easily available, allowing clients to compare law firms and shop around for the best value.

- **Cost.** Businesses are under significant pressure to cut fees paid to outside counsel.

Beginning in the 1990s, companies created and expanded their in-house legal departments. They hired experienced lawyers to staff them. No longer are companies' legal departments overseen by a business executive whose duty is simply to select outside counsel, delegate projects to counsel, follow outside counsel's advice, and authorize payment for legal services.

As in-house legal departments have grown, it has become more efficient for companies to retain more legal work in-house. Additionally, as law has become more specialized and regulatory, it makes more sense for businesses to keep legal work in-house where the attorneys are well versed in the needs of the specific business. Regulatory schemes affecting business have increased, especially since 2008, as have the consequences of non-compliance. Companies have responded by ramping up their internal legal departments.[26] As one General Counsel of a $3 billion-revenue-per-year company explained:

> "An in-house attorney provides a quality and level of service that is difficult, if not impossible, to purchase from an outside law firm, because an in-house attorney is truly part of the business. [In-house counsel is able] to provide legal advice that takes into account the broader business considerations and long-term goals of the company and . . . has a vested interest in making sure good advice is actually implemented, that problems are actually solved. . . . In-house attorneys are better at driving necessary change within our organization because, being part of the business, they must live with the end result."[27]

As attorneys, usually quite seasoned attorneys, in-house counsel are able to effectively evaluate the performance of outside counsel when they send work to outside firms. Their evaluation is aided by publicly available information allowing inter-firm comparison of profits, expenses, and billing rates. As Richard Susskind states, "The old system, one that has allowed lawyers to under-perform and overcharge, [is] displaced by a new model, under which all law firms are subject to far greater scrutiny and competition—on availability, price, performance, and client satisfaction. The free market has come to the world of law."[28]

A 1977 decision by the United States Supreme Court holding that efforts by bar associations and other professional societies to limit attorneys' advertising improperly infringed on First Amendment rights of attorneys[29] brought transparency to attorneys' fees and costs. Once the ban on advertising was lifted and firms began to market themselves, all firms, even those initially reluctant to advertise, found that to compete they had to make publicly available financial information about themselves. Within a few years, the media, primarily *The American Lawyer* and *The National Law Journal,* began reporting law firms' expenses, profits and salaries. Value comparison by clients of law firms became possible.

In a related development, also in the 1990s, billing software became available which enabled clients to track outside counsel's expenses and "to pit one law firm against another."[30] "Preferred vendor" programs became common. In such programs, law firms apply for, qualify, and compete for companies' legal business just as other vendors have long competed for purchase of goods and services.[31]

Evaluating and comparing law firms' productivity has become vitally important to business clients because of the increased pressure on businesses to control costs, including the cost of legal services. When the 2008 recession hit, controlling costs became imperative for many businesses to survive. Companies took significant steps to control all costs, including legal fees. Able to scrutinize the expenses of their outside counsel because of increased transparency, companies refused to pay some expenses they previously had not questioned. Among other things, companies refused to pay for legal services rendered by new associates at law firms on the ground that they did not want to pay for new lawyers to learn how to practice law.[32]

As companies became more informed about the legal costs of outside counsel, it was an obvious cost saving measure to keep more work in-house. The Senior Vice President and General Counsel of Cisco, a top Fortune 100 firm, spoke of frustration with outside counsel's rising legal fees:

> "As Cisco gets bigger, the share of revenue devoted to legal expense gets smaller. Letters from law firms telling me how much billing rates are going up next year are . . . totally irrelevant to me. . . . I don't care what billing rates are. I care about productivity and outputs."[33]

Cisco is not alone. In a recent survey of chief legal officers, fifty-nine percent had fired or were considering firing at least one of their outside law firms as a cost management move.[34]

As part of their cost saving efforts, corporate clients are insisting on alternative fee arrangements (AFAs) to billable hour billing. This move to AFAs is not surprising. The billable hour system contains no incentive for lawyers to control costs; in fact it encourages the opposite. Under a billable hour system, law firms have the incentive to work as slowly, laboriously, duplicatively, and repetitively as possible. As Richard Susskind notes, "At worst, hourly billing can tempt lawyers to dishonesty. At best, it is an institutional disincentive to efficiency. To put it more crudely, hourly billing often rewards the inefficient practice that milks the work given to it and it penalizes the well run legal businesses whose systems and processes enable it to conclude matters rapidly."[35]

Law firms are responding to clients' insistence on AFAs. The Hildebrand 2012 survey of law firms found that "the percentage of total firm revenues attributable to AFAs has been rising steadily since 2008 and is projected to hit 13.4 percent in 2012."[36] There are risks to law firms using AFAs. Firms must accurately estimate the time and costs they will expend on a matter. Law firms that mis-judge, mis-quote or submit a low AFA to compete with other firms, will lose money. Whereas the billable hour system never imposed financial risk on law firms, AFAs place financial risk squarely on law firms. Metric tools using predictive analysis can be invaluable to law firms in accurately establishing AFAs[37] (See Chapter IV (4)(A)(ii)(1) *infra*).

There are professional responsibility issues posed by the growth of in-house counsel departments, including: When is in-house counsel the "client" of outside counsel? Should opposing counsel be barred from contacting in-house counsel if outside counsel has been retained? May a former in-house lawyer pursue a wrongful discharge claim against her former employer and client? How is client information protected in such a situation?[38] To what extent are in-house counsel and outside counsel in competition for the legal work of corporate clients? To what degree is it appropriate for outside counsel to divert legal work from in-house counsel, and vice versa?[39]

Summary: Changes in Behavior of Business Clients

The convergence of multiple, independent trends over the past few decades have changed business clients' needs and preferences for legal advice. These trends include:

- *Passage of increasingly complex regulations with significant consequences for non-compliance has prompted growth of in-house counsel departments.*

- *Internal pressure on businesses to cut costs and the desire that lawyers they use understand their business concerns, has led to companies to move more work away from law firms to in-house legal departments.*

- *There is less loyalty by businesses to law firms. Greater sophistication by corporate clients, through expanded in-house departments, access to financial information about law firms' operations, and the availability of computer tools to assess such information, encourage businesses to shop around for the best value in legal services.*

As William D. Henderson and Rachel M. Zahorsky note, these changes mean that "[t]he balance of power has shifted from . . . law firms towards clients."[40]

B. Individual Clients

Business clients are not the only clients whose needs for law services have changed. The high cost of legal services and ready access to information about law and legal issues through the Internet have forever altered the legal needs and perceptions of individuals who seek legal help. With a national average billable hour rate of $432,[41] lawyers' services have become too expensive for most people to afford. Additionally, anyone with access to the internet has options, many free and reputable, to hiring a lawyer. While some online sites are incomplete, inaccurate and disreputable, many are not. Championed by bar associations concerned about access to justice,[42] pro se forms and services increasingly are available at no charge on the internet or at court house clerk offices.

Government offices provide thousands of websites providing legal forms and instructions.[43] Many commercial sites provide legal forms and instructions for a minimal fee. As a result of this easy and cheap access to legal advice and forms, individuals can complete their own transactions in dozens of areas of law, ranging from divorce, bankruptcy, trusts and wills, and intellectual property.

One consequence of the easy and cheap availability of legal services, abundance of lawyers, and nature of some lawyer advertising[44] is a change in the public perception of lawyers and the value of legal services. Few individuals are able to judge the quality of legal services, or see that their problem is more nuanced than advertisements proclaim. To many individuals, it makes no sense to pay a lawyer hundreds of dollars in fees when they can go online and complete a few forms to seemingly accomplish what an expensive lawyer would do.

4. THE SUPPLY OF LAWYERS

The supply of lawyers in the United States has more than doubled in the past fifty years. In 1960, there were 285,933 lawyers in the United States (.159% of the population). By 1990, there were 755,694 lawyers in the United States (.303% of the population). In 2012, there were 1,268,011 lawyers in the United States (.404% of the population).[45]

One reason for this proliferation of lawyers is the increased number of American law schools. In 1995, the United States Department of Justice and the American Bar Association (ABA) entered into a consent decree resolving charges that the ABA's process of accrediting law schools violated antitrust laws.[46] This settlement made it easier for for-profit law schools to become accredited.[47] In 1964, there were 135 law schools in the United States, with total enrollment of 51,079 students. By 2013, there were 202 accredited law schools with total enrollment of 128,641 students.[48] Adding to this supply of lawyers graduating from American law schools is growth in the number of lawyers offshore who provide legal services through global internet services.

5. WHAT DO THESE CHANGES MEAN FOR LAW FIRMS?

As a result of the changing needs and expectations of clients, increased supply of lawyers, and emerging legal services and products, law firms are less stable creatures. The changes in private practice affect partners, associates, and new lawyers differently. Consider the following:

- Throughout the past four decades, 55–58% of law school graduates were employed by private law firms upon graduation.[49] In 2012, just over half, 50.7%, of law school graduates took employment at private law firms.[50]

- Since 2008, law firm profits have stagnated as measured by revenue per lawyer.[51] It has become more difficult for law firms to collect their fees from clients.[52] More law firms are dissolving and merging as firms seek to shed or add lawyers or practice groups.[53]

- The business model of private law practice is evolving from the "Cravath pyramid" model, to a "diamond," and now to a "starfish."

A. Evolving Law Firm Business Models

The "Cravath" business model dominated American law firms from the late 1800s until the twenty-first century.[54] Under the "Cravath" model, named for Paul Cravath, a renowned New York attorney, a law firm seeks to hire the best new lawyers it can, train its new hires in the firm's culture, promote only from within a firm, and reward associates with the "golden key" to partner status after the associates have proven themselves. Under Cravath model, associates receive valuable mentoring from partners but work long hours for years following partners' dictates and direction. Many associates leave their law firms in favor of a less intense work life or more independence. Other associates are edged out as it becomes clear they are not "partner material." Under the Cravath model, clients are loyal to the firm. Partners pass their clients to associates once they become partners, securing the firm's link to the client. The Cravath business model resembled a pyramid.[55]

Under the Cravath model, partners' billing rates were roughly the same, and partners shared equally in the firm's profits. Equal distribution of firm profits maintained stability of the firm, provided continuous employment of partners throughout their careers, and enhanced a firm's culture and "brand." Cravath-model partners tended to ease out of the intense practice of law as associates made partner and took over client contact and service. During 1980s and 1990s, the Cravath model evolved to include a breakdown of "senior associates" and "junior partners" reflecting differences in responsibility and compensation, but the pyramid structure of the Cravath model of law firm structure remained intact.

"Pyramid" Business Model

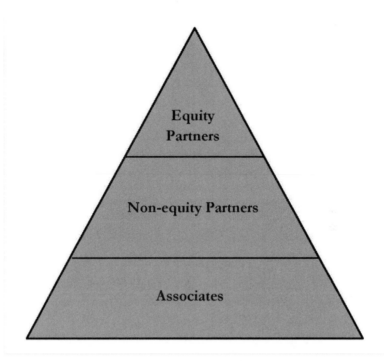

Problems with the Cravath model began to develop when some legal services became more profitable than others. The value of various legal specialties has always been cyclical, but the equal sharing of firm profits under the Cravath system kept law firms stable throughout the cycles. A partner with a large real estate practice, for example, may bring in more clients and have higher billings during boom years and less during recessions, but his cycles would have been off-set by work performed by other partners.

However, as corporate clients have become more sophisticated and cost-conscious, and as some legal specialties have become more commoditized, various legal specialties are less profitable than others. General business, regulatory compliance, trusts and estates, for example, have become more commoditized, lending themselves to the greatest amount of comparative shopping by clients for the best value.[56] Other specialties, such as real estate during the 2008 recession and aftermath, experience cycles in which they simply do not have enough work. Some specialties are insensitive to comparative shopping and economic downturns. White collar practice, where criminal liability for a company or its officers and directors is at stake, is not an area in which companies shop around for the best value. Similarly, mergers and acquisitions, and intellectual property are other areas which businesses are willing to pay whatever firms ask. "When corporate legal departments need a trusted hand to fend off a hostile takeover or win a critical court battle, few general counsels will nitpick over whether a key lawyer is charging $900 an hour or $1,150 an hour."[57]

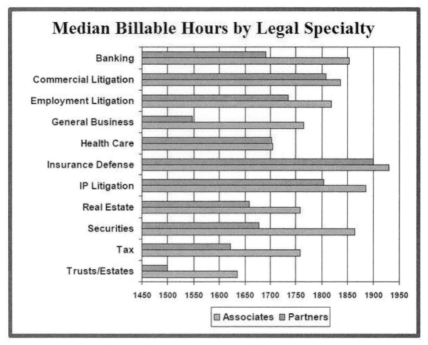

Source: Altman Weil 2002 Survey of Law Firm Economics

Given this dynamic of uneven profitability among legal specialties, one firm partner can command $1000 per hour, bill hundreds of hours, and keep several other attorneys in the firm busy on his cases. Meanwhile, another partner with the same seniority and just as able in his field but now subject to commoditization and comparative shopping by clients, may be able to command only $275 per hour and unable to bill enough hours to keep himself busy, much less other firm lawyers.

Despite a sense of loyalty to each other and their firm, if wildly fluctuating profit margins among practice areas continue for long, partners tend to allocate a greater share of the firm profits to lucrative partners. Stakes are raised when other law firms seek to lure lucrative partners away with promises of a "better deal" (a higher salary, higher percentage of firm profit, more associates, more paralegals, greater firm resources that make the partners' life easier). Wooing of lucrative partners and practice groups is the major reason for the many lateral moves by lawyers among firms. Unheard of in the Cravath business model, lateral hiring is rampant in law firms today.[58]

Because of the instability lateral moves bring to law firms, lateral hires destroy the Cravath model. Associates can no longer assume that a firm's partners or clients will remain at a firm, or even that the firm will continue to exist. Without these assurances, associates are less willing to work long hours for years to become partner. As Henderson and Bierman note: "The increased reliance on lateral hiring undercuts the perception by associates that they are being groomed for partnership."[59]

Lateral hiring impairs a firm's ability to provide continuous, consistent, quality legal services to its clients. Again, as Henderson & Bierman note, movement of partners in and out of a firm "dilute the level of service that can be provided to demanding corporate clients," leaving firms "vulnerable to boutique and regional law firms, who offer greater value."[60] When a key partner leaves her firm and takes associates with her, the disruption to her firm is greater than just the loss of one partner. When an entire practice group leaves a firm, the firm can no longer service its clients in that area and will have difficulty attracting future clients who may have legal needs in that specialty.

The flow of partners, practice areas, and associates in and out of firms makes it difficult to preserve a firm's "culture." It becomes harder to build a unique brand that helps firms attract new clients and talented new lawyers. The lack of law firm collegiality and culture becomes the impetus for more instability. When partners do not know each other and do not have loyalty to each other, they are more likely to bolt to another firm that offers them a better deal. Associates are more likely to leave when they have paid off their law school debt.

Further eroding the collegiality of law firms are the hierarchies within firms created by differences in profitability among law specialties. In most of today's law firms, categories and subcategories of partners exist. For starters, there are "equity" and "non-equity" partners. Potentially, a partner could move among categories as her duties with the firm, expertise, and practice area evolves. Law firm consultant Thomas Clay has described the types of law partners as follows:

> "Equity partners share in the profits of the firm. They have potential for greater income, as well as greater risk for firm liabilities. Equity partners also determine the governance of the firm, including the setting of salaries and bonuses, hiring, and allocation of firm resources to attorneys and projects. Non-equity partners may be perceived as "partners" by the outside world but they work on salary and have a limited role in the management of the law firm."[61]

Types of Law Firm Partnerships

- **Entrepreneurial:** This partner "drives the firm brand," is able to keep many attorneys busy, maintains relationships with key clients and within the firm among partners. This type of partner is rare.

- **Business Generating:** This partner is able to generate enough legal work to keep himself and one to three additional attorneys in the firm busy.

- **Self-Sufficient:** This partner stays busy but gets a portion of work from others.

- **Service:** This partner is a sophisticated lawyer, delivers good service but does not generate a significant volume of work on her own.

- **Technical Specialist Partner:** This partner is a sophisticated problem solver but is uncomfortable with social interaction.[62]

Despite the possible disruption to firm culture and stability caused by multiple tiers of partnerships within a firm, the flexibility they bring offers advantages for firms, including the following:

- **Way to retain lucrative partners.** Multi-tier partner tracks provide a mechanism for allocating different incomes and prerogatives to the lucrative partners, thereby retaining them at the firm.

- **Provides a mechanism to prune unproductive partners.** Multi-tier partner tracks allow law firms to de-equitize, reduce the equity of, or dismiss partners whose practice area is not profitable or have otherwise ceased to contribute to the financial health of a law firm.

- **Helps avoid "promotion errors."** Longer partnership tracks to full equity partnership allow a longer period of time for firms to evaluate attorneys before conferring full membership in the firm.

- **Way to retain good lawyers who are not partner material.** Non-equity and Of Counsel positions provide a way to keep good attorneys who, under the Cravath model, would have been released from the firm once it was clear that they were not partner material. These attorneys are motivated to say at the firm because they will be able to do interesting work at which they are skilled and although they may not make "stratosphere" incomes, they will make a "handsome" living.[63]

- **Profitable.** Firms which have moved to multi-tier partnerships tend to be more profitable as measured by profits per partner (PPP). Higher PPP enhances a firm's prospects for a merger should the need arise and makes it easier to attract laterals.[64]

- **Lifestyle advantages.** Associates in two-tier firms tend to work less than their counterparts at the few remaining one-tier law firms. In 2001, for example, associates in one-tier firms billed 1.8 hours more per week than associates in two-tier firms.

Multi-tiered partnerships can be disastrous for law firms if they are "poorly designed or executed"[65] because they:

- **Promote poor personnel decisions.** Using tiers to park unproductive partners or promote less-than-competent associates rather than let lawyers go, damages firm morale and jeopardizes a firm's financial vitality.

- **Encourage diminished productivity.** There are some indications that non-equity partner positions may result in too many partners who are content to work less, earn less and not contribute to growing the firm. The 2012 Hildebrant study of top-tier and middle-tier law firms showed that the "productivity levels of income partners (i.e., non-equity partners) have consistently been well below that of equity partners and associates for the past decade— indeed, about 150 hours per year below."[66]

- **Erode firm culture, brand and collegiality.** Depending on how they are used, tiers and hierarchies among lawyers within a firm have the potential to destroy the loyalty necessary to bind firms together through difficult economic times, make it more likely that partners will bolt for more lucrative offers from other firms, undercut firm collegiality and continuity, and encourage associates and clients to leave.

Whereas the Cravath system resembled a pyramid with a bottom-heavy supply of associates and few partners at the top, the current business model with its multiple tiers of partners resembles a diamond, with fewer associates and fewer equity partners.

"Diamond" Business Model

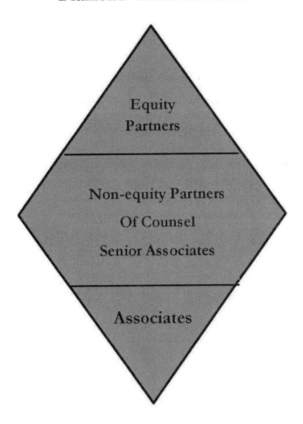

The law firms likely to struggle the most in the years ahead are those that have indebted their firm to pay new laterals exceptionally large salaries and are locked into other high overhead costs. The recent, high-profile demise of national firms exemplifies this. Thelen LLP, a San Francisco law firm with 600 attorneys; Heller Ehrman, also of San Francisco with 500 attorneys; Howrey LLP, a Washington, DC firm with 700 attorneys; and Dewey and LeBoeuf, a New York law firm with 1,400 attorneys, have dissolved and entered bankruptcy in the past few years. All of these firms had aggressively expanded and hired expensive lateral attorneys, committing the firms to large personnel costs.

B. Impact of Evolving Law Firm Business Models on Lawyers' Professional Lives

(i) Impact on Partners

The new legal world has impacted quality of life for law firm partners. As one partner explains, "The hours don't get any better for partners; partners have even more pressure than associates do."[67] Under the Cravath model, partners eased out of an intense life-style when the associates they had groomed became partners and took over the firm. Partners could slow down knowing that their equity in the firm would be continued by loyal lawyers in the firm, the firm's clients would remain loyal to the firm because they would be serviced by the associates, now partners, who had spent years working with the client. Stability prevailed. Partners could scale back their workload, mentor new lawyers, and focus on bar and public service.

Today, however, partners are under pressure to maintain an active role in their firms. If they do not bring in and retain clients, bill a significant number of hours, and keep their firms intact, they risk a breakup of their firm or being de-equitized by other partners who are bearing greater firm responsibility. As one equity partner explained, firms need to: "Cut out the dogs. Get rid of the partner whose practice has died. Every two to three years . . . firm[s] need to look closely and make the hard decisions—look at production versus salary . . . [D]equitize the couch potatoes."[68]

The experience of a number of the largest, most prestigious law firms in recent years demonstrates the new reality for law firm partners. Patton Boggs LLP, a 465-lawyer firm in Washington, D.C., long recognized as "the venerable Washington, D.C., influence-broker," recently dismissed sixty-five lawyers and staff including twenty partners.[69] The firm told "idle partners to step up their performance or find work elsewhere."[70] In light of shrinking revenues, the firm, "hoping to reverse its own decline," determined that it needed to "get rid of the deadwood, slash expenses and direct resources to practices that sync up with the firm's long suit. . . ."[71] Similarly, Weil, Gotshal & Manges, LLP, a 1,200 lawyer firm and one of the most prestigious law firms in the United States,[72] recently notified dozens of partners that their pay would be cut by hundreds of thousands of dollars a year "serv[ing] as a not-so-subtle invitation for lawyers to leave the firm."[73]

(ii) Impact on Associates

The difficult lives of partners affect the lives of associates. One effect is that partners have less time to mentor new associates. Without such mentoring ("royal honey"; See Chapter IV(2) *infra*), associates risk becoming permanent "worker bees," destined to work for others, not growing professionally or learning how to be independent attorneys. Without mentoring, associates do not get opportunities to develop close and nurturing relationships with firm partners. They have less loyalty to a firm and are more likely to leave for better opportunities or when their school loans are repaid. Associates' departures, in turn, render firms less stable, less able to service clients, and less likely to garner long-term loyalty from future associates.

The instability of law firms, corrosive nature of multi-tier partnerships, emphasis on lateral hiring, less mentoring by busy partners, and cost consciousness by clients (*i.e.*, refusal to pay for work done by new associates) mean there are fewer positions in many law firms for associates.[74]

It is "riskier than ever for firms to hire new associates,"[75] because law firms have to invest increasingly rare time and resources training new law graduates. As Daniel Katz states: "Entry-level lawyers are having great difficulty getting a start in traditional legal industry because a hiring mistake by a law firm can be a particularly costly one."[76] One way firms are attempting to minimize this risk is by using lawyer metrics that "forecast the future success of individual lawyers, especially at the entry level." [77] These metrics rely on predictive quantitative tools that measure likely performance and focus on grades in law school, law review experience, clerkships and law school rank, as well as life experience, such as "blue or pink collar work experience, advanced degrees, publications, participation in team sports."[78] (These life experiences are also the characteristics of star performers identified by organizational psychologists (See Chapter IV(5) *infra*)).

As the "traditional Cravath model" law firm associate positions become less available, or, if available, less appealing, other avenues for new lawyers are opening up. For an increasing number of new lawyers who want to enter private practice, contract lawyer positions are available. The instability in today's law firms and unpredictability of firms' workloads make hiring contract lawyers smart business for firms. Firms can hire the number of lawyers they need for a single case, group of cases, or a period of time. Employing contract lawyers is cheaper for law firms than hiring associates because firms generally pay contract lawyers less than they pay associates and cover fewer, if any, benefits. Additionally, contract lawyers have less expectation of mentoring and do not present the complexity of promotion decisions.

"Of Counsel" positions also are an increasingly effective and less risky, staffing strategy for firms. Offering more prestige than contract positions, "Of Counsel" positions provide flexibility for firms and lawyers. Such positions may be offered for a brief period of time or a number of years, at a set salary, a floating salary, with or without benefits, part time or full time, and offered to partners, associates or laterals.

Reflecting these flexible staffing options within law firms, the developing business model for law firms is akin to a starfish. In a starfish business model, the core of the firm consists of equity partners while the starfish points reflect the variety of staffing options: non-equity partners, "Of Counsel" positions, contract lawyers, outsourced services, affiliated law firms, and staff such as paralegals, personal assistants and administrators.

"Starfish" Business Model

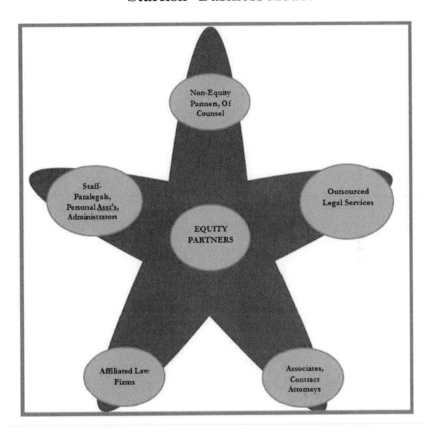

Non-Equity Partners, Of Counsel

Staff-Paralegals, Personal Asst's, Administrators

Outsourced Legal Services

EQUITY PARTNERS

Affiliated Law Firms

Associates, Contract Attorneys

C.   Small Firms and Solo Practices Become Increasingly Viable

Shifts in the legal market are changing the landscape for small firms and solo practitioners, rendering these firms increasingly financially viable and capable of handling complex cases previously handled only by large law firms.[79] The market factors making small firms and solo practices attractive are: changes in client behavior; lower billing rates and billing flexibility small firms and solo practitioners are able to provide; increasing conflicts of interest in large firms as more firms merge; and, quality of life advantages offered by small firms and solo practices. (Chapter Four provides an extended discussion of how newly available tools, technologies and services are enabling small firms to handle complex legal matters previously handled exclusively by large law firms (See Chapter IV (4)(A)(ii) *infra*)).

Client Behavior

Clients, especially large business clients, are moving more of their legal work from large law firms to smaller firms. One General Counsel described this shift: "What has changed for us over the years is how we select and manage outside counsel. We have consolidated the vast majority of our legal work with a smaller number of lawyers who are strategically located around the country."[80] *Corporate Counsel*, a publication by and for corporate counsel, reported on the trend of retaining smaller firms, noting that corporate counsel had "come to think that they were throwing money away by sending all their work to big firms."[81]

In addition, as companies expand their in-house legal offices, they have less need for large firms that can handle cases in multiple jurisdictions. Many of the "largest, most sophisticated buyers of corporate legal services . . . have their own legal teams on the ground . . . and have the ability to coordinate dozens of outside law firms," [82] giving them greater flexibility to choose small law firms. As John Schultz, General Counsel of Hewlett-Packard Co., states: "When I talk to my colleagues, we are all . . . aligned . . . that we hire lawyers, not law firms."

Cost

One of the reasons business clients are moving from large to smaller firms is cost. Companies can replace a large national firm, where attorneys charge $700 per hour, with smaller regional firms whose attorneys charge $325–$450 per hour.[83] Eric Kobrick, Deputy General Counsel for American International Group, Inc., spoke of rate flexibility when discussing AIG's decision to leave large firms for small firms, "Small firms, in general, are more flexible. They're able to use rate flexibility, and still provide excellent service."[84] General Counsel who have switched to small firms cite high-priced first year associates as one of the problems with big firms. Small firms, in contrast, "aren't saddled with the need to train armies of associates on the client's dime."[85] Many large law firms have also priced themselves out of the market with high salaries, debt from commitments to expensive lateral hires, and large overhead costs because of offices located in pricey markets.

Conflicts of Interest

Companies retaining smaller firms find fewer conflicts of interest. Compared to large firms (which are getting larger because of mergers and hiring of lateral partners) small firms rarely have to turn a client away because of conflicts. As law firms acquire lateral partners and practice groups they also acquire conflicts of interest for the existing and potential clients. AIG Deputy General Counsel Kobrick cited the "endless conflicts"[86] at the large firms AIG previously retained as "a key consideration" in retaining smaller firms to serve as outside counsel.[87]

As an aside, it should be noted that conflicts of interest are a problem for lawyers in a law firm as well as a firm's clients. A lawyer who obtains a new client may have to turn away the client because the new matter creates a conflict with existing clients of other attorneys in the firm. This problem has always existed for attorneys in large law firms, but lawyers' options for leaving their firms were more limited. Today, with outsourcing, technology and other resources available to small law firms, small firms can compete with large law firms for cases. This new competitiveness enables lawyers to leave their large law firms and continue handling their clients' complex matters elsewhere (See Chapter IV (4)(A)(ii) *infra*).

Resources

As Professor Oliver Goodenough of Vermont Law School, an expert in the evolving legal market, states: One thing is for sure—technology and law are the wave of the future."[88] Technology has leveled the playing field for small firms and solo practitioners allowing them to provide the same quality of service that previously only large law firms, with their armies of lawyers and full service back-up support, were able to provide. According to a seasoned solo practitioner, "Now with a little creativity and flexibility and a lot of technology, an enterprising solo practitioner can turn what looks like a negative into something positive." [89]

Until a few years ago large law firms, with their unlimited budgets for Westlaw or Lexis, had a significant advantage over small firms. Large firm lawyers could put in hours of research while small firm lawyers and solo practitioners were relegated to clients and cases requiring no or minimal research because of the high cost of research. Today, through bar association membership, any attorney can obtain free access to case law databases such as Fastcase.[90] Previously, large law firms, with their deep pockets, were uniquely able to hire the private investigators needed on complex matters. Today, with Facebook and other social media, it is possible to find almost anyone, anywhere, allowing small firms to conduct thorough investigations on cases.[91] Previously, only large law firms with deep budgets could hire forensic experts, photographers and artists to create necessary trial exhibits. Today, any solo practitioner can create high quality demonstrative evidence through inexpensive word processing platforms and access to public information on the internet.[92]

Previously, operating a law office required considerable staff resources. Today, firms can outsource payroll, bookkeeping, billing and collection. As one seasoned solo practitioner states: "[T]he day-to-day management of the office has become easier. . . . I can attest that in the pre-Internet days, payroll was a major chore that had to be done twice a month."[93] In addition to outsourcing, there are fewer in-office tasks to be done. No one has to spend hours at a photocopier, making copies of exhibits. No one has to take documents to the courthouse or post office. It is no longer necessary to pay expensive postage since almost everything can be sent electronically.

Previously, only large law firms with marketing budgets were able to hire firms to conduct effective and expensive marketing campaigns and business managers to plan client appreciation events. Today, social media platforms allow the smallest firms to create and update their webpages and reach out to potential clients. With such access, a savvy solo practitioner can market herself as effectively as the largest law firm.[94]

Quality of Life in
Small Firms and Solo Practices

"Career satisfaction is not distributed equally throughout the profession. . . ."[95] Small firms and solo practices often offer quality of life advantages over large law firms. Findings from the *After the JD, First Results* project, which tracked 5000 lawyers over a ten year time period from 1994–2004, found that lawyers at larger firms report less satisfaction with their jobs than lawyers at smaller firms:[96]

> "[L]awyers in the largest firms (251+) are . . . substantially more likely to express a desire to work fewer hours, to have less pressure to bill, and to have greater opportunities to shape decisions on matters on which they work. The smaller the law firm, the more likely it is that new attorneys will report relatively high satisfaction with the work that they do."[97]

While attorneys in large law firms tend to be satisfied with "power track" attributes of their jobs ("satisfaction with career opportunities within the work organization, including method of compensation, opportunities for advancement, recognition they receive for their work and performance evaluation"[98]), they are often the least happy,[99] whether associates or partners, regarding life balance issues and control over their lives. [100] The *After the JD, First Results* study found that attorneys "with the highest incomes report relatively less satisfaction with the work they do and the practice settings in which they work than those earning far less from the practice of law."[101]

The *After the JD, Second Phase* project found that more than two-fifths (41%) of attorneys in firms with more than 250 lawyers reported that they worked more than 60 hours per week."[102] Attorneys working in the largest law firms work more hours than lawyers in other private practices or lawyers in government offices.[103] Studies show that associates at large law firms typically bill 2000 to 2500 hours per year and partners average 2000.

It takes a lot of time to bill 2000 to 2500 hours per year. Lawyers typically can bill only two hours for every three hours at the office. One cannot "bill for going to lunch, chatting with colleagues, reading mail, going to the bathroom, filling out time sheets, making a pitch to a prospective client, interviewing a recruit, attending CLE seminars, taking a recruit to a social event, or any personal calls or errands."[104] Professor Schiltz, a law professor at Notre Dame and previously a partner in a large law firm before entering law teaching, explains what is necessary to bill 2000 hours per year:

> "[T]o bill 2000 per year, you will have to spend about sixty hours per week at the office, and take no more than two weeks of vacation/sick time/personal leave. If it takes you, say, forty-five minutes to get to work, and another forty-five minutes to get home, billing 2000 hours per year will mean leaving home at 7:45 am, working at the office from 8:30 am until 6:30 pm, and then arriving home at 7:15 pm—and doing this for *six days per week*, every week."[105]

In short, solo practices and small firms may be the wave of the future in the legal profession, offering increased opportunities for challenging work and enhanced quality of life.

Conclusion

The legal profession is experiencing dynamic changes and needed corrections. It is a robust profession poised to grow more than most sectors of the economy. Lawyers are and will remain among the highest paid professionals in the United States. Most practicing lawyers express satisfaction with their career choice. Changing demographics favor those entering the legal profession today. As the needs and expectations of clients who use legal services are changing, the business models of law practice are evolving. While disruptive for some, these business models offer flexibility for clients and lawyers.

TABLE OF AUTHORITIES

"A Former In-house Lawyer May Pursue a Wrongful Discharge Claim Against Her Employer and Client as Long as the Client Information is Protected." *ABA Formal Opinion* 01-424.

"Big Firm Salaries Drop: What It Means." *The National Jurist* Sept. 21, 2012.

Blumenthal, Jeff. "Bitter Medicine: Law Firms in a Squeeze Increasingly Take Difficult Step of Turning Equity Partners into Nonequity Partners." *Broward Daily Business Review* Dec. 9, 2002, S. Fla. ed.: A9.

Burk, David. "Review of Brian Z. Tamanaha, Failing Law Schools." *Journal of Legal Education* 63 (2013): 348.

"Contact With Inside Counsel of an Organization Regarding a Matter When the Organization is Represented in the Matter by Outside Counsel." *ABA Formal Opinion* 06-443.

"Contingent Fees in Civil Cases Based on the Amount of Money Saved for the Client." *ABA Formal Opinion* 93-373.

Dance, E. Leigh, ed. *Bright Ideas: Insights From Legal Luminaries Worldwide*. Minneapolis: Mill City Press, Inc., 2009.

Epstein, Richard. "The Rule of Lawyers." *Wall Street Journal* May 5, 2013.

Galanter, Marc & Thomas Palay. *Tournament of Lawyers: The Transformation of the Big Law Firm*. University of Chicago Press, 1993.

Galbenski, David. *Unbound: How Entrepreneurship is Dramatically Transforming Legal Services Today*. Unbound Legal, 2009.

Gibson, K. William. "Outsourcing Spotlight: Outsourcing Legal Services Abroad." *ABA, Law Practice* July, Aug. 2008 http://www.americanbar.org.

Goldberg, Elizabeth. "Law Firms Face Gray Area as Boomers Age." *The American Lawyer* Dec. 10, 2007.

Hajavsky, Laura. "Top Ten Proven Tactics to Generate Cost Savings." *Association of Corporate Counsel* http://www.acc.com/legalresources.

Harper, Steven J. "Pop Goes the Law." *Chronicle of Higher Education* March 11, 2013.

Harper, Steven J. *The Lawyer Bubble*. New York: Basic Books, 2013.

Hendersen, William D. & Leonard Bierman. "An Empirical Analysis of Lateral Lawyer Trends from 2000–2007: Emerging Equilibrium for Corporate Law Firms." *Georgetown Journal of Legal Ethics* 22 (2009): 1395.

Henderson, William D. & Rachel M. Zahorsky. "Law Job Stagnation May Have Started Before the Recession—And It May Be a Sign of Lasting Change." *ABA Journal* July 1, 2011 http://www.abajournal.com/magazine/article/paradigm_shift/.

Jones, Ashby & Joe Palazzo. "Law-Firm Slowdown Fuels Cuts at Weil." *Wall Street Journal* June 25, 2013.

Kelley, Robert E. *How To Be A Star At Work*. Random House, 1999.

Kerschberg, Ben. "Legal Services Outsourcing (LSO)—Maximizing Comparative Advantage." May 16, 2011 http://www.forbes.com.

Kirkland, Kimberly. "Ethics in Large Law Firms: The Principle of Pragmaticism." *University of Memphis Law Review* 35 (2005): 677.

Lavagnino, Javier. "Corporate Counsel Facing Budget Cuts and Need to Address Outside Law Firm Costs." *Inhouse: The Findlaw Corporate Counsel Blog* June 5, 2009 http://blogs.findlaw.com.

"Law Firms Wring Costs From Back-Office Tasks." *Wall Street Journal* Oct. 7, 2012 http://online.wsj.com.

"Lawyer Websites." *ABA Formal Opinion* 10-457.

Leipold, James. "The Employment Profile for the Law School Class of 2011." *NALP* www.nalp.org.

Levit, Nancy and Douglas O. Linder. *The Happy Lawyer: Making a Good Life in the Law*. New York: Oxford University Press, 2010.

Melcher, Michael. *The Creative Lawyer*. Chicago: ABA, 2007.

Natarajan, Ganesh. "A Decade of Legal Services Outsourcing." *National Law Journal* Mar. 12, 2012.

Olsen, Dana. "Bye-Bye Big Firm; Is the Exodus of Lawyers From Big Law to Small Firms Here to Stay?" *Corporate Counsel Online* Apr. 1, 2012.

Osofsky, Justin & Lynn Wood. "Crossing the Charles: The Experience, Networks, and Career Paths of Harvard JD/MBA Alumni." http://www.ssrn.com/en/.

"Outsourcing the Law to India." June 14, 2011 http://www.pbs.org.

Palazzolo, Joe. "Law Grads Face Brutal Job Market." *Wall Street Journal* June 25, 2012.

"Protecting the Confidentiality of Unencrypted Email." *ABA Formal Opinion* 99-413.

Regan, Jr., Milton C. *The Fall of a Wall Street Lawyer. Eat What You Kill*. The University of Michigan Press, 2004.

Ross, Michael C. "Law Firm Diet: Reduce Firms—Reduce Costs?" *Altman Weil, Inc. Report to Legal Management* Oct., 2004: 5.

Rubin, Gretchin. *The Happiness Project*. New York: Harper Collins, 2009.

Schiltz, Patrick J. "On Being a Happy, Healthy and Ethical Member of an Unhappy, Unhealthy, and Unethical Profession." *Vanderbilt Law Review* 52 (1999): 871.

Smith, Jennifer. "D.C. Law Firm Tightens Its Belt." *Wall Street Journal* Aug. 9, 2013.

Smith, Jennifer. "On Sale: The $1,150-per-hour Lawyer." *Wall Street Journal* April 10, 2013.

Susskind, Richard. *The End of Lawyers?* New York: Oxford University Press, 2010.

Swaine, Robert T. *The Cravath System and Its Predecessors*. Ad Press, 1948.

Tamanaha, Brian Z. *Failing Law Schools*. Chicago: The University of Chicago Press, 2012.

The American Bar Foundation and the NALP Foundation for Law Career Research and Education. "After the JD: First Results of a *National Study* of Legal Careers." 2004.

The American Bar Foundation and the NALP Foundation for Law Career Research and Education. "After the JD: Second Results From a *National Study* of Legal Careers." 2009.

"The 2012 Law Firm Billing Survey." *National Law Journal* Dec. 17, 2012.

"U.S. Firms Outsource Legal Services to India." *New York Times* Aug. 21, 2007 http://www.nytimes.com.

Weiss, Debra Cassens. "New Career Path for Lawyers." *ABA Journal* Dec. 10, 2009 http://www.abajournal.com.

Welch, Mary. "Skanska USA General Counsel Explains Move Toward a Virtual In-house Law Firm." *Daily Report* Oct. 24, 2012.

Zahorsky, Rachel M. & William D. Henderson. "Who's Eating Law Firms' Lunch?" *ABA Journal* 99 (2013): 32.

Zweig, Jason. "Here Comes the Next Hot Emerging Market: The U.S." *Wall Street Journal* Apr. 20–21: BI.

ENDNOTES

1   *See, e.g.*, BRIAN Z. TAMANAHA, FAILING LAW SCHOOLS (University of Chicago Press 2012); STEPHEN J. HARPER, THE LAWYER BUBBLE (Basic Books 2013).

2   Richard Epstein, *The Rule of Lawyers*, WALL ST. J. A13 (May 5, 2013).

3   *Id.*; David Burk, *Review of Brian Z. Tamanaha, Failing Law Schools,* 63 J. LEGAL EDUCA. 348, 355 (2013).

4   United States Bureau of Economic Analysis, Table 1.1.5 Gross Domestic Product, http://www.bea.gov/iTable/itable.cfm?reqid= 51&step=1#reqid=51&step=51&isuri=1&5102=15 (last visited Feb. 9, 2014).

5   UNITED STATES BUREAU OF ECONOMIC ANALYSIS, Value Added by Industry as a Percentage of Gross Domestic Product, January 23, 2014, http://www.bea.gov/iTable/itable.cfm?reqid=51& step=1#reqid=51&step=51&isuri=1&5 (last visited on Feb. 9, 2014).

6   UNITED STATES DEPARTMENT OF LABOR, *Monthly Labor Review,* www.bls.gov/mlr (last visited Feb. 19, 2014). This compares to a projected growth in health care of 21.4%, *id.* at 84, 14.4% in education, *id.*, 16.5% in community and social services occupations, *id.*, 10.3% in architecture and engineering, *id.* at 86, 19% in life, physical and social science occupations, *id.* at 85, and 12.1% in arts, design, entertainment and media. *Id.*

7   William D. Henderson, Rachel M. Zahorsky, *Law Job Stagnation May Have Started Before the Recession—And It May Be a Sign of Lasting Change,* ABA JOURNAL, July 1, 2011, http://www.abajournal.com/magazine/article/paradigm_shift/ [hereinafter *Stagnation*] (last visited Feb. 19, 2014).

8   Jason Zweig, *Here Comes the Next Hot Emerging Market: The U.S.,* WALL ST. J. BI (Apr. 20–21).

9   *Id.*

10   NALP, *Law School Class of 2012 Finds More Jobs, Starting Rise—But Large Class Size Hurts Overall Employment,* http:// www.nalp.org/classof2012_selected_pr [hereinafter NALP, *Class of 2012*] (last visited Feb. 18, 2014).

[11] UNITED STATES DEPARTMENT OF LABOR, *Occupational Employment Statistics,* http://www.bls.gov/oes (last visited Feb. 24, 2014).

[12] NALP, *Research and Statistics, Class of 2012,* http://www.nalp.org/classof2012 (last visited Feb. 18, 2014).

[13] NALP, *Market for New Law Graduates at Highest Level in 20 Years, Approaching 92%,* http://www.nalp.org/marketfornewlaw graduates (last visited FEB. 18, 2014).

[14] Joe Palazzolo, *Law Grads Face Brutal Job Market,* WALL ST. J., June 25, 2012, http://wsj.com (last vested on March 9, 2014).

[15] U.S. CENSUS BUREAU, POPULATION BY SEX AND SELECTED AGE GROUPS: 2000 AND 2010, http://www.census.gov/popest/data (last visited Feb. 24, 2014).

[16] Elizabeth Goldberg, *Law Firms Face Gray Area as Boomers Age,* THE AMERICAN LAWYER, Dec. 10, 2007, available at http://www.law.com/jsp/article.jsp?id'1197021878240 (last visited on Feb. 18, 2014).

[17] NALP FOUNDATION FOR LAW CAREER RESEARCH AND EDUCATION AND THE AMERICAN BAR FOUNDATION, AFTER THE JD: FIRST RESULTS OF A *NATIONAL STUDY* OF LEGAL CAREERS at 33 (2004) [hereinafter AFTER THE JD: FIRST RESULTS] "The mean number of hours reported for a typical work week was 49 and the median 50— compared with a median of 40 hours for all full-time workers in the United States." *Id.*

[18] *Id.*

[19] *Id.* at 47.

[20] *Id.*

[21] RICHARD SUSSKIND, THE END OF LAWYERS, 269 (Oxford University Press 2010) [hereinafter SUSSKIND, END OF LAWYERS].

[22] Jennifer Smith, *Online Matchmakers Offer New Source of Legal Help,* WALL ST. J. R2 (Dec. 2, 2013).

[23] ABA Formal Op. 10-457, *Lawyer Websites*; ABA Formal Op. 99-413, *Protecting the Confidentiality of Unencrypted Email;* ABA Formal Op. 93-373, *Contingent Fees in Civil Cases Bases on the Amount of Money Saved for the Client.*

[24] SUSSKIND, END OF LAWYERS, *supra* note 21 at 10.

[25] *Id.* at 4.

[26] New rules and regulations put in place after the 2008 economic meltdown make "extraordinary" changed in capital and liquidity requirements for banks operating in the United States; increased penalties for financial violations (JP Morgan Chase paid a record $13 billion in a 2013 settlement with the Department of Justice); "stepped-up government enforcement actions in the labor arena ... aimed at misclassifying workers as independent contractors"; and liability companies face for cybercrime attacks mean "corporate legal departments [are] beefing up internal risk-and-compliance programs." WALL S. J., B6 (JAN. 6, 2014).

[27] Mary Welch, *Skanska USA General Counsel Explains Move Toward a Virtual In-house Law Firm,* DAILY REPORT, http://www.dailyreportonline.com (Oct. 24, 2012) (regarding interview with Clay Hayden, General Counsel of Skanska USA) (last visited Feb. 18, 2014).

[28] SUSSKIND, END OF LAWYERS, *supra* note 21 at 110 (tense in original quotation has been changed).

[29] Bates v. State Bar of Arizona, 433 U.S. 350 (1977).

[30] *Stagnation, supra* note 7.

[31] Michael C. Ross, *Law Firm Diet: Reduce Firms—Reduce Costs?* ALTMAN WEIL, INC. REPORT TO LEGAL MANAGEMENT 5 (Oct. 2004).

[32] *Stagnation, supra* note 7.

[33] Mark Chandler, Speech at Northwestern School of Law's 34th Annual Conference of the Securities Regulation Institute, http://blogs.cisco.com/news/cisco_general_counsel_on_state_of_technology_in_the_law/, discussed in *Results* at 5.

[34] FOURTH ANNUAL CHIEF LEGAL OFFICERS SURVEY, October 2003, conducted by Altman Weil, Inc.

[35] SUSSKIND, END OF LAWYERS, *supra* note 21 at 151.

[36] *Id.* at 12.

[37] Daniel Martin Katz, *Quantitative Legal Prediction—Or— How I Learned to Stop Worrying and Start Preparing for the Data-Driven Future of the Legal Services Industry,* 62 EMORY L.J. 909, 930 (2013) [hereinafter *Quantitative Legal Prediction*].

[38]   ABA Formal Op. 01-424, *A Former In-house Lawyer May Pursue a Wrongful Discharge Claim Against Her Employer and Client As Long as the Client Information is Protected.*

[39]   ABA Formal Op. 06-443, *Contact with Inside Counsel of an Organization Regarding a Matter When the Organization is Represented in the Matter by Outside Counsel.*

[40]   *Stagnation, supra* note 7.

[41]   *The 2012 Law Firm Billing Survey,* NAT'L L. J., December 17, 2012.

[42]   Pro se services have proliferated. Many states and bar associations have led the movement. In an effort to make access to the legal system possible for those with limited funds, they have committed significant resources to providing reliable, accurate forms to the public to assist them in simple, routine legal matters. Secretary of State offices make hundreds of forms available free of charge including divorce petitions and bankruptcy filings. *See e.g.,* www.sos.alabama.gov (Alabama); www.ct.gov/sots (Connecticut); www.dos.ny.gov (New York). *See also* http://www.americanbar.org/groups/delivery_legal_services/resources/pro_se_unbundling_resource_center/pro_se_resources_by_state.html

[43]   SUSSKIND, END OF LAWYERS, *supra* note 21 at 18.

[44]   Rachel M. Zahorsky & William D. Henderson, *Who's Eating Law Firms' Lunch,* 99 ABA J. 32, 37 (2013) [hereinafter *Who's Eating Law Firms' Lunch*].

[45]   http://associatesmind.com/wp-content/uploads/2013/08/Historical-Lawyer-Growth-Data (listing number of lawyers in U.S. in 1960, 1990 and 2012); http://www.censusscope.org/us/print_chart_popl.html (listing population in U.S. in 1960, 1990 and 2012) (both sites last visited on April 28, 2014).

[46]   UNITED STATES DEPARTMENT OF JUSTICE PRESS RELEASE, June 27, 1995, http://www.justice.gov/atr/public/press_releases/1995 (last visited Feb. 18, 2014).

[47]   *Id.*

[48]   American Bar Association discussed at http://www.thefacultylounge.org/2013/02/historical-data-total-number-of-law-students (last visited Apr. 28, 2014).

[49]   NALP, *Law School Class of 2012 Finds More Jobs*, http://www.nalp.org/classof2012_selected_pr (last visited Feb 5. 2014).

[50]   *Id.*

[51]   *Stagnation, supra* note 7.

[52]   CITI PRIVATE BANK HILDEBRANDT INSTITUTE, 2012 CLIENT SURVEY.

[53]   *Id.* at 13. Mergers of law firms have increased significantly in recent years, up 67% in 2012 over 2010. An "intriguing development" in this increased merger activity is mergers in global markets. The Hildebrant study found that "mergers outside the U.S. jumped to 54 in 2011, as compared to 44 and 48 in 2010 and 2009, respectively," some of which were Aquite significant in size. *Id.* at 18. Hildebrant predicts more of these cross-border merges especially in emerging global markets as world economic activity moves from the west and north to the east and south. *Id.*

[54]   William D. Hendersen & Leonard Bierman, *An Empirical Analysis of Lateral Lawyer Trends from 2000–2007: Emerging Equilibrium for Corporate Law Firms*, 22 GEO. J. OF L. ETHICS 1395, 1417 (2009) [hereinafter *Lateral Lawyer Trends*].

[55]   Steven J. Harper, *Pop Goes the Law*, CHRONICLE OF HIGHER EDUCATION (Mar. 11, 2013).

[56]   *Lateral Lawyer Trends, supra* note 54 at 1412.

[57]   Jennifer Smith, *On Sale: The $1,150-per-hour Lawyer*, WALL ST. J. B1 (Apr. 10, 2013).

[58]   *Lateral Lawyer Trend, supra* note 54 at 1423.

[59]   *Id.* at 1424.

[60]   *Id.* at 1422.

[61]   Jeff Blumenthal, *Bitter Medicine: Law Firms in a Squeeze Increasingly Take Difficult Step of Turning Equity Partners into Nonequity Partners*, BROWARD DAILY BUS. REV. (S. Fla.) Dec. 9, 2002 at A9.

[62]   *Id.*

[63]   *Lateral Lawyer Trends, supra* note 54 at 1424.

[64]   *Id.* at 1422.

[65]   *Id.*

[66]   Kimberly Kirkland, *Ethics in Large Law Firms: The Principles of Pragmaticism,* 35 U. MEM. L.REV. 631, 639 (2005) [hereinafter *Ethics in Large Law Firms*].

[67]   *Id.* at 683.

[68]   *Id.* at 678 (internal quotation marks and brackets deleted).

[69]   Jennifer Smith, *D.C. Law Firm Tightens Its Belt,* WALL ST. J. B1 (Aug. 9, 2013).

[70]   *Id.*

[71]   *Id.*

[72]   Ashby Jones & Joe Palazzolo, *Law-Firm Slowdown Fuels Cuts at Weil,* WALL ST. J. 1 (June 25, 2013).

[73]   *Id.* at A1 & A6.

[74]   *Lateral Lawyer Trends, supra* note 54 at 1424.

[75]   *Quantitative Legal Prediction, supra* note 37 at 934.

[76]   *Id.* at 934

[77]   *Id.* at 935.

[78]   *Id.*

[79]   AFTER THE JD, FIRST RESULTS, *supra* note 17 at 25.

[80]   Mary Welch, *Skanska USA General Counsel Explains Move Toward a Virtual In-House Law Firm, Daily Report,* http://dailyreportonline.com quoting Clay Hayden, General Counsel of Skanska USA, a $3 billion revenue per year company (last visited Feb. 18, 2014).

[81]   Dana Olsen, *Bye-Bye Big Firm; Is the Exodus of Lawyers From Big Law to Small Firms Here to Stay?,* CORPORATE COUNSEL ONLINE (Apr. 1, 2012) (last visited Feb. 18, 2014).

[82]   Jennifer Smith, *Lawyers All Over? No, Thanks,"* WALL ST. J. B1, B7 (Nov. 11, 2013).

[83]   Javier Lavagnino, *Corporate Counsel Facing Budget Cuts and Need to Address Outside Law Firm Costs,* INHOUSE: THE FINDLAW CORPORATE COUNSEL BLOG, http://blogs.findlaw.com (June 5, 2009).

[84]   *Id.*

[85]   *Id.*

86 *Id.*

87 *Id.*

88 *Who's Eating Law Firms' Lunch, supra* note 44 at 35.

89 K. William Gibson, *Flying Solo*, http://www.americanbar. org/publications/law_practice_magazine/2014/january-february/flying-solo.html (last visited on Feb. 18, 2014).

90 *Id.*

91 *Id.*

92 *Id.*

93 *Id.*

94 *Id.*

95 Patrick J. Schiltz, *On Being a Happy, Healthy, and Ethical Member of an Unhappy, Unhealthy, and Unethical Profession,* 52 VAND. L.REV. 871, 886 (1999) [hereinafter *Happy, Healthy, Ethical*].

96 AFTER THE JD, FIRST RESULTS, *supra* note 17 at 48.

97 *Id.*

98 *Id.* at 49.

99 *Id.* at 888, citing Margaret Cronin Fisk, *Lawyers Give Thumbs Up*, NAT'L L.J. S2 (1990).

100 THE AMERICAN BAR FOUNDATION AND THE NALP FOUNDATION FOR LAW CAREER RESEARCH AND EDUCATION, AFTER THE JD: SECOND RESULTS FROM A *NATIONAL STUDY* OF LEGAL CAREERS, at 49 (2009) [hereinafter AFTER THE JD: SECOND STUDY].

101 *Id.*

102 *Id.*

103 *Id.*

104 *Happy, Healthy, Ethical, supra* note 95 at 894.

105 *Id.* (emphasis in original).

CHAPTER IV

HOW TO SURVIVE AND THRIVE IN TODAY'S LEGAL MARKET

1. INTRODUCTION

As discussed in Chapter Three, the legal profession is experiencing dramatic, structural changes. It is a difficult time for those who fail to adapt, and a time of opportunity for those who do. As Daniel Katz of Michigan State University School of Law notes: "The very dynamics that create peril for some create possibility for others."[1] The key to success is responding "creatively and forcefully to the shifting demands of what is a rapidly evolving legal marketplace."[2]

New lawyers are the best positioned to seize and develop these opportunities. Unlike many currently practicing attorneys, young lawyers are well-versed in the technology which is driving many of the changes in the legal profession. Additionally, new lawyers are not invested in the traditional ways of practicing law and are able to think creatively about responding to the changes afoot. There is much to embrace in the evolving practice of law for many of the new opportunities offer quality of life improvements over current ways of practicing law.[3]

This chapter picks up where the last chapter left off. Chapter Three addressed the economic and technological forces that are changing the legal profession and their consequences for attorneys. This chapter addresses the future, discussing what law students and lawyers, new and experienced, can do to survive and thrive in the legal world ahead.

2. LAW STUDENTS: GET THE "ROYAL HONEY"

Law students need a job when they graduate. They also need a job that is challenging and enjoyable, at least most of the time. No job is challenging and enjoyable *all* of the time but for the kind of people who tend to go into law, binding oneself to a job that is not fulfilling in some way will exact a high personal cost (See Chapter I (M) *supra*). Nurturing one's career means more than just "getting a job." To get a job that is challenging and enjoyable, law students need the "royal honey."

Bees begin life genetically identical. All bees' diet is the same during their first three days of life. They all get "royal honey," which is secreted from the heads of the worker bees and consist of B vitamins and protein, especially royalactin. After the third day, drone and worker bees get no more royal honey. Only bees destined to become queens continue to receive royal honey. Like bees, and athletes (David Thorpe has developed the concept of royal honey in the context of athletes), new lawyers need royal honey to thrive professionally. Royal honey for new lawyers consist of choice assignments; mentors; opportunities to build skills, including EQ skills; and promoters.

It has become harder for new lawyers to get royal honey as corporate clients balk at paying for work done by new associates, law firms become less stable, and law firm partners mentor less because of their pressure to bill more hours and bring in more clients (See Chapter III (5)(B) *supra*). There are, however, two ways law students can get royal honey. The first is choosing law school experiences wisely. The second is savvy navigation of one's path immediately after law school.

A. What to Do While in Law School

(i) Mentors

Everyone enjoys helping eager law students. Students should take advantage of this willingness to help while they can. Seek out mentors, whether professors or practicing attorneys. Register for courses taught by respected adjunct faculty who are also practicing members of the bar or bench. Do well in your classes, speak up during class, and visit with your professors before or after class. Go by your professors' offices. Correspond with them about course coverage. Seek career advice.

Stay in touch with lawyers you shadow and those you work with during the summers of law school. Offer to continue to work on projects once you have left your summer position and returned to law school. Don't over-commit or take on more than you can handle but if you can work on small projects during the school year, do so. Such projects will give you an opportunity to build your relationship with a lawyer and law office. Offer to do these projects, especially if they are small, on a volunteer basis. Your willingness to do so will signal your interest in the lawyer and firm, as well as your industriousness and work ethic. Explore your family and friend connections. Who do you know who knows an attorney? Ask family members and friends to inquire of their attorney friends if they would be willing to meet with you, or permit you to shadow him or her. Follow up the inquiry.

(ii) Shadow Programs

Most law schools have "shadow" programs in which lawyers volunteer to allow law students to follow them for a day or more to observe what the lawyer does. Do this as much as possible while in law school, either through your law school program or through opportunities you locate. When shadowing, make a point to observe and comply with the unspoken rules of etiquette and expectation within the law office (See Chapter IV (3) *infra.*) If the lawyer you have shadowed seems receptive, ask if you may return to shadow again, thereby further solidifying a relationship with him or her.

(iii) Clinic Courses

Seek out clinic programs and courses. In these courses, you will develop client interviewing and litigation skills. You will see a bit about the "real world" of lawyering. You will get opportunities for one-on-one mentoring. You will be able to observe different types of law practices and the life styles they offer.

(iv) Employment During Law School

Even if you do so as a volunteer, seek out part-time employment at a law office while you are in law school even if

it is only during a semester break. You will begin learning
lawyering skills and the "intangibles" of law practice. You will
make contacts. You will have the opportunity to impress the
lawyers and the offices in which you work, meet potential
employers and impress them with your dedication and work
ethic.

B.   First Jobs After Law School

Recall the discussion in Chapter Three regarding law firms
and the dynamics of who and why firms hire attorneys (See
Chapter III (3) *supra*). Law firms want experienced lawyers
with established clients. They don't have the voluminous, high-
volume, discovery work they previously had for new associates
to work on (See Chapter IV (4)(A)(ii)(2)). Associates in law
firms no longer have as many opportunities to develop
lawyering skills or obtain valuable mentoring. These facts
mean that to compete for jobs in private practice, law students
need to obtain experience, lawyering skills, and client
development abilities *before* going into the job market. Thus, it
is wise to look at the first few years of one's career after law
school graduation as an investment in the rest of one's career.
Obtaining experience through "high leverage learning
opportunities" (See Chapter IV (5)(A)(1)(d) *infra*)) is the way to
obtain career advantages for a lifetime. "High leverage"
opportunities include government and public interest law
offices, private practice options to being a salaried employee,
dual training, and pursuit of law-related professions.

(i)   Government and Public Interest Offices

Government and public interest law jobs present a number
of advantages for new lawyers. These positions have always
provided unique opportunities to do meaningful work, but now
as law firms become less able to provide mentoring,
government and public interest positions stand out. Unlike
partners at law firms who are under increasing pressure to bill
more hours, maintain clients, and spend less time mentoring
new lawyers, senior attorneys at government and public
interest offices are liberated from billable hour and client

development expectations and have more time to mentor, train and advise new attorneys.

In addition, with a few exceptions, most new lawyers at government and public interest offices get more responsibility than new associates in law firms. Even the least senior lawyer in government and public interest offices is soon handling her own cases, making her own decisions about a case, preparing and trying her own cases, conducting mediations, drafting significant and complicated contracts, and negotiating with seasoned and experienced lawyers on the other side. Lawyers who get such responsibility will become better lawyers than their peers who do not.

Lawyers at government and public interest offices tend to work fewer hours than lawyers in practice. The *After the JD: First Results* project, a study of 5000 attorneys over the first ten years of their practice, found that "[t]hose least likely to report . . . long hours [60+ hours per week] are working in government and public interest."[4] This confirms data gathered by the ABA in previous longitudinal studies of attorneys.[5]

The premium placed on government and public interest employment by the private sector is reflected in law firm compensation. Lawyers with government law experience are valuable lateral hires. In a study of lateral moves by lawyers within large law firms, Hendersen and Bierman found:

> "The data supports the observations that non-law firm employment in government, private industry, or another setting (*e.g.,* education or non-profit organization) enhances the value of lawyers' human capital. . . ."[6] In particular, government attorneys command a price vis à vis lateral partners who join through other practice settings such as law firms."[7]

Data from large (Top Five) legal markets gathered by Henderson and Bierman show that lawyers with experience at the U.S. Department of Justice and U.S. Attorney's Offices, for example, garner salaries up to $150,000 per year higher than other lateral hires.[8] Although government employment generally offers a lower beginning salary than many law firms, salaries in government positions are quite respectable. In 2010,

the nationwide median salary at government civil legal
services offices was $42,000; public defenders' office, $47,500;
local prosecuting attorneys' offices, $50,000; and public interest
organizations, $45,000. Attorneys with eleven to fifteen years
at these offices had a national median salary of $62,550;
$76,160; $77,500; and $70,875, respectively.[9] These figures
compare to a median starting salary of $61,245 at private law
firms.[10] The often generous employment benefits one earns
when in the public sector (retirement, health care coverage,
vacation time) can make the overall financial package of public
sector employment more advantageous than many private firm
positions.

Additionally, most government and public interest
employment qualifies for federal loan forgiveness programs.
Under these programs, repayment of qualifying school loans is
annually capped based upon one's salary so that monthly
repayments are not burdensome, and after a period of time,
usually ten years, the balance of one's loan is forgiven partially
or totally, depending on loan terms.

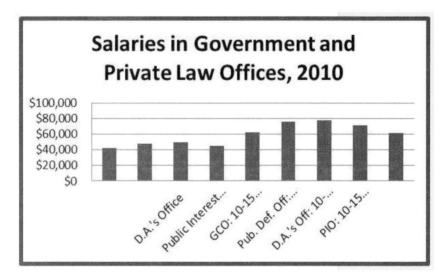

(ii) Private Practice Options

There are increasingly diverse private sector options to becoming a salaried associate at a law firm.[11] As noted, Of Counsel, contract attorney, and non-equity partnerships in firms offer attorneys flexibility while still providing a handsome living and stimulating work (See Chapter III (5) *supra*). Also noted in Chapter Three and as discussed in more detail below, solo and small firm practices are increasingly viable (See Chapter III (5)(C) *supra* and Chapter IV (4)(A)(ii)(b) *infra*).

In today's legal world, forming one's own LLC and contracting with several law firms is a viable business plan that provides a good living and considerable flexibility. Increasingly, it makes sense for law firms and businesses to contract out specialized legal work that arises periodically but does not justify full staffing. Law firms can cut overhead costs by trimming lawyers and practice groups that are not profitable. Firms can continue providing these legal services to clients by affiliating with niche law firms for the specialized services these attorneys previously provided. Similarly, businesses with established in-house counsel offices may find it cost-effective to contract out small or specialized matters that do not arise often enough to justify hiring additional in-house attorneys. The Association of Corporate Counsel advises companies that a "top ten" strategy to cut legal costs is to send work to specialists.[12] For these reasons, lawyers with LLCs providing specialized services are now the "starfish points" in the "starfish" business model of modern law firms.

In short, forming one's own LLC and contracting with several law firms or businesses on a regular basis allows one to make a very handsome living while maintaining considerable autonomy over one's work schedule. Practicing solo or in small firms is easier than ever because of outsourcing services, technology and guidance tools readily available[13] (See Chapter IV (4)(A)(ii)(b), *infra*). A number of recent ethics opinions setting forth guidelines for attorneys who serve simultaneously as a partner in, "Of Counsel," or otherwise affiliated with multiple law firms,[14] are further indicator of the increased viability of lawyer affiliations with multiple law offices.

(iii) Dual Training; Law-Related Careers

Dual training in business and law, engineering and law, nursing and law, technology and law, or any number of combinations can leverage one's career. As Richard Susskind states, lawyers of the future need to be "hybrid professionals."

Business

A JD degree or joint JD/MBA degrees are valuable in the business world. A survey of Harvard JD/MBA students from 1971 to 2004 showed that such training increased the networking and career opportunities available in both the legal and business fields, creating a "boundaryless career."[15] The percentage of recent law graduates going into business and industry has tripled over the past twenty years.[16] In 2012, 17.9% of lawyers are employed in the business world.[17]

Business training is valuable in the legal world. In fact, given the volatility of the legal market, it is inconceivable how lawyers in private practice today can create and sustain a law practice without a business background. As Richard S. Granat and Stephanie Kimbro, note:

> "Law firms fail, whether large or small, because often lawyers have no understanding of the business planning process. A law firm is both a professional practice and a service business." [18]

Granat and Kimbro know of what they speak. Both are founders or members of law practices with unique business models. Both have been recognized for excellence in lawyering by the ABA.[19]

Technology

Numerous experts in legal profession note the increasingly interwoven relationship of law and technology. As Professor Goodenough of Vermont Law School states: "Legal practice isn't going away. It is just going to forms of delivery that can combine the competence and flexibility of an old-fashioned firm with the efficiency and scale of a just-in-time-cloud-computing company." [20]

There are tremendous opportunities for optimizing technology in the delivery of legal services (See Chapter IV(4) *infra*). These opportunities allow traditional law firms to transform themselves to meet the needs of clients and adjust to the new legal landscape. They also represent opportunities for law or law-related careers for new lawyers. As Daniel Katz of Michigan State University observes: "Legal information technology is the arbitrage opportunity for entrepreneurially minded law schools, law students, and practicing lawyers."[21]

Law Enforcement

A Juris Doctor degree opens doors in many law related and non-law careers. For example, law enforcement, especially at the federal level, is an excellent career path for attorneys. Many FBI, IRS, DEA and other federal law enforcement agents are licensed attorneys. Lawyers with prior law enforcement experience are hot commodities within law firms as more companies turn to law firms instead of forensic investigators to uncover security breaches and conduct internal investigations. When Penn State needed a top-to-bottom internal investigation following the Jerry Sandusky scandal, it hired Louis Freeh, former FBI Director and attorney. Freeh is a partner at the law firm, Pepper Hamilton LLP. He is also the Chairman of Freeh Group International Solutions, Inc., a company that "work[s] closely with ... client[s] to efficiently assess their circumstances, provide independent counsel, and jointly develop or enhance effective risk mitigation strategies."[22]

Law firms can offer something forensic investigators cannot: attorney client privilege. Such confidentiality is the reason Nationwide Mutual Insurance Company, as one example, retained the law firm of Ropes & Gray, LLP, to conduct an internal investigation of a computer breach of its files in which personal data of one million people were stolen.[23] As the *Wall Street Journal* reported, Nationwide "hired Boston-based Ropes & Gray LLP . . . in part because the law firm could offer something a forensic firm couldn't: attorney-client privilege and the secrecy it confers."[24]

Companies that experience computer breaches or other internal malfeasance often face lawsuits by customers whose personal details have been disclosed or suffered other losses. In these situations, as Mike Dubose, the head of Kroll Advisory Solutions' cyber investigations practice, explained, "what a company does not want is its investigation or due diligence, undertaken with the best of intentions, to be used against it in litigation."[25] Attorney-client privilege can help companies maintain the confidentiality of the internal investigations they undertake.

Additionally, law firms can "help companies navigate the patchwork of federal and state laws governing public disclosures of data breaches."[26] Increased regulation and pressure by the SEC on companies to disclose cyber-attacks on their networks,[27] means that the internal investigation of cybersecurity is a "developing practice area."[28] As Steve Nelson, a recruiter at executive-search firm McCormick Group, Inc., explains, "law firms are increasingly looking for prosecutors with cybercrime experience to beef up incident-management-and-response practices."[29]

Sports

Consider the experience of Derrick Crawford, Managing Director of Enforcement, NCAA. Crawford joined the FBI immediately after law school. In this capacity he worked on complex fraud and public corruption cases in New York. Crawford then served as an Assistant Attorney General for the state of Alabama before being tapped by the NCAA to become an NCAA Compliance Investigator. Crawford was recruited from the NCAA to join the NFL General Counsel's office where he served for eight years before moving to senior administrative positions at colleges. The NCAA reached out to Crawford while he was in academia to return to the NCAA as a Director of Enforcement. As Crawford's career demonstrates, a JD provides tremendous opportunities to marry one's love of sports and the law.

The enforcement division of the NCAA is dominated by lawyers, where over two-thirds of the professional staff are JDs. This makes sense. NCAA investigators use the same skill set as prosecutors who learn how to investigate cases, separate poor decisions from actual violations, and summarize cases orally to fact finders. NCAA investigators present cases to the NCAA Committee on Infractions, an independent body composed of individuals from NCAA member institutions. Their presentations require the same analytical, organizational and oral skills trial attorneys use in the courtroom. Starting as an investigator in the NCAA is a stepping stone to enforcement and management positions at colleges and universities. Ten percent of the NCAA investigative staff turns over each year as investigators leave to go to NCAA member schools.[30]

Higher Education

A JD opens doors in higher education. Many colleges consider a Juris Doctorate to be a "terminal" degree, equivalent to the Ph.D. generally prized in academia. Joining a college faculty to teach business law, criminal justice or other law-related courses is a career path available to attorneys, especially those who have had primary or secondary teaching experience prior to law school.

(iv) Be Creative

As Deborah J. Long, Executive Vice President, Secretary and General Counsel, Protective Life Corporation, advises law students and new lawyers, "The most important thing you need to know is that you're going to have to be creative. No one can give you a list to do. You have to be willing to think in different ways how to do things."[31]

Law students will be judged on more than academic performance when they enter the working world. Today, it takes more than good grades to stand out among all other talented, hard-working, newly minted JDs with good grades. As Mark Drew, Managing Shareholder at Maynard, Cooper & Gale, P.C., states, "If all you are doing is going to college, going to law school, and making good grades, that's not enough."[32] Employers are looking for character traits such as resilience, resourcefulness, social acumen, and problem-solving abilities. Practical experience is a way to develop these traits and demonstrate to employers that one possesses them. Law firms like other businesses increasingly use metrics to assess the potential for success in prospective hires. These predictive analyses focus on real world experience such as participation in team sports and part-time work during school years.[33] Studies by organizational psychologists show that character and work ethic, not IQ, cognitive ability, awards or accolades, separate star performers from average performers (See Chapter IV (5) *infra*).

Mailing a cover letter (however engaging) and a resume (however sterling) to dozens of employers simply adds one's resume to the stack. Savvy law students supplement these efforts by developing mentors, nurturing contacts throughout law school, and seeking opportunities that demonstrate interpersonal skills and traits of character, good judgment and work ethic to future employers.

For this reason, law students who do not secure a paying summer position while in law school or obtain employment immediately after graduating from law school, should consider volunteering at a law office (even if doing so means working at night bartending or cleaning offices to pay the bills). Such commitment and work ethic makes a great impression. Any employer will think, "If John is cleaning offices at night so he can volunteer at my office during the day, he must really want this job." Additionally, by volunteering, "John" will be present, in view, and on the mind of attorneys in the office when a position becomes available.

If a law firm you are interested in does not hire you, consider proposing an alternative to their up-or-down hiring decision. Offer to work as a contract lawyer or as a volunteer for a trial period. Doing so will demonstrate your resourcefulness and desire. Your initiative will separate you from the other applicants who are content simply to send cover letters and resumes.

3. EXCEL AS A NEW LAWYER

Whether working part-time during law school or full time as a new lawyer, follow the advice from experienced attorneys (and one rock star) on how to succeed.

A.   Know When It Is "Show Time"

We should all take a lesson from Mick Jagger.

Many years ago, when I was an impoverished law student, a neighbor, Pete (a pseudonym), worked for a concert promoter. One of Pete's tasks was to ensure that a licensed physician was available on site for performing bands and entourages. At the time I knew several friends who were medical residents at the teaching hospital in town. As residents, they were also poor and more than happy to get free admission to concerts in return for taking a doctor's bag to concerts and being available should a medical need arise.

I recruited several medical friends to attend concerts as the "on site physician." For my services as the "fixer," I also got to attend the concerts free. It was great fun. We always had seats in the front row balcony box. For a bunch of in-debt, stressed-out, exhausted law students and medical residents, this was heaven. We attended a number of concerts and were becoming quite accustomed to our prime seats without any medical needs ever arising. Until the Rolling Stones came to town.

During the Stones' warm-up band's ear-drum-busting performance, Pete ran to our box, frantic. "Mick's sick!" he yelled. My medical-licensed friend, Joe (a pseudonym), grabbed his doctor's bag and ran off with Pete. Before that day, we had joked about what in the world do you put in a doctor's bag to treat band performers? We were about to find out. We couldn't wait until Joe returned to tell us all about it. Half an hour later Joe returned and told us about meeting Mick Jagger.

With Pete leading him behind stage, Joe walked into a dressing room that had the feel of a bank board room. He saw Keith Richards, Ronnie Wood and Mick Jagger, each sitting in separate couch areas in the huge room, huddling with different sets of people. The room was hushed. Everyone was calm and speaking softly. A large buffet table covered with a white table cloth sat in the middle of the room. It was filled with flower arrangements and delicacies of boiled shrimp, sliced beef tenderloin, fruits, vegetables and cheeses.

Mick Jagger sat at the back of the room, talking quietly with two clean-cut men in business suits. All of them, Jagger included, had briefcases open and spread-sheets out. They were discussing stocks, bonds, and investments. Joe stood to the side until they finished. He was introduced as the physician on call. Mick said that he had a sore throat. Joe looked inside Mick's throat. It was raw, red and covered with white patches of infection. Joe dug into his doctor's bag for a topical anesthetic spray. Mick took the bottle and carefully read the ingredients on the label. He gave it back. "Thanks, Mate, I think I'll go with what I've got." From under the spread sheets in his briefcase, Mick pulled out a spray bottle, opened his mouth, and sprayed. He stood up and said, "It's show time." The rest of the band began gathering themselves.

By the time Joe had reached our box and told us the story, the Rolling Stones were on stage. For the next three hours, they put on an intense show of music, lights, special effects and athleticism. Mick Jagger jumped from one elevated and moving stage to the next, strutting, dancing, gyrating, singing, and seemingly having the time of his life.

Here's what I learned. Mick Jagger is a professional. He may be a mild-mannered businessman in part of his life (he did attend the London School of Economics, after all) and he may have felt puny with an infected throat that night, but when it was show time, he knew how to flip the switch.

Attorneys are professionals. When it is our show time, we must behave as calm, logical, wise counselors. That's what we are paid for. That's why people come to see us. Clients seek advice from lawyers on matters of critical importance such as whether they're going to jail, what the rest of their lives and their children's lives will be like after a divorce, and how to structure or salvage the business of their dreams. Many clients are at the darkest, saddest, scariest point of their lives when they seek legal advice. They need a wise, discrete counselor. They deserve such.

Today, because of social media, it is *always* show time. Our professionalism or lack thereof will be judged 24/7. Idiotic pictures of half-clad law students or lawyers, dressed in ridiculous clothes, intoxicated, acting and saying stupid things on Facebook, in tweets, or texts, or any other social media, will undercut anyone's professional reputation. Thanks to iPhones, anything we do or say can be seen, by anyone, including clients, colleagues, hiring partners, judges and General Counsel, anytime, anywhere, *for years.*

The informal, colloquial, abbreviated spelling and sloppy grammar we may use in texts, tweets or emails with friends or family, has no place in correspondence with any attorney, client, prospective client, colleague, or in any business venue.

The same goes for anger. Petulance has no place in professional communications. Do not email, text, tweet or return phone calls relating to any professional matter in anger (good tip for life in general). Take a lesson from the emails (now public) exchanged by partners of Dewey & LeBoeuf, LLP, the 650-attorney law firm based in New York that filed for bankruptcy in 2012, in which partners called another "pathetic," "little prick," "assholes," "squat, ignorant, motherf---er."[34] No wonder the firm failed.

Law students and lawyers who are tech savvy have a tremendous advantage in the legal world ahead. However, do not let your "tech comfort" allow you to develop communication patterns that are inappropriate in a professional world. Your communications should reflect professionalism. Always. No one hires or consults an attorney because of antics on Youtube or sensational tweets. Not everyone can be a lawyer. Treasure your professionalism.

Follow one simple rule and you can never go wrong. If you would be embarrassed to have something you say, do, write, print, post or pose, show up on the front page of a newspaper, don't say it, do it, write it, print it, post it or pose for it.

B. Figure Out Who the "Stars" Are and Do What They Do

"Dress like them, watch their behavior at [office] functions . . . copy them."[35] This is advice from a law firm associate about the stars at his law firm. It is good advice. As discussed *supra* (Chapter IV (5)), industrial psychologists who study the performance of "brain-powered" workers have identified traits that separate star performers from average performers. These traits and strategies can be observed, taught, and learned. New lawyers and law students, actually anyone new to a law office even the most sought after new lateral hire, would do well to watch the successful lawyers in the firm and how they "interact with opposing counsel, judges, clients, other lawyers in the firm and staff. . . . Watch how they practice law and how they treat people. . . . Look for examples of good writing . . . whether it be a loan document, a pleading, or correspondence to a client."[36]

One star strategy is to treat staff with respect. Staff are as much a part of a team as are attorneys. An assistant, legal secretary, paralegal and other support personnel "can make or break you early in your career. . . ."[37] As one experienced attorney said, "Remember, you are not nearly as important as you think you are."[38] Do not, as another experienced attorney said when speaking of new lawyers, behave as "swaggering braggarts cross[ing] the threshold of their career so utterly convinced of their own importance that they become intoxicated with an exaggerated sense of self-worth."[39] Heed the advice from Kira Fonteneau, Public Defender for Jefferson County, Alabama:

> "No one will fault you for being a young lawyer. Everyone will fault you for being an arrogant, new lawyer who thinks they know everything. Ask the stupid questions and don't be afraid to admit you do not know. This advice is particularly helpful when dealing with court clerks, secretaries and paralegals, but will also gain you the respect of your clients and other lawyers."[40]

C. Be Available

As one equity partner advises, "You have to be available. You can't say no."[41] New lawyers should also be wary of what is told and what is expected. One associate explained:

> "The rhetoric coming from the firm to summer associates was that quality of life was very important. We were told that if associates worked too many hours,

the firm would lock the door to their offices and tell them that they could not come in. But when you looked at who was successful it was the people who were working long hours. . . . No partner at the firm would ever say 'you need to work this weekend,' but the people who were succeeding were working weekends. Whenever partners mentioned associates favorably, they mentioned those who were working incredibly long hours. The people who were making it, the associates a partner would mention at a meeting—'Jeff did a great job on this'—were the highest billers among the associates. The 'go to' associates never said no to an assignment. These were the people who were first in, in the morning, and last out at night."[42]

D.   Master Your Craft

Being a good lawyer is the first step in achieving professional success. Competence is the baseline. As one equity lawyer explained:

"[B]eing a good lawyer is not enough to make equity partner in today's large firms, and in a number of firms, it is also not enough to make non-equity partner. Large firms view good lawyers as expendable. . . . By the time a lawyer is being considered for partner, 'being a good lawyer is off the table,' meaning the 'good lawyer' criterion has been met, and other criteria will be the deciding factors."[43]

E.   Know the Expectations of the Lawyers for Whom You Work

An equity partner gave the following example: "A junior partner may think the partner wants him to bill 2,500 hours a year, but in reality that partner would like to see that lawyer bill 2,200 hours and spend 300 hours chairing an ABA committee."[44]

Fournier J. "Boots" Gale, III, founding member of the law firm, Maynard Cooper & Gale, PC, and General Counsel,

Regions Bank, tells how he learned about expectations of lawyers he worked with early in his career:

To Eat or Not to Eat

"In the first year of the practice of law, I was having lunch at my desk when one of our senior partners, Mr. Joseph F. Johnston, one of my early mentors and a very well-rounded gentleman with many interests, came into my office and made the point that eating lunch at my desk was not a good habit to develop. Mr. Joe told me that lawyers should try to take a mid-day break for lunch and share a meal and engage in conversations with others.

"He stressed the need to engage with others, especially non-lawyers, and said that over lunch with different people you could develop a broader perspective of the community and could learn from others what they were engaged in and what was happening in the city, state, etc. He discussed the obvious benefits of being involved in one's community and the advantage of getting to know a broad variety of people. I remember his saying that even if you don't have a lunch companion, you should get up from your desk, go outside and stretch your legs and mind. He told me that Birmingham had a very fine art museum and that an occasional visit there would be enjoyable. Mr. Joe said you will almost always see someone you know on the street and can find out interesting things by being around different people.

"Having an external vision, he stressed, will aid in keeping your legal work in perspective. He suggested that having lunch out of the office even with co-workers is much better than eating alone at your desk with work in front of you."[45]

If you are unclear about expectations at the office where you work, watch, listen and ask. Ask savvy staff, lawyers with a few years of experience, and the most senior lawyers their advice on how best to build your career.

F. Be Loyal to the Lawyers
with Whom You Work

Loyalty includes not revealing a colleague's mistakes. As one equity partner explained: "I don't want someone who is backstabbing me. I had an associate who worked for me . . . who would then go work for another partner and tell him what I screwed up. Why do I need that?"[46]

Loyalty does not include failing to address, or if necessary, disclosing another attorney's oversight, error or malfeasance. A lawyer risks her law license if she fails to reveal wrongdoing, or aids, assists, or helps conceal wrongdoing by an attorney with whom she works.[47]

G. Manage Perceptions

While staying true to oneself, it is important to know how to behave in different situations. Know how to manage others' perceptions of you. The following description by one associate about another is helpful in this regard:

"It became clear that the good associates developed a partner face, when they talked to the partners they were different than when they talked to other people. For instance, when Jim sat down and talked to associates it was like sitting in a high school locker room. However, when he talked to a partner he was a completely different persona and the switch was totally natural; he didn't seem to have to think about it, he just moved into it naturally. The associates loved this guy, he was succeeding but he was one of them. The partners also loved this guy, it seemed like he was always at the firm, always available. . . . I was in Jim's office at one point when a partner called him asking him to work on another project and he said to the partner, "I'm really busy, can you tell me more about this project" and he would thereby create the impression that he was busy but he would take on this project to work with this partner because he really liked working with him. I don't think that that Jim was all that busy when he said this, however, this was totally natural to him, it wasn't as if he was scheming."[48]

H. Cultivate a "Promoter"

To make partner or otherwise advance in a law firm, associates need someone who is willing to lend his or her stature, good will and time to promoting the associate within the firm. In part, this is due to the hierarchy among partners in many firms (See Chapter III (5) *supra*). As one equity partner stated, "Now that fewer and fewer partners have the power to demand that their candidates be promoted to equity partner, the enthusiastic support of one or more equity partners is not enough."[49] You must have someone champion you.

An equity partner gave an example. He had just received a call from another equity partner, asking him to support the election of a particular associate to equity partner. The partner was calling every equity partner in the firm of more than 700 lawyers, asking them to support that associate for promotion.

4.   NEW AND EVOLVING OPPORTUNITIES FOR LAWYERS—EVERY LAWYER IS AN ENTREPRENEUR

The fact is every lawyer, young or old, new or experienced, is an entrepreneur in today's practice of law. Even if one works as a salaried employee in a law firm, her value is measured by how much business she brings into the firm; revenues realized from her clients; hours she bills; profitability of alternative billing systems she quotes; difficulty collecting bills from her clients; leads for clients she pursues; amount of time those leads take; whether those leads yield clients. Lawyers' metrics are compared to other lawyers within a firm and among firms. Job security, salary and perks such as office location and staff assistance are allocated based upon these metrics. Law firms are not stable creatures. Lawyers and practice groups regularly move from firm to firm, altering the financial picture for the lawyers left behind. Firms merge and dissolve. In private practice, one is always going to have to justify his or her salary, equity share, perks, and existence within a law firm.

Lawyers who work in a government or public interest law offices also have to prove their worth. Government offices experience furloughs. Public interest offices lose funding. There are no guarantees or job security in any field. Retention, choice assignments, transfers, promotions, and raises go to those who are of value to an organization.

Lawyers of the future will succeed only by managing themselves as businesses, whatever their practice venue. As Richard Granat and Stephanie Kimbro note: "More than any generation of lawyers, the next generation . . . will have to be entrepreneurs rather than employees working for someone else." [50]

"Who in the world am I?
Ah, that's the great puzzle."
(Alice, arriving in Wonderland)

Previously, a position at a prestigious law firm was the road to stability, wealth and prestige. That remains true for fewer and fewer lawyers today.

Previously, starting one's own law firm was undertaken primarily by small town lawyers or those who wanted to practice simple, high-volume work. Today, technology allows the smallest firms, wherever located, to compete successfully against the largest firms in the most complex cases.

Previously, only foreign law graduates willing to do tedious document review worked for outsourcing firms. Today, outsourcing firms offer interesting work, flexible schedules, good career paths, and better pay than many law firms. They are also expanding in the U.S. In 2011, Pangea3, for example, was purchased by Thomson Reuters and opened a 400-seat office in Carrollton, Texas.[51] Novus Law, based in Chicago, hires new law graduates at "significantly higher salaries than the $60,000 median published by NALP for 2011 law graduates."[52]

Previously, accepting a job in a government or public interest law office meant financial hardship. Today, the financial package of salary, loan repayment, retirement benefits, and health insurance make many government and public interest practice options financially competitive with many private practice options. As noted *supra,* prior government experience carries salary premiums for lawyers moving from government experience to private practice (See Chapter IV (2)(B)(i) *supra*). Given the freedom from client development expectations and billable hour requirements, and the available mentoring and interesting, "high leverage" work opportunities, government and public interest jobs are now highly sought after.

Like Alice, lawyers are in a new world. Discussed below are some of the new and evolving professional opportunities in the legal profession and law-related professions. They are exciting. Many are uniquely available to new lawyers entering the profession.

A. Law and Technology

Technology is driving most of the changes in the legal profession. The ABA recognized this reality in 2012 when it added Comment 8 to Professional Code of Responsibility Model Rule 1.1 which requires that attorneys practice with competence. Comment 8 states "To maintain the requisite knowledge and skill, a lawyer should keep abreast of changes in the law and its practice, including the benefits and risks associated with relevant technology. . . ."

(i) Online Legal Services

> Bill is a forty year old married father of two who earns $45,000 per year as an assembly line worker. Bill and his wife, Sarah, went to a retirement party for a co-worker of Bill's. They stayed for two hours. Bill ate a burger and drank three beers. When driving home, Bill made a rolling stop, was pulled over by a police officer in an unmarked car, and asked to take a Breathalyzer test.
>
> Bill took the Breathalyzer, confident that he was a sober and legal driver because of the amount of time since he had consumed beer and because he ate food with his alcohol. Bill tested at .095, which is over the

.08 legal limit. The officer issued Bill a "citation" that directed Bill to appear in court on a specific date. The officer allowed Bill to leave the scene with Sarah driving.

To say the least, Bill is concerned about a number of issues, including whether he will lose his job. Early the next day, Bill calls the Public Defender's office and learns that given his income, he does not qualify for legal assistance from that office. Bill made a few embarrassed calls to trustworthy friends and obtained the name of two lawyers in town. Bill visited their webpages.

The webpage of one of the lawyers, Adam Anderson, invited users to visit links on the webpage. The links explain the types of cases Anderson handles. Bill clicked on the DUI link. He found a questionnaire and completed it in a few minutes. The questionnaire worked much like TurboTax. When Bill clicked an answer, the link took him to another question. Each question provided brief information about the topic raised in the question.

By the time he completed the questionnaire, Bill had learned quite a bit about what happened at the scene (his "citation" was a non-custodial arrest); his rights to challenge the Breathalyzer test; his rights in the workplace; and the likely procedure, time, cost and consequences of pleading guilty or contesting the Breathalyzer results.

Adam Anderson's webpage invited users to contact him by phone or email. Bill was impressed. He called Anderson and retained him to represent him in resolving the matter.

The above is an example of a "legal services app," also called an "automated interview," "legal apprentice software," "software based legal assistance," "legal knowledge tool," and "interactive online legal services." Such systems have evolved from the more simple online, low-cost services such as

LegalZoom, LawGuru, LawDepot, and RocketLawyer [53] that provide legal forms and minimal legal guidance to users.

"Legal services apps" blend advice and guidance with access to forms that can be individualized. A number of firms are now using such products to attract and support clients. For example,

- Allen & Overy, a law firm based in London, has created a databank with complex loan documents, allowing it to produce and amend documents as transactions evolved, and to do so more quickly and cheaply than other firms.[54]

- Richard Granat, based in the United States, offers online family law services with access to forms and information, and access to lawyers.[55]

- Firms have created databases to integrate into client systems, allowing, for example, a client's human resources department to log on, fill out a questionnaire, and generate reliable employment contracts automatically.[56] One such example is Business Integrity, a legal software dealer in England that has created contracts available online for salesmen to complete and obtain in real time attorney review. Richard Susskind explains how this works:

  > "[A] salesman out in the field can often generate an agreement for a customer, with no direct contact with lawyers and yet heavily constrained by the rules embodied in the system. The answers entered by such a salesman may be such that the contract is generated immediately. Alternatively, it may be that the answers suggest problem areas or possible legal risks, so that a document can be automatically routed to a lawyer for review. If the lawyer is comfortable, or has changes to recommend, their feedback is injected back into the standard life cycle."[57]

- Microsoft is a leader in the use of online legal advice. In 2004, Microsoft's legal department adopted license agreement templates that permit Microsoft lawyers to individualize the template allowing variations in law and jurisdictions.[58] Other in-house legal departments are incorporating online document production as a best practice. As one corporate General Counsel notes:

  > "With the introduction of forms or templates to streamline the contract process, and provision of training on the company's legal positions in contracts, low value/low risk contracts can be assigned to professional non-attorney resources skilled in contract drafting and negotiation. By shifting this work to non-attorney resources, the internal contract attorneys will have more time to focus on higher value and higher risk contracts. This will . . . create opportunities to handle in-house contract work that had previously been outsourced to outside counsel, creating a measurable cost savings."[59]

- A handful of law schools now offer law and technology clinics where students build computer applications to assist low and middle income individuals with legal problems such as eviction,[60] determining one's rights to and legal consequences of a same-sex marriage,[61] bankruptcy,[62] gift tax,[63] music copyright,[64] compensation claims resulting from vaccine related injuries.[65]

Until recently, the cost of developing and maintaining online legal assistance applications has been prohibitive. However, as computer technology evolves, developing online legal systems is becoming financially feasible.[66] Software such as A2J[67] and Neota Logic[68] permit those without computer programming skills to create legal assistance apps.[69] Design of such apps requires the skill set all lawyers use regularly: understanding legal issues of the client; separating simple from complex situations; explaining the issue in lay terms; accessing the relevant law to the applicable facts; and predicting outcomes and consequences.[70] With available software, any attorney can create programs to attract and assist clients in any type of case.

(ii) Outsourcing

As Ben Kerschberg notes, "Legal services outsourcing is transforming the legal marketplace."[71]

> *After working at a large law firm for eight years, Carl and David, friends since law school and law partners since graduation, decide to open their own law firm. They thought about the decision long and hard. One of their concerns was whether a small firm could specialize in complex commercial litigation, the only area of law in which they had experience. Traditionally only large firms could handle such cases because of the ebbs and flows of the work load, detailed billing reports, and the armies of lawyers needed at different stages of the cases. However, Carl and David were encouraged by the recent trend of corporate clients shifting complex cases from large firms to smaller firms. They decided to give it a go.*

> *Carl and David are also encouraged by the availability of high quality outsourcing firms. They are confident they can outsource their business needs to a back office firm, obtain discovery and research assistance for their cases, and secure expertise they may lack. With the help of outsourcing services, they believe it is realistic for their two-lawyer firm to handle the same type of cases they had handled at their 250-lawyer firm.*

> *Fortuitously, one of Carl and David's law school friends, Ed, started a back office outsourcing firm after law school. Carl and David engaged Ed's firm. Within thirty days, Ed's firm had everything in place: lease signed for office space; office equipment rented; malpractice insurance obtained; an LLC created.*

Ed recommended several outsourcing companies for other services Carl and David would need. Ed directed them to relevant provisions of applicable professional codes of conduct regarding communication with current clients about their plans to open their own firm.[72] With Ed's advice, and guidance provided by their state bar, Carl and David properly notified the clients with whom they had worked at their large law firm. Ed explained to Carl and David the quickly evolving law regarding "limited scope representation" and how they could utilize it to their and their clients' advantage (See Chapter IV (4)(B) infra). Ed provided a directory of online CLEs which covered limited scope representation and how to build it into one's law practice.

(a) Outsourcing Back Office Support

Ed's firm contracted with Carl and David to provide all of the back office support they would need. A number of back office outsourcing services have developed in response to changes in the legal profession. Firms of all sizes are finding that outsourcing their back office work to specialty firms is convenient, efficient, and saves costs.[73] As one attorney who recently established his own practice said, a back-up office support specialist makes it "easier than ever to get a firm up and running."[74] NexFirm, a business founded in 2008 to provide back-office support to law firms, offers to help launch a law firm in thirty days. NexFirm has doubled its business every year since it opened.

As Carl and David discovered from working with Ed, a back office support firm can provide the following assistance:

- **Office space, equipment and staff.** Because much of Carl and David's legal work could be done remotely, Ed suggested that they work primarily from home offices and use a local business incubator facility when they needed physical office space such as a conference room. The incubator facility Ed recommended had been established by the local Chamber of Commerce. For a minimal

monthly membership fee, members acquired access
to conference rooms and office staff.

Ed provided Carl and David guidance on IRS
deductibility requirements for home offices. The
income tax deduction Carl and David obtained
more than offset their incubator membership, in
essence reducing their office overhead cost to zero.

- **Internal office data management.** Ed's firm
  established systems to manage data at Carl and
  David's firm including client files, business files,
  financial accounting, emails, and memoranda. Carl
  and David are in good company. Small and large
  firms are turning to data management specialists
  for internal record keeping. For example, in 2013,
  Baker Donelson, a national firm with 1500
  employees including 675 attorneys, contracted with
  Recommind, a back office service, to provide data
  management service, connecting all eighteen of
  Baker Donelson's world-wide offices.[75]

- **Marketing.** Ed's firm is able to provide Carl and
  David guidance on marketing issues ranging from
  effective use of social media; developing and
  maintaining firm webpages including interactive
  links for prospective clients; and creation of "legal
  services apps" for firm clients. Particularly helpful
  has been the guidance Ed's firm provided about
  professional code prohibitions and limitations
  regarding social media.

  Ed's firm is also able to provide Carl and David
  with marketing experience and expertise that
  allows them to accurately measure which
  marketing efforts yield the most prospective clients
  and greatest revenues.

- **Law firm metrics.** As Carl and David knew from
  their experience at their prior firm, a firm's ability
  to quote AFAs (alternative billing arrangements)
  instead of hourly rates is appealing to clients.
  However, as they also well knew, they would need

to quote accurate fees because they will bear the financial risk of low estimates. AFAs are increasingly important in a competitive legal market. As noted in Lexis/Nexis's 2013 legal management trends report, "Overall, the battle to win business is being won by . . . firms . . . will[ing] to offer, use and implement AFAs that meet client needs.[76] Using sophisticated software that includes predictive analysis, Ed's firm provided data on the actual cost of providing various legal services, enabling Carl and David to quote accurate rates for AFAs as well as accurate traditional retainers and hourly billings. Carl and David quickly garnered a large number of corporate clients[77] in part because of their ability to quote flexible and accurate AFAs.

(b) Outsourcing E-discovery and Other Legal Services

Carl and David believed that one way they could be successful in their new practice was by capitalizing on the revolution in case discovery. As they knew from working at the large law firm, the world of discovery had changed within the past few years, and this had changed the practice of law.

Modern rules of civil procedure provide for broad discovery by making relevant any information that "appears reasonably calculated to lead to the discovery of admissible evidence."[78] Rules of civil discovery also require parties to produce electronically stored information.[79] These two rules, along with the advent of digital data, have led to the transformation of civil litigation. Digital data did not exist twenty years ago. Today, "[o]ver 90 percent of all new information . . . created is digital and 70 percent never gets put on paper."[80] Approximately 144 billion emails are sent from 2 billion email accounts worldwide *per day*.[81]

Because of digital data, it is no longer practical, accurate, or cost-effective to conduct case discovery manually. As Clay Rankin explains: "Simple math verifies this conclusion. Assuming 6,000 documents per gigabyte and a lawyer review rate of 40 documents per hour, a one gigabyte manual review takes 150 hours and, at $200 per hour, results in a $30,000 legal fee."[82] Nor is manual discovery accurate. Examples abound. In one instance, Firemen's Fund hired Novus Law, an e-discovery review firm, on a test basis to redo discovery on 30,000 documents already reviewed by the Fund's outside counsel. Novus Law "identified a missing key document and saved [Firemen's Fund] $100,000 in outside lawyers' fees on the matter." Fireman's Fund began using Novus Law, "saving 15–30% per case on outside counsel fees."[83]

Until recently, large law firms were able to hire many new associates, confident they would need them to conduct discovery. Discovery was the cash cow of large law firm practice, providing jobs, high salaries, and training for new associates. The cash cow is now gone.[84] Law firms failed to recognize or adjust to changes brought by digital data and the void was filled by offshore entrepreneurs. Today, business clients and law firms outsource much of their discovery needs to firms that specialize in e-discovery, onshore or offshore. The e-discovery business market is huge and growing. Bloomberg estimates that the e-discovery market will grow 35% per year, from $16.9 billion in 2012 to $22.8 billion by 2016.[85] Novus Law, the outsourcing firm hired by Fireman's Fund and based in Chicago, estimates that eighty percent of its work was previously done by large law firms.[86]

Reasons for the growth of outsourcing firms include: businesses' experience and expectations; cost; access to expertise; timeliness; and convenience.

Reasons for Growth in Firms Providing Outsourced Legal Services

- **Client Experience.** Many companies have been outsourcing services such as IT for years. They are comfortable doing so and have readily embraced opportunities to outsource legal services.[87] Outsourcing routine legal services such as e-discovery is becoming a best practice among corporate counsel. A recent survey by *Financial Times* found that 43% of corporations and 72% of law firms surveyed used or were planning to use legal outsourcing services. Decisions to outsource have ripple effects. For example, in 2011, the U.S. Securities and Exchange Commission contracted with the company, Recommind, to manage data collection on one-hundred cases it is investigating, making it helpful, obviously, for the companies being investigated (and the law firms that represent them) to use the same data storage and mining tools.[88]

- **Cost.** The cost savings offered by e-discovery are huge. Document review that costs $1 per page in India costs $7–10 per page in the United States. Rio Tinto, a global mining corporation and early proponent of outsourcing document review, for example, estimates that it saved $14 million in legal costs within a few months by switching to an Indian legal services company.[89] General Counsel for another large corporation described the following experience with an outsourcing legal services firm. He requested his company's outside counsel prepare a residential lease which could be customized for use in all fifty states. The law firm quoted an estimate of $400,000. The General Counsel found an outsourcing firm in India that did the work, excellent quality, for $45,000. The corporation has been working with the Indian law firm since.[90]

- **Access to expertise.** Outsourcing can provide access to expertise law firms or clients may lack, enabling them to accept projects they otherwise would have to decline. Artificial intelligence, a niche specialty that is can be of enormous help to law firms and clients, is one example of a valuable expertise that is easily outsourced. Quantitative legal analysis permits predictions on questions clients want to know like, "Do I have a case? What's my likely exposure? What are the chances of settlement? On what terms? As Daniel Martin Katz explains, computer-based predictive analysis is now feasible because of increases in computing power, decreases in data storage costs, and artificial intelligence innovations.[91] As Katz notes, whereas the most experienced attorneys may base their judgment on hundreds of cases, perhaps a thousand, a well-designed predictive outcome program can, within seconds, analyze *millions* of cases, without the cognitive bias of humans.[92]

- **Convenience.** Outsourcing e-discovery, legal research, preparation of trial exhibits and other legal tasks helps firms manage peaks in work flow. As Rio Tinto's managing counsel noted: "In a big litigation matter or regulatory review, the work is subject to sudden and dramatic peaks that corporate legal departments and their external counsel may not be able to handle."[93] Outsourcing also makes twenty-four hour and multi-lingual service possible. An attorney in the United States, for example, could leave her office at 6PM having emailed a research assignment to Mumbai, and have a memorandum by email when she returns to work the next morning. Outsourcing firms, including Pangea3, Thomson Reuters and Mindcrest, offer services in Spanish, German, French, Chinese, Japanese, Korean, Dutch, and Tagalog with offices worldwide.[94]

Ethical Considerations When Outsourcing

There are ethical and regulatory considerations when outsourcing legal services. ABA Model Rule 1.15 requires that attorneys safeguard client property when using cloud based technology. Rule 1.18 discusses counsel's duties to prospective clients when outsourcing. Rules 5.1 through 5.3 address responsibilities of supervisory lawyers, including supervision over nonlawyer assistants. Other applicable rules pertain to conflicts of interest (ABA Model Rule 1.7–1.10), preserving attorney client privilege (ABA Model Rule 1.6), and ensuring data security (ABA Model Rules 1.6, 1.9). Ethical obligations vary depending on whether "substantive legal support services" or "administrative support" such as transcription and document coding is sought.

Specific professional responsibility questions that may arise when outsourcing legal services include:

- How much legal work may lawyers outsource on cases for which they remain responsible? What duty of disclosure is owed to clients regarding outsourced services?[95]

- When may lawyers subject to the Model Rules divide legal fees with lawyers practicing in jurisdictions that do not follow the Model Rules (*i.e.*, allow the division of legal fees with non-lawyers)?[96]

- What sort of supervision is a lawyer or firm required to exercise over companies that provide information technology services and have access to confidential databases?[97]

- May a lawyer form a partnership with an individual in a foreign jurisdiction if the individual is admitted to practice law only in the country in which the individual resides?[98]

- If a lawyer practices in one jurisdiction that forbids forming partnerships with non-lawyers and in another that does not, which ethical rules apply?[99]

- Under what circumstances, if any, can a lawyer contract to obtain legal research services from a corporation on a contingent fee basis, *i.e.*, could the lawyer agree to pay the corporation a portion of the contingency fee the lawyer expects to receive from a client?[100]

(iii) E-learning

From the first day of law school, it was clear Linda was theatrical. She was funny, with exquisite timing for comedic one-liners, usually whispered under her breath so those around her started laughing at inappropriate times during class while Linda sat angelic and seemingly attentive. While in law school, Linda performed stand-up comedy a few nights a month at a bar in town. Her audiences were packed.

After law school, Linda worked as an associate at a small law firm and performed in Community Theater in the evenings as her time permitted. Invited at the last minute to serve as a stand-in for one of her partners who was to give a CLE, Linda brought down the house. She received more requests to present CLEs. Within a few years she joined an established CLE provider as a regular presenter. She traveled nationally to give CLEs and developed dozens of first-rate materials on CLE topics. Linda's law firm viewed her transition into the CLE industry as excellent visibility for the firm and negotiated an Of Counsel position for her that provided gave Linda scheduling flexibility, a salary reflecting referrals that originated from her CLEs, and health care and other employment benefits. It was a win-win situation.

Continuing Legal Education (CLE), which all attorneys must obtain every year to maintain law licenses, is more vital than ever as lawyers struggle to keep abreast of the changing legal landscape. Technology has revolutionized the delivery of CLEs just as it has revolutionized other aspects of the practice of law by making remote and multi-media delivery viable. Creation, production and delivery of CLEs is a growing "cottage industry." It is likely to grow even more as practicing attorneys strive to stay current and mentoring becomes more difficult for new lawyers to find. Technological advances such as podcasts and other interactive media make large-scale commercial CLE services viable. [101] This burgeoning area presents opportunities for those with film, recording, acting, writing, performing, and teaching skills.

(iv) Online "Closed Communities" for Clients

There are opportunities, largely untapped, for delivery of legal services through online "closed communities" for clients. Such tools are being used in other professions. As described by Richard Susskind, a visionary in the legal profession, these communities have tremendous potential for law firms to maximize service to their clients. A user-generated online community similar to a Wikipedia model, is limited to a client or group who discuss and share professional concerns.[102] Sermo, comprised of 50,000 physicians, is one such online community.[103] Access to Sermo is restricted to licensed physicians who pose questions and obtain answers from other Sermo physicians.

Law firms could establish such online communities for niche clients, such as construction companies or health care providers.[104] An online closed community could also be established for a single client with many legal needs. To do so the various law firms that represent a corporate client, for example, would affiliate to establish a "panel" of attorneys from the various firms that work with the client on the client's many legal issues, working together to coordinate coverage and ensure there are no overlaps or gaps in services,[105] thereby saving the client time and expense in presenting the same facts to multiple firms.

Professional responsibility issues that may arise with online "closed" communities include general issues of competency as well as specific issues of maintaining confidentiality of communications discussed in the online community.[106]

(v) Fun and Games

How would you like to have a career creating online law games? One of the most intriguing untapped avenues for growth in the legal profession is in the development of law games. William E. Hornsby, Jr., staff counsel at the American Bar, in a fascinating 2013 article, makes the point that while "[t]he legal profession is experimenting with online quizzes and educational games at the grade school and high school levels . . . little effort is being advanced to use online games . . . to engage the general public in legal matters and in ways that can demonstrate the advantages of participation in the legal system." [107]

Hornsby's major emphasis in his gaming article is improving access to legal services. He points to data showing that cost is only one hurdle in getting legal services to those who need such services.[108] Hornsby argues that online games can improve access to legal services by helping individuals who are unaware that they have legal problems see that they do, encouraging those who know that they have legal problems but do not believe that the legal system can help them seek relief in the legal process, and informing citizens how and where to go to obtain legal help.[109] Hornsby cites data from a recent legal needs survey:

> "About 87% of households with legal problems did not seek legal assistance. A key reason for not [doing so] is lack of understanding of the legal nature of the problem. . . . Among households that did nothing, the main reason given . . . included that they did not know that he problem was a legal problem (18%), believed nothing could be done about the problem (16.7%), did not want the hassle (7.5%), or did not know where to go for help (7.1%)."[110]

There are a number of online games available for elementary and middle-school students aimed at civic facts and stories. For example, Justice Sandra Day O'Connor's iCivics program offers a game, *Vindicate the Constitution*, aimed at seventh and eighth graders in which players "[d]ecide if potential clients have a right, match them with the right lawyer, and win the case. The more clients you serve and the more cases you win, the faster your law firm grows."[111]

However, as Hornsby points, out there is very little else available in online law games. As Hornsby notes, "the legal profession has . . . no virtual presence. That is, the law has not yet surfaced in a meaningful way as a source of entertainment on the Internet."[112]

It is surprising that the law game genre has not yet been tapped. The public is fascinated with law-themed entertainment. Consider the following:

- "Over ten million people a week watch *Judge Judy*, making the show the second highest rated syndicated program on television."[113]

- "Dramas such as *To Kill a Mockingbird* and *Twelve Angry Men* are found on the list of all-time best movies."[114]

- Television series focusing on the law such as *Perry Mason, LA Law, Law & Order, Ally McBeal, Boston Legal, JAG* are among the highest rated, long running television series in history.

- Legal thrillers by authors such as John Grisham, Scott Turow, Michael Connelly, Richard North Patterson and others dominate fiction book sales.

Consider also the widespread use of the internet:

- Eighty-five percent of American adults use the Internet and engage in a wide variety of online behaviors, including using search engines to find information, sending and receiving e-mail, checking the weather, receiving news, reading about politics, and maintaining a social media profile. For younger Americans, the numbers are even higher, with 98% of adults between the ages of 18–29 going online."[115]

Lastly, consider the appeal of online games:

- "Sixty-nine percent of all heads of households play computer and video games."[116]

- "Ninety-seven percent of youth play computer and video games."[117]

- "Forty percent of all games are women" and "[o]ne out of four games is over the age of fifty."[118]

- "Most gamers expect to continue playing for the rest of their lives."[119]

Given these data points: the appeal of law-themed entertainment, widespread use of the internet, and popularity of online games, growth in law-themed gaming is inevitable.

All that is needed is entrepreneurial spirit, enthusiasm of new lawyers, and angel investors. Development of online games may be a classic example of "doing good by doing well."

B. Limited Scope Representation

Integrally tied to all changes taking place in the practice of law is the growth of "limited scope representation" (LSR), also called "unbundling."[120] LSR simply means that a client retains an attorney to handle one aspect of the client's legal problem. As explained by the New York Civil Courts, "unbundled" legal services occur when "the lawyers provide only the agreed upon tasks, rather than the whole 'bundle,' and the clients perform the remaining tasks on their own." [121] Corporate clients do this, and have done so for years, when they handle some aspects of a legal matter in-house and retain outside counsel to research or handle other aspects, or when they partition their legal matters to multiple law firms. Over forty states have amended their rules of civil procedure and codes of professional conduct in recent years to encourage similar "limited scope representation" for individual clients. For example, in 2012, the Alabama Supreme Court adopted changes to Alabama Rules of Professional Conduct permitting a lawyer and client to agree "to limit the scope of . . . representation with respect to a matter."[122]

Access to legal service for underserved individuals has driven much of the recent LSR movement. The high cost of legal fees has priced legal services out of the reach of most individuals. Additionally, the availability of online legal forms and guidance allows many individuals to handle some aspects of their legal problems adequately without counsel.

LSR is good for lawyers as well as clients because of the opportunities it creates for attorneys to expand and control their practices. LSR expands the client base for attorneys, frees attorneys to step out of client relationships before they become dysfunctional, and helps attorneys minimize uncollectible fees.

In states which have adopted LSR rules, lawyers have profitably marketed an LSR practice to middle-income individuals who otherwise are not able to pay for full legal services and would not retain an attorney, either ignoring their legal problem or handling (or mishandling) it themselves. This is especially true in the area of family law, where motions regarding child support, visitation, and custody are suitable for both in-court and out-of-court limited-scope representation."[123] With LSR, a client who cannot afford thousands of dollars to retain an attorney to handle her case may be able to afford a few hundred dollars to handle one aspect of her legal problem.

LSR helps a lawyer terminate a dysfunctional relationship with a client. Firing a client can be hard to do. Once counsel has entered an appearance, court permission is needed to terminate the relationship. Even when court appearances have not yet been entered, attorneys face legal obligations, if not moral, in terminating a client relationship with a client who is in the midst of a legal problem. LSR helps resolve this dilemma by giving attorneys a mechanism to clarify and limit counsel's role in the matter from the beginning.

LSR also helps attorneys avoid uncollectible fees. An attorney experienced in LSR explained:

> "[S]ince LSR replaces big retainers with a pay-as-you-go business model, cash flow is affected. A lawyer who brings in an initial retainer, only to be unable to withdraw from the case when the client runs out of money, may run up thousands of dollars in uncollectible fees before getting out of the case. Limited-scope representation eliminates that problem because there aren't any accounts receivable."[124]

It is hard to overstate the significance of LSR in the delivery of legal services, especially when combined with other changes in the legal profession.

There are important considerations in making a LSR relationship succeed. These include:

- Carefully define the scope of the representation.
- Advise clients of their right to seek counsel on issues outside the scope of the limited representation.

- Be wary of LSR in highly complex or technical cases.

- Be wary of LSR with clients who may have a difficult time with self-representation because of mental health issues, language barriers, or emotional attachment to achieving an unrealistic outcome.

- Memorialize in writing any changes in the scope of representation, as they occur.

- "Let the client know when your involvement has ended," and "[i]f you have entered an appearance, serve and file a Notice of Completion."[125]

- Be cognizant of professional code of conduct issues such as when a lawyer is obligated to disclose that limited legal services have been provided to a party, for example, to a litigate pro se.[126]

Conclusion

The development of all of the above: online legal services, outsourcing firms, e-learning businesses, online communities, and limited scope representation are just some of the new ways delivery of legal services and law-related services are revolutionizing the legal profession. They present exciting and practical ways for lawyers and law firms to adapt to the changes afoot in the legal market. They demonstrate, as Richard Susskind states, "unparalleled opportunit[ies] . . . for innovative law firms to extend their ranges of services beyond traditional reactive work to a fundamentally different, proactive suite of services."[127] Importantly, each of the above also present career opportunities for entrepreneurial lawyers who want to pursue law and law-related careers establishing or operating such services.

5.   FREE AGENCY: HOW TO BE AN EFFECTIVE FREE AGENT THROUGHOUT ONE'S CAREER

Currently, the average lawyer changes jobs seven times in a legal career.[128] This frequency is likely to increase as the legal profession becomes more fluid in the years ahead. When these changes occur, we want to be in control of our careers rather than having changes foisted upon us by others or by unanticipated situations. To be in control of one's legal career, a lawyer must know how to be an effective free agent within the legal marketplace.

Professional athletes who find themselves no longer affiliated with a team, whether by choice or not, go into the market as a free agent. They hope to be picked up by a new team and with a favorable contract within the free agency based marketplace. During their free agency status, athletes make known the strengths, abilities and talents they can bring to a new team. Most professional athletes expect to be free agents several times during their professional careers. Athletes prepare for free agency by maintaining their skills and fitness, and by staying informed (at least through their agents) about budget, personnel and other business issues of their sport that will impact contract negotiations.

Until recently, few lawyers were "free agents." Stability prevailed. Lawyers tended to stay with the same law firm for their entire careers. Today all lawyers, new and experienced, are likely to be called upon, throughout their careers, to demonstrate the value they bring to an office and to clients. Hiring and retention decisions will be made throughout one's career as firms disband and merge. Opportunities arise in business, government or law-related professions as quickly as other opportunities disappear. Most attorneys of the future will be free agents multiple times throughout their careers.

A.   Star Performers

In 1974, the United States Department of Justice filed suit against AT&T, the telecommunications giant, alleging that AT&T engaged in illegal monopoly practices.[129] The suit was settled in 1982 and required the break-up of AT&T into seven regional telecommunications companies. For decades prior to the AT&T break-up, AT&T's Bell Laboratory, with its 250 scientists, had been one of the premiere research laboratories in the world with Nobel Prize winners and innumerable patents and inventions.

AT&T's leadership was concerned that the break-up of the company would make it difficult to sustain the quality of Bell Laboratory. AT&T management hired Robert E. Kelley, a professor at Carnegie Mellon University and an expert in industrial psychology, to study, assess, and recommend how AT&T could continue after its transition to select Bell Lab "star performers."[130] The "Bell Labs" study of two hundred scientists resulted and stands as one of the most thorough analyses of excellence in the workplace.

Kelley's research team first selected the "star performers" and "average performers" at Bell Lab. They did so by surveying Lab scientists and managers and evaluating awards, bonuses, and performance evaluations. Only individuals identified as star performers or average performers by both their peers and by supervisors were chosen for the study. Kelley's team then worked with Bell Lab managers and scientists to develop a list of forty-five characteristics by which they would measure the star and average performers, identify what separated the two groups, and thereby guide Bell Lab management in selecting star performers as its future scientists.[131]

The forty-five characteristics included cognitive factors such as IQ, logic and reasoning abilities; personality factors such as self-confidence, ambition, a sense of control over one's destiny; and social factors such as interpersonal skills. Kelley's team administered a two-day battery of tests to the two hundred scientists in the study. They analyzed their data for four months and came up with nothing.[132] There were "no appreciable cognitive, personal-psychological, social or environmental differences between stars and average performers."[133] The research team, AT&T's leadership, and the Lab leaders were surprised and disappointed by the study's findings.[134]

But Kelley and AT&T were not ready to give up. They had, after all, discovered something "critically important" . . . that the factors they thought were basic to star performance were not. This led Kelley to the next question: "If these people are so similar, what makes some of them perform professionally much better than others?"[135] To answer this question, Kelley and his team embarked on a two-year, "mind-numbing" study of watching the star and average performers work.[136] According to Kelley, by the end of the study his "personal definition of hell is being forced to watch brain-powered workers do their jobs day in-day-out, in minute detail, for all eternity."[137]

The results of the research team's efforts are revealing. Kelley's team found clear differences in the work strategies of the star and average performers. Specifically, the star performers used nine work strategies that the average performers did not. As Kelley said, "It wasn't what these stars had in their heads that made them stand out from the pack, it was how they used what they had."[138]

The nine star performer strategies, ranked in order of importance, are: initiative, networking, self-management, perspective, followership, leadership, teamwork, organizational savvy, show-and-tell. These strategies are applicable to any "brain-powered" worker. They have been studied, adopted and taught for years in the business world.[139] They are equally applicable to the legal profession.

The last two strategies, organizational savvy and show-and-tell, are at the "outer edge" of star performers strategies because they are "finishing skills."[140] The opportunity to use them generally arises later in the workplace than the preceding work strategies.[141] All nine strategies are closely integrated, and none exists without using the others.[142] For example, "it is impossible to demonstrate a high-powered initiative without also using other strategies such as perspective, leadership and organizational savvy."[143] As Kelley describes, "Stars need to demonstrate all nine work strategies. . . . Mastering a few is not enough."

Strategies of Star Performers:
Nine Work Strategies That Separate
Star Performers and Average Performers

- *Initiative*
- *Networking*
- *Self-management*
- *Perspective*
- *Followership*
- *Leadership*
- *Teamwork*
- *Organizational Savvy*
- *Show-and-Tell*

Kelley's study revealed interesting facts about performers' use of these nine strategies. One was that the average performers' understanding of these strategies was a *mis*understanding.[144] For example, average performers "inverted the ranking of strategies, believing that show-and-tell and organizational savvy were the core strategies."[145] Second and relatedly, the average performers' misuse of these strategies hurt their performance.[146] Third, when these nine strategies were taught to average performers, the average performers' effectiveness in the workplace improved.[147] Fourth, the star performers had a better quality of life than the average performers. They got more critical work done in less time and worked fewer hours than average performers.[148]

Comparing Work Strategies of Star Performers and Average Performers

- *Strategies of star performers are closely related; none exists without using the others.*

- *Average performers are aware of these strategies but misunderstand them.*

- *Average performers can learn these strategies; when they do, their performance increases.*

- *Star performers work fewer hours than average performers.*

- *Star performers use the nine work strategies to improve their quality of life as well as their performance at work.*

(i) Initiative

Initiative is the fundamental star performer work strategy. All of the Bell Lab scientists surveyed in Kelly's study understood the importance of initiative; however, the average performers' understanding and implementation of initiative differed from that of star performers. Average performers viewed initiative as "[c]oming up with ideas that help me do my job better and get me noticed" and "[v]olunteering to do the little extras in the workplace."[149] In contrast, star performers viewed initiative as "[g]oing above and beyond the accepted job description or busting out of everyday work routines to offer new, often bold, value-adding ideas . . . doing so for the benefit of coworkers or the entire organization and following through diligently to ensure the implementation of those ideas."[150] Small, day-to-day efforts had the same impact over time as did "big bang" initiatives on star performers' work quality.[151]

Kelley provides the following example of how average performers and star performers view initiative differently:

> "An employee had been assigned to attend a series of long meetings, prepare a summary of the meetings for her boss, and brief the rest of her team about the meetings. The employee decided to record the meetings and use the recordings to supplement her summary and brief for the others to insure she did not miss important details. The employee thought that taking the extra step of recording the meetings showed initiative. However, as noted by the star performers when presented with this example, this employee was not demonstrating initiative. She was just doing her job. *How* she chose to do her job (take notes, record the meetings, rely on memory) was up to her. But doing her job is not initiative."[152]

According to Kelley, star performers show initiative in the following ways: They "seek out responsibility above and beyond the expected job description;"[153] "undertake extra efforts for the benefit of coworkers or the larger group;"[154] "stick tenaciously to an idea or project and follow it through to successful implementation;"[155] and "assume personal risk in taking on new responsibilities."[156]

Ways to Demonstrate Initiative in Law Offices

- **Look for opportunities to present an internal CLE or presentation.** Be thinking about how you would prepare and present a CLE as you research a case or topic that would be relevant to other attorneys. There are many such "recycling" opportunities on any matter you work on. Keep a "CLE" file as you research specific cases.

- **Get a proofing buddy.** Offer to proof memos for other attorneys. Ask others to proof your work.

- **Send follow-up information.** Look for opportunities in conversations, whether on topics of work or pleasure, to follow up by sending information.

- **Offer to meet with the high-maintenance client everyone tries to dodge.** Your colleagues will be grateful to you and view you as "taking one for the team." To protect your schedule, structure meetings or phone conversations with difficult clients with an exit strategy (pre-arranged phone call requiring your presence) and corroboration of conversations (follow-up email confirming any discussions).

- **Look for unmet needs in your office.** These may include establishing and maintaining a document bank for your office, firm, and/or clients; creating, assisting with, or revising a firm blog; generating a "closed" on-line community for clients.

- **Offer to help with law firm recruiting.** Remember: it may be wise to "pay your dues" assisting in recruiting efforts when your life is relatively uncomplicated.

- **Suggest an alternative work arrangement.** If you are interested in working less than full time, or on a non-standard compensation system, approach your firm with a proposal. Firms are increasingly open to such arrangements. You may, for example, prefer that a portion of your salary be contingent on cases you bring into the office rather than receiving a set salary, or vice versa. Valued attorneys may be able to negotiate reduced firm commitments to spend more time with family, serve as an elected official, develop one's own book of business, train as a triathlete, or for any number of reasons. *Law and Reorder* by Deborah Epstein Henry and published by the American Bar Association, contains excellent suggestions and practical tips for negotiating such arrangements, as well as issues firms should consider in creating flexible work arrangements.[157]

(ii) Networking

Both average and star performers identified networking as an important work strategy but like initiative, average performers interpreted this strategy differently than star performers. The average performers thought of networking as "[b]uilding a communications grapevine so that I am 'in the loop' on the latest office gossip."[158] Networking as interpreted by star performers was more sophisticated. They viewed networking as knowing their own strengths and those of their contacts and collaborating with colleagues to compensate for each other's weaknesses.[159] Star performers admit what they don't know[160] and use networks to "overcome their knowledge gaps."[161] There were also differences in the effectiveness of the networks of the average and star performers. Star performers' networks worked better. The quality of knowledge in their networks was higher than those of average performers and their networks were faster. It took an average performer three to five hours to get an answer through her network for every hour it took a star performer.[162]

(a) Participate in Bar Associations

Meeting other lawyers is important. Many, if not most, referrals of clients will come from other attorneys. Opportunities for lateral career moves come from other lawyers. Other lawyers are potential mentors. The most efficient (and also fun) way to network with other lawyers is through bar associations. There are local, state and national bar associations. Your type of practice and professional goals will make some bar associations more relevant to you than others.

**Tips for Effective Networking in
Bar Associations**

- **Choose your bar associations strategically.** Some types of bar associations are more relevant than others to various practices. For example, if you have a general practice in a small firm, participation in the local bar will yield greater referral opportunities than attending a national ABA meeting. If your practice involves national corporate law, attendance at an ABA meeting will yield greater referral opportunities than at a local bar association meeting.

  Different types of bar associations are also more relevant to certain career paths. For example, if your goal is to sit on the local trial bench, participation in local bar and state bar associations will be key. If you want to run for public office, local and state bars are also key. If you seek to impact public policy, participation in local, state, or national bar associations will be relevant depending your policy interest.

- **Sequence your participation in bar associations.** If you decide all levels of bar associations serve you well, choose one to focus on at a particular point in your career. Allow five to ten years for active participation in a particular bar association. This will give you the opportunity to become involved, identify your areas of interest, and serve in leadership positions.

- **Be efficient in your bar association activities.** Get the biggest bang for your buck. Assess which bar events have the largest turnout, or are most relevant to you. For example, "Law Day" events of local bar associations generally have the greatest attendance of the year. This is an event to attend. In some local bar associations, the state and federal trial judges host a coffee once a month. If you are a trial lawyer practicing in these courts, this is an event you should attend. If you practice corporate law, it is not. Most bar associations, especially at the state and national levels, have sections tailored to practice areas. If you practice family law, for example, you should attend the state bar's Family Law Section's annual CLE weekend at the beach, both for substance and networking purposes.

The point is, if you do not have time to attend all bar events, and few of us do, choose wisely which to attend.

(b) Maintain Good "Networking Etiquette"[163]

Star performers appreciate that obtaining knowledge from others is a privilege that must be earned. They do not take for granted that anyone should take time to give them information.[164] Star performers are aware that the people they find the most valuable are also in demand by others. They are solicitous of their contacts' time.

(c) Reciprocate to Network Contacts

Star performers recognize that networking is a *quid pro quo*. Star performers demonstrate their value to their networks. For example, a star performer might send a research memo she has completed to a contact who is interested in the topic. Such communications demonstrate a performer's area of expertise to her contacts. Star performers "have something worth trading in order to attract trading partners."[165]

(d) Expand Your Network

Star performers add people to their networks. They evaluate speakers at conferences as potential contacts, and keep up contacts with school friends, professors, and colleagues from prior work experiences. Star performers gather information from others by asking friends, "When you need quick information on _____, who do you ask?"

(e) Nourish Networks

Star performers build and maintain their networks. As Robert Kelley says, "The worst time to be building your network is when you need it to work for you now. Star performers try to get their networks in place well before they might ever need them."[166]

(f) Use "Vouchers"[167]

Star performers recognize the importance of "vouchers" when seeking knowledge from someone they do not know. Star performers ask others to make an introduction. They do not call a contact cold. As Kelley notes, the practice of "vouching may be even more appropriate in today's high-technology, need-it-yesterday business environment, where experts in networks are inundated with requests for information and forced to choose carefully in order to salvage time for their own work."[168] Star performers know that "those without vouchers seldom get access."[169]

(g) Prepare Before Approaching Contacts

Star performers do their homework before reaching out to their networks, including:

- Doing a "quick self-study on as much of the general subject area as possible to save the expert's having to run through basics before tackling the specific problem."[170]

- Summarizing to contacts attempts to solve the problem or find information.

- Spending time framing questions for their contacts.

- "Link[ing] the problem to an area of interest that intrigues the expert."[171]

(h) Show Appreciation and Share Credit

Star performers "lavishly"[172] thank those who give them advice, help, and information, both privately and publicly. They send notes of thanks upon receiving information from a contact, and again upon achieving some goal with the help of the contact's information. They highlight the contribution of their contacts in conversations with others, public presentations, and group correspondence. As Kelley says, "[T]here are no reputations worse than being pegged as an idea thief, as a pseudo-star who stands on stage and acts as if there were no supporting players. . . ."[173]

(i) Optimize "Newness"

Most people are more than happy to help someone who is new in a position and seeking advice from those more experienced. Once "newness" wears off, requests for advice become burdensome, if not irritating. Star performers optimize their "newness," but also know when to cease relying on such status.[174]

(j) Pay Back Promptly

Star performers begin network traffic by giving. This helps build their networks for when they need them. Star performers are careful not to do "a lot of one-way trades." Star performers recognize that using their networks is "not without an eventual price." They "offer something of value back as quickly as possible."[175]

(k) Set up a Regular Networking Group, or Two or Three

Maintain law school contacts after graduation by putting together a lunch group of law school friends that meets periodically, four or six times a year. Pick a place that everyone can get to easily and provides ready parking, is quiet enough to hear each other, and permits reservations so there is no delay waiting for a table. Keep the group to four to eight persons. Select lunch dates weeks in advance so everyone can put the date on their calendar. Choose a date by listing four or five possibilities, send an email to check everyone's availability, and select the date that works for the most people. Send a "mid-way reminder" (two weeks or so in advance) and a reminder the day prior to the lunch gathering. Set no agenda for lunch. Treat it as a gathering of friends to touch base. Keep the lunches to one hour so everyone can get back to work and won't avoid them in the future because they take so long. Encourage participants to bring a friend.

Assess your interests as you think of other ways to establish networking groups. For example, create a workout group, whether at the gym, jogging at noon, or in your neighborhood. Put together a group of friends that meets regularly after work. Email, texts and twitter make regular gatherings easy to pull together. The regularity of meetings builds bonds.

(l) Set Aside Time for "Networking Catch-Up"

Keep a "network to-do" list. Go through your "to do" list in a weekly "networking catch-up" appointment with yourself. If you had a conversation about hiking with someone at a reception several days prior, send her the hiking information you mentioned. If you used tips or information from a contact for a project, send the contact an update on the completed project noting how his contribution helped. If you met a new person during the week, send her an email telling her you enjoyed meeting her and make some reference to a matter you discussed.

(m) Network at All Activities in Which You Are Engaged

Use your first and last name when you introduce yourself. Look for opportunities to follow up on conversations by sending relevant information to individuals you spoke with. When you follow up, use your work email address that identifies who you are and where you work. Future clients or employment opportunities are just as likely to come from friends or acquaintances as from other lawyers.

(n) Know How to Network at Big Events[176]

Put the name you go by on your name tag. Use a single phrase or sentence when you meet people that identifies where you work and what you do. Keep it simple, and keep your conversations brief. Know how to initiate and wrap up conversations so you can converse with more people. One easy exit to conversations is to exchange business cards, then move on with an exit line of "Nice to meet you" or "Nice visiting with you." After events, make notes on the business cards you've collected about people or conversations. Follow up conversations with emails.

(iii) Self-Management

While both star and average performers recognize that self-management is important, star performers' view of self-management is more nuanced. Average performers view self-management as organizing their time to ensure they accomplish tasks. Star performers view self-management as evaluating their to-do list and assessing whether the tasks on their list lead to their goals. As one star performer stated:

> "I first thought I was productive because I got through all the items on my to-do list each day. Then one day I realized that I wasn't sure how things ended up on my list. What I discovered was that many of my activities were reactive responses to things my manager or coworkers wanted. I was okay with that for a while, until I realized that just because they wanted me to do something, it didn't mean it was on the critical path. So I took control of my to-do lists."[177]

Tips for Effective Time Management

- **Evaluate to-do lists.** Star performers constantly assess whether the items on their to-do lists further *their* short-term and long-term goals.

- **Triage to-do lists.** Star performers prioritize their tasks, assessing what is important and what is less important; what has to be done immediately and what can wait; what will take more concentration and when best to do such tasks; and what can be accomplished in conjunction with other tasks.

- **Know yourself and what you enjoy.** Star performers are self-aware. They know what they enjoy and navigate their way to get there. As Kelley describes, star performers "use their self-management skills to ensure they stay with the type of work they enjoy, or to develop a plan to move into the work they wanted to do."[178] The Bell Labs study confirms Mihaly Csikszentmikalyi's scholarly research on "flow" (See Chapter I (M) *supra*). Star performers find a way for their work to be meaningful and enjoyable to them.[179]

- **Develop systems to minimize interruptions.** When they need to accomplish tasks, star performers use techniques to avoid interruptions, such as wearing headphones, or slipping away to somewhere besides their office where no one can interrupt them. As Kelley says:

  > "Brain-powered work can be compared to launching a spaceship. The greatest amount of fuel is used and the greatest stress is incurred ... at takeoff.... The same is true for brain-powered workers. The hard part is getting into the flow. Once you are there, it is like floating in space. When flow is interrupted, then you waste all that time and energy taking off again."[180]

- **Manage your time and tasks in ways that works for you.** As Kelley explained, "Every star developed a self-organizing plan that took their individual makeup into account."[181] For example, messy desk star performers don't try to keep clean desks; they have a system for managing their messy desks.

- **Know how to say no.** Star performers say no and have techniques for doing so. One is delay. They do not agree immediately to participate in something. They buy time to think through requests and opportunities. When star performers say no, they do so tactfully, acknowledging the value of the opportunity they have been given to participate.[182]

- **Build in "mistake-recovery time."**[183] Star performers build "mistake recovery" time into their projects. For lawyers, this means *always* taking time to proof one more time. Get a "proofing buddy," someone who proofs your work while you proof theirs.

- **Prepare for the days that will not be as productive.**[184] Star performers save up small tasks for the days when they have multiple meetings with only small blocks of time available.

- **Have a five-year plan.** Star performers stay in charge of their lives. Long-term plans help do this by maintaining ownership of one's career path (See Chapter I (G) *supra*).

(iv) Perspective

Star performers maintain perspective by having a context for their work. Average performers have a more difficult time seeing the big picture and how everyone's role fits into it. Average performers think it is important to communicate and prevail on their views in the work place. Star performers, on the other hand, believe it is important to see a project or problem through the eyes of others, including clients, competitors, coworkers, and bosses.[185] Star performers have the ability "to discern the changing games and their changing rules,"[186] to think outside the box, to see connections and patterns, and to make intuitive leaps. Star performers gather more information and a different type of information in building and maintaining perspective than do average performers.

Bell Lab CEO and Nobel Prize recipient, Arno Penzias, spoke about the importance of gaining perspective:

> "[Average performers] have an inability to consider multiple perspectives. [This] is the most frequent reason that many highly intelligent researchers never manage to break from the ranks of the average. They get involved in 'work for its own sake,' digging one hole, boring in, and getting more and more fascinated by less and less."[187]

Kelley's study found that one of the ways star performers main perspective is by putting themselves "in high-leverage learning situations." They engage in a personal review process, analyzing their mistakes and learning from situations and missed opportunities. Star performers look for opportunities to learn new skills. They actively "push themselves up the experience curve by practicing new skills of their craft."[188]

Star performers also maintain perspective by looking at problems and projects through the eyes of co-workers, clients, competitors, employees, and superiors. They look for patterns: How have things changed in the workplace? Who has been impacted by the changes? Who will benefit from the changes? How can I benefit?

(v) Followership and Teamwork

Both star performers and average performers see the value of good teamwork, but their views of what constitute "good teamwork" vary.[189] In the Bell study, average performers described effective teamwork as "doing one's part on a team and working cooperatively with others." Star performers viewed good teamwork more comprehensively as "taking joint ownership of goal setting, group commitments, work activities, schedules and group accomplishments, helping everyone feel part of the team, dealing with conflict, and assisting others in solving problems."[190]

Not surprisingly given these different views of team work, average and star performers view the role of a "follower" differently. Average performers view the role of "follower" derogatorily, as sheep blindly following a leader's direction. Average performers tend to be "yes" people telling leaders only what they want to hear; "alienated" followers who undercut the leader; or "pragmatic followers" who avoid offering valuable contributions because it is more expedient to "go along."[191] Star performers recognize that in some situations they will be leaders and in others they will be followers. Star performers view service as a follower constructively and as a way to help their careers advance.[192]

Star performers take more ownership in a team project than do average performers. They bring independent judgment to their role as follower.[193] Star performers are "actively engaged in helping their organization succeed while exercising independent, critical judgment of goals, tasks, potential problems, and methods."[194] Star followers "work cooperatively with leaders to accomplish the organization's goals, even when there are personality or workplace differences."[195]

Strategies of Effective Followers

- **Understand a leader's perspective and concerns.**[196] Star performers recognize that leaders may have to choose between a series of bad options and may have pressures a follower does not.[197] Star performers see it as part of their duty to provide leaders with information that may not have come to their attention or which may not have been fully appreciated.

- **Relate to leaders as equals.**[198] While deferential to the demands on a leader, star performers relate to leaders as equals, not as underlings. This confidence identifies star performers as potential leaders for future endeavors. It also promotes effective communication, making it easier for leaders to make suggestions to and receive suggestions from followers.

- **"Disagree agreeably."**[199] If conflicts arise with a leader, star performers "try to curb their own egos so they don't get in the way of progress. They distinguish between their own preferences and an honest assessment of the ideas under discussion."[200]

- **Play by the system.**[201] Star performers recognize that "most organizations have norms and protocols for airing disagreements. . . . [They] realize that . . . leaders take the procedures they've put in place to deal with these issues very seriously. They find out what these are before taking any action. Then they go the system route first, usually trying to work the issue out privately with the leader who is directly involved."[202]

- **Exercise "self-leadership."** Star performers execute duties as followers without hand-holding. They are proactive in completing their assigned tasks. Average performers, in contrast, need specific directions and confidence building.[203]

- **Turn in competent work.** Star performers get their job done and do it well. Average performers do not consistently do so. As Robert Kelley noted, "[s]ome of the most enthusiastic, most committed, nicest workers can also be the most incompetent, the most lacking in useful work skills."[204]

- **Serve as an ethical watchdog.** Star performers exercise "courageous conscience."[205] They view their responsibility as not only avoiding or correcting obvious wrongs, but also as "championing a worthy idea . . . in the face of strong organizational resistance . . . or deal with a problem before it grows into a crisis."[206]

(vi) Leadership

Both average performers and star performers recognize the value of effective leadership but they describe effective leadership differently. Average performers view leadership as "an inborn trait . . . being in charge . . . the power to make key decisions and to delegate whatever does not interest me."[207] Star performers view effective leadership as being collegial and cooperative and "helping a group of people come together and accomplish a task."[208]

Strategies of Effective Leaders

- **Assume the administrative burdens of a project.** Star performers take on the administrative burdens of leadership such as preparing agendas, setting meeting times, maintaining momentum, and preparing drafts of reports or other work products of the group.[209]

- **Turn to others with expertise.** Star performers find out what expertise others have and assign projects and tasks requiring such expertise to these individuals.

- **Are solicitous of others' views and needs.** Star performers solicit other's views and are attentive to others' needs. For example, before assigning roles to committee member, one star performer took time to check with a colleague about a previously expressed interest in a particular area. After confirming the colleague's continued interest, the star performer assigned the colleague tasks in that area.[210] Star performers checked on others' needs even if they thought they knew what they were. Demonstrating such concern for others helps build team loyalty as well as confirms information.

- **Work discretely with those who may run into difficulties.**[211] Star performers recognize that everyone will make mistakes and miscalculations, and that everyone appreciates being treated respectfully when they make mistakes. This builds good will and support. Sometimes is it necessary to draw a colleague's attention to their error; sometimes it is not. When it is necessary, star performers treat colleagues in a way that allows them to keep their dignity about the situation.

Rarely is it necessary to inform others about a colleague's error. Remedying the problem and moving on generally suffices. The golden rule is a wise business strategy in these situations. Star performers have the ability and self-discipline to practice it.

- **Praise others generously. Highlight others' contributions.**[212] Everyone appreciates being recognized for their efforts. Star performers praise others generously, publicly and privately. Statements of recognition that identify how individuals contributed are important. Pro forma, insincere comments about others' contributions are ineffective, and may be demeaning or insulting. Again, the golden rule is a helpful guide. Star performers thank others in ways they would appreciate if the roles were reversed.

- **Treat team members as equals.**[213]   When in leadership roles, star performers treat team members as equals, recognizing that roles are regularly reversed as one colleague, then another, serves as a committee chair or project manager.

  Star performers treat staff such as administrative assistants, secretaries, paralegals, and runners as part of the team. Especially in the legal field, and especially for new lawyers, these individuals are likely to know more about practical, day-to-day and important matters than lawyers. No matter how renowned a star performer may be, they recognize that staff are crucial to an office's efficiency or division's productivity. Talking down to staff is a sure way to alienate others them and those who observe such demeaning behavior.

(vii)   Organizational Savvy

New workers are often shielded from the nuances of organizational dynamics.[214] This is why organizational savvy is an "outer" ring of the work strategies practiced by star performers.[215] Failure to practice organizational savvy generally will not impair one's performance until later in one's career, after one has mastered the previous strategies. If organizational savvy is not mastered, however, one will not progress in an organization despite outstanding professional skills.[216]

Every organization has a "formal" organizational chart as well as an "underground" organizational chart that describes the "topography of the organization closer to reality . . . where the real power centers are."[217] The topography of an organization includes its institutional personality, culture, norms of behavior, unwritten company taboos, and etiquette.[218] Average performers are not adept at perceiving or navigating these subtleties. Star performers are. For lawyers, good organizational savvy is crucial, whether one is a new lawyer or lateral hire.[219] Successful integration into any law office requires mastery of an organization's culture.

Strategies for Building Organizational Savvy Within a Law Office

- **Be aware of your image.** Star performers are aware of the image they present and tailor it as needed.[220] Recall Mick Jagger (Chapter IV (C)(1) *supra*) and Jim, the associate (Chapter IV (C)(7) *supra*).

- **Focus on forging consensus.** "Aware that it is better to avoid conflicts than to win them,"[221] star performers know when it is best not to address a problem directly and find ways to raise a problem discretely.[222]

- **Pay attention to the symbols of the organization.** Among the most powerful symbols in any law office is the image the firm strives to present to the outside world. New hires understand and perpetuate this office image.

- **Understand the hierarchy within the organization.** Clues to the hierarchy in a law office include whether associates walk into partners' offices without being summoned; whether attorneys take their assistants out for lunch or bring them gifts; whether attorneys go out for lunch together, eat at their desks, go to the gym, or meet others for lunch; whether firm personnel socialize after work.

- **Learn the etiquette of the firm, especially regarding access.** Star performers learn the unspoken rules of etiquette in an office. For example, does an "open door" policy really mean it is okay to walk into someone's office to chat? Do people visit in the halls? Star performers respect office etiquette. They are considerate. Before interrupting a colleague, they ask, "Do you have a minute?" or "Is this a good time or bad time?" Many of the Bell Lab average performers "were severely etiquette-challenged." They were known as "chronic bargers."[223]

- **Establish a personal relationship with coworkers.** Even in organizations where colleagues do not socialize outside of work, relationship building is important. This includes knowing something of colleagues' personal lives and expressing interest in them.

- **Create a niche.** Star performers find a niche in an area of interest to them that also adds value to the organization.[224] Star performers market their niches internally as well as externally.[225] One way to "advertise" within one's organization is by offering to help others who are dealing with an issue within your expertise. Star performers respect the niches of colleagues.[226] Star performers consult with colleagues on areas within the colleagues' expertise.[227]

- **Develop mentors.** The *After the JD: First Results*, a joint ABA-NALP study which followed 5000 lawyers during the first ten years of their practice, discussed the importance of mentors for new lawyers:

> "While law schools are the formal training ground for new lawyers, once they graduate from law school and begin working, mentors (in and out of the workplace) are often the source for insight and advice into legal practice. The topic of mentoring is one of the more difficult ones to probe in studies of legal careers. Mentoring is often informal, casual, and difficult to quantify and recognize. The results may also be elusive. Mentoring can be a key to success, and it may be a way to cope with, and perhaps accept, repeated disappointment. . . . [M]entoring . . . is central in the career of new lawyers."[228]

Star performers recognize that some people are more "mentor worthy" than others. They seek mentors who will be direct with them, have the time and inclination to serve as a mentor, and are savvy organizational citizens.[229]

Star performers do not abuse the mentor relationship. They recognize that good mentors are busy people. Star performers do not overstay their welcome or impose on a mentor unnecessarily.[230] Star performers also recognize a mentor's expectations of a mentor relationship. In law offices, mentors may be looking for "protégés who will become fiercely loyal and competent and will work like hell for the mentor in return for being taken under the mentor's wing."[231] Star performers are aware of the *quid pro quo*.

Star performers are strategic when approaching a potential mentor. Once star performers identify someone as a good mentor, they assess the best way to develop a mentor relationship. Directly asking whether an individual would serve as a mentor can be off-putting.

Subtlety may be more appropriate. For example, one can create an informal mentoring relationship by periodically asking a person for advice, seeking assignments where one would work with a potential mentor, or volunteering to serve on committees or teams where a potential mentor also serves.[232]

Star performers develop alternative mentoring methods by exposing themselves to experiences in different areas in their office or community. As Robert Kelley explained:

> "Some star performers we studied were so constrained by their organizations that they could manage only brief expeditions out of their rigidly marked areas, mostly to work on a project or represent their section on a committee. Even within these constraints, when these opportunities were put on the docket, the stars lobbied to get the assignment. When they moved into an unfamiliar area, the stars grounded themselves thoroughly the work being done there and identified a knowledgeable colleague who would respond well to questions."[233]

New lawyers can create alternative mentoring opportunities by seeking pro bono cases (See Chapter I (M) *supra*) and by becoming active in bar associations (See Chapter IV (5)(A)(ii)(1) *supra*).

(viii) Show-and-Tell

Like organizational savvy, show-and-tell is an "outer" ring star performer strategy that arises after use of the other strategies.[234] As practiced by star performers, show-and-tell is "selecting information to pass on to others and developing the most effective, user-friendly format for reaching and persuading a specific audience."[235] Show-and-tell skills are important to use with groups of all sizes and with multiple audiences: colleagues, CLE audiences, community boards, and volunteer organizations.

There are fundamentals of effective "show and tell." The first is to know your audience and shape your message to it.[236] Star performers pitch their message to the audience to whom they are speaking. They vary their message with their audience. They contact audience members ahead of time to get a sense of expectations and to solicit advice on what would be helpful to the full audience.[237]

Kelley provides an example of a labor relations manager for a Fortune 500 corporation who demonstrated this strategy of tailoring his message to different audiences. The manager was asked to develop a plan for reducing health care costs in a new contract to be negotiated with unions. He presented his plan to lower-level union officials in "bit-size chunks over a week of meetings on their home turf, and provided them with clear, easy-to-read handouts that could be duplicated and handed out to rank-and-file members with reasonable expectations of being understood."[238] When this manager presented the same plan to the CEO and vice-presidents of the company, he used a different presentation style. He delivered the information in one meeting, rather than multiple meetings, and his delivery style was a "no-nonsense" and well-documented, with a detailed report on recommendations for future decisions."[239]

Star performers recognize there are two steps for every presentation. Average performers do the first step only, if that. Star performers do both. The first step is to collect, organize, research, understand, and learn the material. The second step is to determine how to best present the material to the audience. Star performers strive for a way to present their material that will grab and keep an audience's attention.[240] Effective speakers don't just transmit information. They tell a story. [241] Star performers use props when helpful. They know how to use power point effectively, which can be hard to do. Power point presentations require dimmed lights, which can put an audience to sleep. They also always run the risk of technical glitches. Star performers are prepared to "wing it" if their power point presentation can't be accessed. Once an audience is lost, it's hard to recapture it.[242]

An adult's average attention span is ten to fifteen minutes. Ninety percent of communication is non-verbal. Star performers appreciate these two facts. They keep their presentations short, switch segments every ten to fifteen minutes, and move around. They use their hands, smile, and maintain eye contact. Star performers do not read their talk. They do not attempt to memorize their presentations. They are conversational and involve their audiences. They ask questions and use role play. Star performers give their audience a road map, providing direction such as: "I will cover the following three points. The first is _____. The second is _____, and the third is _____." Star performers signal transitions with tag lines like, "Moving on to point two," or "Are there any questions before I move on to point two?"

B. Six Steps in a Lawyer's Free Agent Playbook

(i) Preparation

Begin your free agent preparation while in law school by understanding the changing landscape of the legal profession (Chapter III). Raise and nourish your EQ (Chapter I). Get your financial house in order (Chapter II).

(ii) Choose "High Leverage" Learning Opportunities

Get experience. Lots of it. You will grow as an attorney only when you have opportunities to learn through "high leverage" learning opportunities (Chapter I (K); Chapter IV (5)(A)(iv)).

(iii) Publish in Bar Journals

Bar journals, published by state or city bar associations or by specialty groups within the bar such as corporate counsel or trial lawyers, are excellent places for practicing lawyers to publish. The articles are short and practical. Generally, bar journals are happy to receive high quality submissions, which means it is feasible for new lawyers to get their articles accepted for publication. Bar journals are widely read, which is why they are career boosters. Not many lawyers read law review articles, but almost every lawyer will at least scan relevant bar journals as soon as they receive them. In many states and cities, every member of the bar receives the bar journal. Every attorney who practices in an area will receive that specialty's journal. Exposure is extensive.

When working on seminar papers in law school or memos during a summer clerkship, keep your eye out for topics that might be converted into articles for professional journals. There are dozens of such journals. Peruse these journals while in law school or early in your practice so you can get a feel for their tone, coverage and length.

Save your law school era work product. When you are in practice, pull out your work product, update it, and edit it into a publishable article. Submit it to a bar or specialty journal. While in practice, think about the research projects you are working on, or research you need done. Turn these projects or needs into a bar journal article. It's a good bet that if it is research you need, an article on the topic will be helpful to other lawyers. When your bar journal article is published, send its link or reprints of it to co-workers, former law school classmates, clients, and potential clients. Add it to your firm's webpage.

The career boost from publishing in bar journals is good for lawyers in government and public interest law offices as well as lawyers in private practice. Publishing can help any lawyer obtain choice assignments, increase one's value internally, and add to one's value as a lateral hire throughout a career.

(iv) Become a Faculty Member for Continuing Legal Education Programs or a Law School Adjunct Faculty Member

Serving as a CLE faculty member gives lawyers significant visibility within the legal profession, establishes expertise and builds referral pipelines. It is important to know that generally, one does not "sign up" to be a CLE speaker. One is invited. To obtain invitations to serve as a CLE presenter, volunteer for service on a local, state, or national bar association's CLE committee or for the planning committee of law day programs. Serve on such committees for a couple of years and observe how CLE speakers are selected. Realistically, once you have served on such a committee for a few years and are recognized as knowledgeable in your field (especially if you have published a bar journal article or two), you will be invited to serve as a CLE speaker.

Do an excellent job when you speak and prepare helpful, thorough written materials to accompany your CLE. Written materials are required of CLE speakers. Do *not* submit as your CLE materials copies of motions, memos you have authored, or photocopies of court opinions. Although done by some speakers, this is poor form and will hurt your chances of being asked to serve again as a CLE speaker.

(v) Participate in Bar Associations

Meeting other lawyers is important. Many, if not most, referrals of clients will come from other attorneys. Opportunities for lateral career moves come from other lawyers. Other lawyers are potential mentors. The most efficient (and also fun) way to network with other lawyers is through bar associations. There are local, state and national bar associations. See Chapter IV (E)(1)(b), *supra,* for tips on optimizing bar association opportunities.

(vi) Cultivate Mentors

Mentors are essential for any field, but especially for something as nuanced and fluid as the legal profession. See Chapter IV (5)(A)(g), *supra,* for tips on developing mentor relationships.

Conclusion

The legal profession is in a state of flux. In recent years, most notably since the 2008 recession, there have been profound changes in the relationship between lawyers and their clients, the internal structure of law firms, and employment opportunities for new lawyers. These are structural changes, not cyclical. They have forever changed the legal profession. The legal market of today requires that new lawyers approach entry into the profession with different strategies and that practicing lawyers think differently about their delivery of legal services. As Richard Susskind says, "The game is afoot."[243]

TABLE OF AUTHORITIES

American Bar Association. Code of Professional Responsibility. (2014).

American Bar Association, Formal Opinions:

- "Access of Nonlawyers to a Lawyer's Data Base." *ABA Formal Op.* 95-398.

- "Acquiring Ownership in a Client in Connection with Performing Legal Services." *ABA Formal Op.* 00-418.

- "Breaking Up is Hard to Do: Ethics Concerns When Your Firm Splits Up or When a Lawyer Leaves for Another Firm." *ABA Formal Opinion 99-414*; https://www.americanbar.org/newsletter/publications/gp_solo_magazine_home/gp_solo_magazine_index/breakingup.html.

- "Disclosure of Client Files to Non-Lawyer Supervisors." *ABA Formal Op.* 95-393.

- "Division of Legal Fees With Other Lawyers Who May Lawfully Share Fees with Nonlawyers." *ABA Formal Op.* 13-464.

- "Duty to Protect the Confidentiality of E-Mail Communications with One's Client." *ABA Formal Op.* 11-459.

- "Fee Sharing with Business Corporation for Legal Research and Analysis Services." *ABA Informal Op.* 86-1519.

- "Forming Partnerships with Foreign Lawyers." *ABA Formal Op.* 01-423.

- "A Lawyer's Obligations When Outsourcing Legal and Nonlegal Support Services." *ABA Form Op.* 08-451.

- "Lawyers Practicing in Limited Liability Partnerships." *ABA Formal Op.* 96-401.

- "Lawyer Serving as Director of Client Corporation." *ABA Formal Op.* 98-410.

- "Relationships Among Law Firms." *ABA Formal Op.* 94-388.

- "Sharing Legal Fees with a For-Profit Corporate Employer." *ABA Formal Op.* 95-392.

- "Undisclosed Legal Assistance to Pro Se Litigants." *ABA Formal Op.* 07-446.

Ashley, Kevin. "Teaching Law and Digital Age Legal Practice with an AI and Law Seminar." *Chicago Kent Law Review* 88 (2013): 783.

Bibb, Julian L., IV. "The Modern Justice's Dilemma: How to Harness Social Media to Garner [Reelection] Support While Maintaining Ethical Propriety." *Journal of the Legal Profession* 38 (forthcoming, Spring, 2014).

Callaway, Henry A. "Alabama's New Limited-Scope Representation Rules." *Alabama Lawyer* (2012): 262.

Federal Rule of Civil Procedure 26(b)(1).

Federal Rule of Civil Procedure (a)(1)(A)(ii).

Freeh Group International Solutions, http://www.freehgroup.com (last visited on Feb. 10, 2014).

Galbenski, David. *Unbound: How Entrepreneurship is Dramatically Transforming Legal Services Today.* Unbound Legal, 2009.

Hajavsky, Laura. "Top Ten Proven Tactics to Generate Cost Savings." *Association of Corporate Counsel* http://www.acc.com/legalresources.

Hendersen, William D. & Leonard Bierman. "An Empirical Analysis of Lateral Lawyer Trends from 2000–2007: Emerging Equilibrium for Corporate Law Firms." *Georgetown Journal of Legal Ethics* 22 (2009): 1395.

Henderson, William D. & Rachel M. Zahorsky. "Law Job Stagnation May Have Started Before the Recession—And It May Be a Sign of Lasting Change." *ABA Journal* July 1, 2011.

Henry, Deborah Epstein. *Law and Re-order.* American Bar Association, 2010.

Hornsby, William E. "Gaming the System: Approaching 100% Access to Legal Services Through Online Games." *Chicago Kent Law Review* 88 (2013): 917.

"Jobs in Business and Industry—Two Decades of Change." *NALP Bulletin* (Nov. 2013) http://www.nalp.org/1113research?s=jobs%20in%20business%20and%20industry (last visited on Feb. 25, 2014).

Johnson, Conrad & Brian Donnelly. "If We Only Knew What We Know." *Chicago Kent Law Review* 88 (2013): 729.

Katz, Daniel Martin. "Quantitative Legal Prediction." *Emory Law Journal* 62 (2013): 909.

Kelley, Robert E. *How to Be a Star Performer*. Times Business, 1999.

Kelley, Robert & Janet Caplan. "How Bell Labs Creates Star Performers." *Harvard Business Review* 4 (July 1993): 128.

Kerschberg, Ben. "Legal Services Outsourcing (LSO)—Maximizing Comparative Advantage." http://forbes.com May 16, 2011.

Kirkland, Kimberly. "Ethics in Large Law Firms: The Principle of Pragmaticism." *University of Memphis Law Review* 35 (2005): 631.

"Law Firms Wring Costs From Back-Office Tasks." *Wall Street Journal* October 7, 2012 http://online.wsj.com.

"Law School Class of 2012." http://www.nalp.org/classof2012_selected_pr (last visited on Feb. 26, 2014).

Lupinacci, Timothy M. "Edge of Glory: Practical Tips for Young Associates." *Alabama Lawyer* (September 2011): 385.

Mason, Thomas B. & Semra Mesulam. "Legal Polygamy: Ethical Considerations Attendant to Multiple Law Firm Affiliations." *ABA/BNA, 29 Lawyers' Manual on Professional Conduct* No.3 (Jan. 30, 2013).

Matthews, Christopher M. "Law Firms Tout Cybersecurity Cred." *Wall Street Journal* April 1, 2013.

"Median Private Practice Salaries for Class of 2011 Plunge." http://www.nalp.org

"New Findings on Salaries for Public Interest Attorneys." *NALP Bulletin* (Sept. 2010).

Olsen, Dana. "Bye-Bye Big Firm; Is the Exodus of Lawyers From Big Law to Small Firms Here to Stay?" *Corporate Counsel Online* Apr. 1, 2012.

Osofsky, Justin and Lynn Wood. "Crossing the Charles: The Experience, Networks, and Career Paths of Harvard JD/MBA Alumni." http://www.ssrn.com/en/.

"Prohibition of Partnerships with Nonlawyers: Extrajurisdictional Effect." *ABA Formal Op.* 91-360.

Rankin, A. Clay, III. "What Every Litigator Needs to Know About Using Web-Based Electronic Document Review Services." *Alabama Lawyer* 75 (2014): 36.

Rostain, Tanina, Roger Skalbeck & Kevin G. Mulcahy. "Thinking Like a Lawyer, Designing Like an Architect: Preparing Students for the 21st Century Practice." *Chicago Kent Law Review* 88 (2013): 743.

Schiltz, Patrick J. "On Being a Happy, Healthy, and Ethical Member of an Unhappy, Unhealthy, and Unethical Profession." *Vanderbilt Law Review* 52 (1999): 871.

Susskind, Richard. *The End of Lawyers* Oxford University Press, 2010.

Stewart, James B. "The Collapse." *The New Yorker* October 14, 2013.

Talia, M. Sue. "Expanding Your Practice Using Limited-Scope Representation." *Alabama State Bar Addendum* (June 2012): 5.

Timmons, Heather. "Legal Outsourcing Firms Creating Jobs for American Lawyers." *New York Times* June 2, 2011.

"U.S. Firms Outsource Legal Services to India." *New York Times* Aug. 21, 2007 http://www.nytimes.com.

Walker, Vern R., A.J. Durwin, Philip H. Hwang, Keith Langlais & Mycroft Boyd. "Law Schools as Knowledge Centers in the Digital Age." *Chicago Kent Law Review* 88 (2013): 879.

Zahorsky, Rachel M. & William D. Henderson. "Who's Eating Law Firms' Lunch." *ABA Journal* 99 (2013): 32.

BLOGS/WEBSITES/BOOKS
ADDRESSING QUALITY OF LIFE AMONG
LAW STUDENTS AND YOUNG LAWYERS

http://abovethelaw.com/

Above the Law is one of the most popular and most comprehensive sites by lawyers, for lawyers. It has content about law firms, big and small, law schools, and more. The content runs the gamut from law school gossip/big firm gossip, to law school critiques, to weighty commentary.

https://www.alabar.org/alap/. . ./lawschool_stress.pdf

This is a booklet called "The Hidden Sources of Law School Stress: Avoiding the Mistakes That Create Happy and Unprofessional Lawyers" by Lawrence Krieger. It focuses on identifying law school stressors and suggests actions students can take to prevent these stressors from undermining their law school experience.

http://www.thebestcolleges.org/the-50-best-blogs-for-law-students/

This is a web site that aggregates "The 50 Best Blogs for Law Students". It has links for blogs that address current legal issues, advice and resources for being a law student/lawyer, law and technology, and humor.

http://www.lawschoolasp.org/students/wellness.php

This is the "wellness" page of the Law School Academic Success Project." It is an aggregate of web resources and literature addressing quality of life in law students.

http://www.law.fsu.edu/academic_programs/humanizing_law school/images/tenthings.pdf

This is a link to the article: "What We're Not Telling Law Students—And Lawyers—That They Really Need to Know: Some Thoughts-in-Action toward Revitalizing the Profession from its Roots" by Lawrence S. Krieger. The article addresses workable approaches to improving the legal profession by improving internal motivations and attitudes of individual students and attorneys.

http://www.law.fsu.edu/academic_programs/humanizing_law school/studentresources.html

This web site provides great resources and guidance for improving the quality life of law students.

http://lawyerist.com/

This blog/forum is mostly dedicated to giving tips about how to "lawyer" better, and the tips are helpful. But the "Law School" tab also has good information about how to navigate your career services office better, "what I wish I had known in law school" tips, etc.

http://happygolegal.com/

This web site provides resources and guidance for law students and lawyers seeking fulfilling, challenging, and balanced careers. She blogs on work-life balance and career planning to "help new lawyers create successful and sustainable career paths."

http://www.nalp.org/may2011research_exp_learning

This web site has more of a hiring and professionalism focus than a quality of life focus, but it has some helpful information for law schools and law students about navigating the legal job market.

http://associatesmind.com/category/law-school/

This web site offers tips for young lawyers on finding a job, transitioning from law school to law practice, finding mentors, developing business and becoming a better lawyer.

http://www.betterlegalprofession.org/leadership.php

This is the web site for a grass roots movement called "Building a Better Legal Profession." It aggregates data from law firms in an effort to provide law students a new set of rankings to help them decide where to work after graduation—based on the quality of life at a firm.

http://thegirlsguidetolawschool.com/about/

This web site is intended to help female law students get what they want from their law school experience. Although it is directed at women, there is useful information for male students as well.

Endnotes

[1]　Daniel Martin Katz, *Quantitative Legal Prediction,* 62 Emory L.J. 909, 964 (2013) [hereinafter *Quantitative Legal Prediction*].

[2]　*Id.* at 269.

[3]　*Id.* at 17; David Galbenski, Unbound: How Entrepreneurship is Dramatically Transforming Legal Services Today (Unbound Legal 2009).

[4]　American Bar Foundation and the NALP Foundation for Law Career Research and Education, After the JD: First Results from a *National Study* of Legal Careers (2004) [hereinafter *After the JD, First Results*].

[5]　Patrick J. Schiltz, *On Being a Happy, Healthy, and Ethical Member of an Unhappy, Unhealthy, and Unethical Profession,* 52 Vand. L.Rev. 871, 892 (1999).

[6]　William D. Hendersen & Leonard Bierman, *An Empirical Analysis of Lateral Lawyer Trends from 2000–2007: Emerging Equilibrium for Corporate Law Firms,* 22 Geo. J. of L. Ethics 1395, 1417 (2009) [hereinafter *Lateral Lawyer Trends*].

[7]　*Id.* at 1419.

[8]　*Id.* at 1420.

[9]　NALP, *New Findings on Salaries for Public Interest Attorneys,* NALP Bulletin, Sept. 2010, http://www.nalp.org (last visited on Feb 26, 2014).

[10]　NALP, *Median Private Practice Salaries for Class of 2011 Plunge,* http://www.nalp.org (last visited on Feb 26, 2014).

[11]　Professional responsibility issues that arise with imaginative business models include: How can a lawyer use particular business entities to limit personal and vicarious liability? ABA Formal Op. 96-401, *Lawyers Practicing in Limited Liability Partnerships.* When a lawyer has a nonlawyer supervisor, how can organizational responsibilities be balanced with maintaining client confidentiality? ABA Formal Op. 95-393, *Disclosure of Client Files to Non-Lawyer Supervisors.* Can lawyers who work with start-up companies acquire an ownership stake as part of, or in lieu of, their fee? ABA Formal Op. 00-418, *Acquiring Ownership in a Client in Connection with Performing Legal Services.* Ethical standards that

apply as law firms seek to meet the challenges of the market by pooling resources and developing new forms of association? ABA Formal Op. 94-388, *Relationships Among Law Firms.* May a lawyer represent a corporate client and serve on its board at the same time? If so, how can a lawyer prevent the dual roles of director and counsel from generating conflicts of interest? ABA Formal Op. 98-410, *Lawyer Serving as Director of Client Corporation.* Under what circumstances can corporate in-house counsel supply legal services to a third person? Is the lawyer's corporate employer entitled to any portion of the fee for the legal services? ABA Formal Op. 95-392, *Sharing Legal Fees with a For-Profit Corporate Employer.*

[12]   Laura Hajavsky, *Top Ten Proven Tactics to Generate Cost Savings,* Assoc. of Corp. Counsel http://www.acc.com/legal resources.

[13]   *See, e.g.,* ABA, Solo, Small Firm and General Practice Division, http://www.americanbar.org/aba.html (last visited on Feb 26.2014).

[14]   Thomas B. Mason & Semra Mesulam, *Legal Polygamy: Ethical Considerations Attendant to Multiple Law Firm Affiliations,* ABA/BNA, 29 *Lawyers' Manual on Professional Conduct* No.3 (Jan. 30, 2013).

[15]   Justin Osofsky and Lynn Wood, *Crossing the Charles: The Experience, Networks, and Career Paths of Harvard JD/MBA Alumni,* SSRN.com.

[16]   *NALP: Jobs in Business and Industry—Two Decades of Change,* NALP Bulletin, November, 2013, http://www.nalp.org/1113research?s=two%20decades%20of%20change (last visited on Feb. 25, 2014).

[17]   NALP, *Law School Class of 2012,* http://www.nalp.org/classof2012_selected_pr (last visited on Feb. 26, 2014).

[18]   Kevin Ashley, *Teaching Law and Digital Age Legal Practice with an AI and Law Seminar,* 88 Chi. Kent L.Rev. 783, 787 (2013).

[19]   *Id.*

[20]   Quoted in Rachel M. Zahorsky & William D. Henderson, *Who's Eating Law Firms' Lunch,* 99 ABA J. 32, 35 (2013). [hereinafter *Who's Eating Law Firms' Lunch*].

[21]   *Quantitative Legal Prediction, supra* note 1 at 965.

[22]   Freeh Group International Solutions, http://www.freeh group.com (last visited on Feb. 10, 2014).

[23]   Christopher M. Matthews, *Law Firms Tout Cybersecurity Cred,* WALL ST. J. B1 (Apr. 1, 2013).

[24]   *Id.*

[25]   *Id.*

[26]   *Id.*

[27]   *Id.*

[28]   *Id.* at B8.

[29]   *Id.*

[30]   Derrick   Crawford,   Managing   Director   of   NCAA Enforcement, Presentation, The University of Alabama School of Law, February 3, 2014.

[31]   Presentation, "The Business of Being a Lawyer," The University of Alabama School of Law, February 21, 2013.

[32]   *Id.*

[33]   *Quantitative Legal Prediction, supra* note 1 at 935.

[34]   James B. Stewart, *The Collapse,* THE NEW YORKER 80, 85 (Oct. 14, 2013).

[35]   Kimberly Kirkland, *Ethics in Large Law Firms: The Principle of Pragmaticism,* 35 U. MEM. L.REV. 631, 691 (2005) [hereinafter *Ethics in Large Law Firms*].

[36]   Timothy M. Lupinacci, *Edge of Glory: Practical Tips for Young Associates*, ALA. LAWYER 385 (Sept. 2011).

[37]   *Id.* at 387.

[38]   *Id.*

[39]   Charles Gillis, Executive Director of Munsch Hurdt Kopf & Harr, P.C, Dallas, Texas.

[40]   Kira Fonteneau, *Dear New Lawyer,* Jan. 11, 2008, http:// kirafonteneau.typepad.com (last visited on March 9, 2014).

[41]   *Ethics in Large Law Firms, supra* note 35 at 680.

[42]   *Id.* at 681–82.

[43]   *Id.* at 690.

[44]   *Id.* at 686.

[45]   Fornier J. "Boots" Gale, III, *To Eat or Not to Eat,* 68 ALA. LAW. 184 (2007).

[46]   *Id.* at 689.

[47]   See ABA Rule 1.13(b) (Organization as a client); Rules 5.1, 5.2, 5.3, 5.4 (Law firms and Associations).

[48]   *Ethics in Large Law Firms, supra* note 35 at 692 (internal brackets deleted).

[49]   *Id.* at 690.

[50]   *Teaching Law, supra* note 18 at 762.

[51]   Heather Timmons, *Legal Outsourcing Firms Creating Jobs for American Lawyers,* N.Y. TIMES, June 2, 2011 [hereinafter *Creating Jobs*].

[52]   *Who's Eating Law Firms' Lunch, supra* note 20 at 35.

[53]   Document and form providers cover dozens of legal specialties, and are growing. In its first ten years in business, LegalZoom generated more than 1 million customers. In 2012, 20 % of all LLCs created in California were formed with LegalZoom. William D. Henderson & Rachel M. Zahorsky, *Law Job Stagnation May Have Started Before the Recession—And It May Be a Sign of Lasting Change,* ABA JOURNAL, July 1, 2011 [hereinafter *Stagnation*].

[54]   RICHARD SUSSKIND, THE END OF LAWYERS 102 (Oxford University Press 2010) [hereinafter SUSSKIND, THE END OF LAWYERS].

[55]   *Id.* at 123.

[56]   *Id.*

[57]   *Id.* at 139.

[58]   *Id.* at 104.

[59]   Laura Hajavsky, *Top Ten Proven Tactics to Generate Cost Savings,* ASSOC. OF CORP. COUNSEL http://www.acc.com/legalresources (last visited on Feb. 26, 2014).

[60]   Columbia University School of Law; *See* Conrad Johnson & Brian Donnelly, *If We Only Knew What We Know,* 88 CHI. KENT L.REV. 729 (2013).

[61]   Georgetown School of Law; *See* Tanina Rostain, Roger Skalbeck & Kevin G. Mulcahy, *Thinking Like a Lawyer, Designing*

Like an Architect: Preparing Students for the 21ˢᵗ Century Practice, 88 CHI. KENT L.REV. 743 (2013) [hereinafter *Thinking Like a Lawyer*].

[62]   *Thinking Like a Lawyer, supra* note 61 at 744–745 (regarding program at Chicago Kent School of Law).

[63]   *Id.* at 745 (regarding a program at New York University).

[64]   *Id.*

[65]   Vern R. Walker, A.J. Durwin, Philip H. Hwang, Keith Langlais & Mycroft Boyd, *Law Schools as Knowledge Centers in the Digital Age*, 88 CHI. KENT L.REV. 879, 904 (2013) (regarding program at Hofstra School of Law).

[66]   SUSSKIND, THE END OF LAWYERS, *supra* note 54 at 103.

[67]   William E. Hornsby, *Gaming the System: Approaching 100% Access to Legal Services Through Online Games*, 88 CHI. KENT L.REV. 917, 932 (2013). A2J Software was developed with funding from a Technology Initiative Grant (TIG).

[68]   Neota Logic is a private company based in New York that "creates interactive software applications for law firms, financial institutions, and Fortune 500 companies," http://www.neotalogic.com (visited on Feb. 1, 2014).

[69]   *Thinking Like a Lawyer, supra* note 61 at 744–745.

[70]   *Teaching Law, supra* note 18 at 803–815; *Thinking Like a Lawyer, supra* note 61 at 745–751.

[71]   *Ben Kerschberg, Legal Services Outsourcing (LSO)—* Maximizing Comparative Advantage. http://forbes.com (May 16, 2011) [hereinafter *Legal Services Outsourcing*] (last visited on Feb. 26, 2014).

[72]   *See, e.g.,* ABA, Model Rules of Prof. Conduct 1.4, 2.3, 8.4; ABA Formal Opinion 99-414, ABA, FORMAL ETHICS OPINIONS (Oct. 2013).

[73]   *Law Firms Wring Costs From Back-Office Tasks*, WALL ST. J. http://online.wsj.com (Oct. 7, 2012). For example, Boston-based Bingham McCutchen LLP is moving its finance, accounting, human resources and other administrative functions to Lexington, Kentucky. Pillsbury Winthrop Shaw Pittman, a 700-person law firm, is moving its operations services to Nashville, Tennessee, where it will have 160 employees. In a related move, and one that is likely to expand, firms are outsourcing their back office services to firms that specialize in

providing such services. Foley & Lardner, a 900-lawyer firm based in Milwaukee moved all of its business services to William Lea, a company which specializes in such services.

[74]   Dana Olsen, *Bye-Bye Big Firm; Is the Exodus of Lawyers From Big Law to Small Firms Here to Stay?*, CORPORATE COUNSEL ONLINE (Apr. 1, 2012).

[75]   Recommend Press Release dated August 20, 2013, http://www.recommind.com/company (last visited on Feb 26, 2014).

[76]   LEXIS NEXIS, 2013 ENTERPRISE LEGAL MANAGEMENT TRENDS REPORT, http://www.lexisnexis.com/counsellink/documents/Counsel link-EIM-web.pdf (last visited Apr. 28, 2014).

[77]   *Quantitative Legal Prediction, supra* note 1 at 930 (discussing TyMetrix, "an analytics platform used by clients to determine an acceptable rate to pay for a given legal service.) TyMetrix, for example, issues a "Real Rate Report" that analyzes $42 billion in legal spending, $398 million hours of legal services, $105 million activities, 17,000 law firms and vendors and 286,000 individual billers and time keepers to determine the real rates charged for specific legal services. *Id.* Such software provides small firms access to the sophisticated and costly business planning previously available only to large law firms which could hire a business manager.

[78]   Federal Rule of Civil Procedure 26(b)(1).

[79]   Federal Rule of Civil Procedure (a)(1)(A)(ii).

[80]   A. Clay Rankin III., *What Every Litigator Needs to Know About Using Web-Based Electronic Document Review Services,* 75 ALA. LAW. 36, 36 (2014) [hereinafter *What Every Litigator Needs to Know*].

[81]   *Quantitative Legal Prediction, supra* note 1 at 944.

[82]   *What Every Litigator Needs to Know, supra* note 80 at 37.

[83]   *Who's Eating Law Firms' Lunch, supra* note 20 at 33.

[84]   *Quantitative Legal Prediction, supra* note 1 at 943–944.

[85]   Heather Timmons, *Legal Outsourcing Firms Creating Jobs for American Lawyers,* N.Y. TIMES, June 2, 2011 [hereinafter *Creating Jobs*].

[86]   *Who's Eating Law Firms' Lunch?, supra* note 20 at 33.

87   http://www.pbs.org. *Outsourcing the Law to India*, June 14, 2011 (last visited on March 9, 2014).

88   *Creating Jobs, supra* note 85.

89   *Legal Services Outsourcing, supra* note 71.

90   *U.S. Firms Outsource Legal Services to India*, N.Y. TIMES (Aug. 21, 2007) http://www.nytimes.com (last visited on Feb. 26, 2014).

91   *Quantitative Legal Prediction, supra* note 1 at 910–917.

92   *Id.* at 928–929. The Supreme Court tournament which pitted renowned experts (elite lawyers and law professors) against a predictive analysis program to predict the outcome of Supreme Court decisions in the 2002–2003 term (the computer won), demonstrated the viability of predicting by quantitative analysis outcomes in legal cases. *Id.* at 938. Ian Ayers discusses this tournament in IAN AYERS, SUPER CRUNCHERS: WHY THINKING BY THE NUMBERS IS THE BEST WAY TO BE SMART (Bantam Books 2007).

93   *Legal Services Outsourcing, supra* note 71 *quoting* Leah Cooper, Managing Attorney of Rio Tinto and Director, Legal Services, CLP Global.

94   *What Every Litigator Needs to Know, supra* note 80 at 38, discussing SaaS ("software as a service").

95   ABA Form Op. 08-451, *A Lawyer's Obligations When Outsourcing Legal and Nonlegal Support Services.*

96   ABA Formal Op. 13-464, *Division of Legal Fees With Other Lawyers Who May Lawfully Share Fees with Nonlawyers.*

97   ABA Formal Op. 95-398, *Access of Nonlawyers to a Lawyer's Data Base.*

98   ABA Formal Op. 01-423, *Forming Partnerships with Foreign Lawyers.*

99   ABA Formal Op. 91-360, *Prohibition of Partnerships with Nonlawyers: Extrajurisdictional Effect.*

100   ABA Informal Op. 86-1519, *Fee Sharing with Business Corporation for Legal Research and Analysis Services.*

101   *Id.* at 115.

102   SUSSKIND, THE END OF LAWYERS, *supra* note 54 at 131.

103 *Id.*

104 *Id.* at 132. Legal ethics issues of attorney-client privilege, work product and client intellectual property concerns could be addressed in establishing such a resource for firm clients.

105 *Id.* at 135. Such collaboration, like an online community of clients, would necessitate resolution of attorney client privilege, work product and intellectual property issues.

106 ABA Formal Op. 11-459, *Duty to Protect the Confidentiality of E-Mail Communications With One's Client.*

107 William E. Hornsby, *Gaming the System: Approaching 100 % Access to Legal Services Through Online Games,* 88 CHICAGO-KENT L. REV. 917 (2013) [hereinafter *Gaming the System*].

108 *Id.* at 921.

109 *Id.*

110 *Id.* at 920.

111 *Pocket Law Firm,* http://itunes.apple.com/us/app/pocket-law-firm (last visited March 8, 2014).

112 *Gaming the System, supra* note 111 at 935.

113 *Id.* at 935.

114 *Id.* at 935.

115 Julian L. Bibb, IV, *The Modern Justice's Dilemma: How to Harness Social Media to Garner [Reelection] Support While Maintaining Ethical Propriety*, 38 J. LEGAL PROF. ___ (forthcoming, Spring, 2014).

116 *Id.* at 940.

117 *Id.*

118 *Id.*

119 *Id.*

120 For discussions of how LSR is transforming the practice of law, *see, e.g., Teaching Law, supra* note 18 at 706; Henry A. Callaway, *Alabama's New Limited-Scope Representation Rules*, ALA. LAWYER 262 (2012); M. Sue Talia, *Expanding Your Practice Using Limited-Scope Representation*, ALABAMA STATE BAR ADDENDUM 5–6 (June 2012) [hereinafter *Expanding Your Practice*].

[121]   *Definitions,* NEW YORK CITY COURT, http://www.nycourts. gov/courts/nyc/civil/definitions.shtml#u (last visited on Feb. 26, 2014).

[122]   AL R. Prof. Conduct 1.1, 1.2(c); *Expanding Your Practice, supra* note 124 at 6.

[123]   Henry A. Callaway, *Alabama's New Limited-Scope Representation Rules,* ALA. LAW. 262 (July 2012).

[124]   *Expanding Your Practice, supra* note 124 at 5.

[125]   *Expanding Your Practice, supra* note 124 at 6; *Cf.* M. Sue Talia, *Got Clients?* PROGRAM MATERIALS, ALABAMA STATE BAR ANNUAL MEETING, July 20, 2012; *Cf.* AL R. C. P. 1.1, 1.2(c).

[126]   ABA Formal Op. 07-446, *Undisclosed Legal Assistance to Pro Se Litigants.*

[127]   SUSSKIND, THE END OF Lawyers, *supra* note 54 at 226.

[128]   It is unclear what data supports this figure, but it is the most widely cited number for career changes. WALL ST. J., Sept. 4, 2010, http://online.wsj.com Larger averages are cited for those earlier in their careers. *See, e.g.,* a 2012 United States Labor Department study showed that the "average person born in the latter years of the baby boom (1957–1964) held 11.3 jobs from age 18–46," with nearly half held between ages 18 to 24. U.S. DEPT. OF LABOR, BUREAU OF LABOR STATISTICS, NEWS RELEASE, July 25, 2012.

[129]   United States v. AT&T, 522 F.Supp. 131 (D.D.C. 1982).

[130]   ROBERT E. KELLEY, HOW TO BE A STAR AT WORK v, 4–10 (Times Business 1999) [hereinafter, KELLEY, STAR AT WORK].

[131]   *Id.* at 3–10.

[132]   *Id.* at 9.

[133]   *Id.* at 8.

[134]   *Id.* at 9.

[135]   *Id.*

[136]   *Id.* at 27.

[137]   *Id.* at 299.

[138]   *Id.* at 10.

[139]   Robert Kelley & Janet Caplan, *How Bell Labs Creates Star Performers,* 4 HARV. BUS. REV. 128–39 (July 1993).

[140]   KELLEY, STARS AT WORK, *supra* note 134 at 235.

[141]   *Id.* at 214.

[142]   *Id.* at 249.

[143]   *Id.* at 43.

[144]   *Id.* at 30–35.

[145]   *Id.* at 30.

[146]   *Id.* at 21.

[147]   *Id.* at 39–41, 302–308.

[148]   *Id.* at 40.

[149]   *Id.* at 31.

[150]   *Id.*

[151]   *Id.* at 56.

[152]   *Id.* at 58.

[153]   *Id.* at 55.

[154]   *Id.*

[155]   *Id.*

[156]   *Id.*

[157]   DEBORAH EPSTEIN HENRY, LAW AND RE-ORDER (ABA 2010).

[158]   KELLEY, STARS AT WORK, *supra* note 134 at 32.

[159]   *Id.*

[160]   *Id.* at 76.

[161]   *Id.* at 78.

[162]   *Id.* at 83.

[163]   *Id.* at 91.

[164]   *Id.* at 86–88.

[165]   *Id.* at 88.

[166]   *Id.* at 90.

[167]   *Id.* at 91.

[168]   *Id.*

[169]   *Id.*

[170] *Id.* at 93.

[171] *Id.*

[172] *Id.*

[173] *Id.* at 94.

[174] *Id.* at 95.

[175] *Id.*

[176] DEBORAH EPSTEIN HENRY, LAW AND RE-ORDER 321–323 (ABA 2010).

[177] KELLEY, STARS AT WORK, *supra* note 134 at 103.

[178] *Id.* at 107.

[179] *Id.* at 110.

[180] *Id.* at 110–111.

[181] *Id.* at 106.

[182] *Id.* at 112.

[183] *Id.* at 119.

[184] *Id.*

[185] *Id.* at 125; 133–147.

[186] *Id.* at 148.

[187] *Id.* at 125.

[188] *Id.* at 131–132.

[189] *Id.* at 33.

[190] *Id.*

[191] *Id.* at 155–56.

[192] *Id.* at 154.

[193] *Id.*

[194] *Id.*

[195] *Id.* at 151.

[196] *Id.* at 161.

[197] *Id.* at 163.

[198] *Id.* at 160.

199   *Id.* at 166.

200   *Id.*

201   *Id.* at 169.

202   *Id.* at 169–170.

203   *Id.* at 162.

204   *Id.* at 161.

205   *Id.* at 163.

206   *Id.* at 164.

207   *Id.* at 33.

208   *Id.*

209   *Id.* at 188–89.

210   *Id.* at 183.

211   *Id.* at 182–187.

212   *Id.* at 186.

213   *Id.*

214   *Id.* at 214.

215   *Id.* at 214.

216   *Id.*

217   *Id.* at 216.

218   *Id.* at 216–218, 224.

219   *Id.* at 232.

220   *Id.* at 213.

221   *Id.* at 228.

222   *Id.* at 217–218.

223   *Id.* at 224.

224   *Id.* at 229.

225   *Id.*

226   *Id.* at 230.

227   *Id.* at 230–31.

[228] AMERICAN BAR FOUNDATION AND THE NALP FOUNDATION FOR LAW CAREER RESEARCH AND EDUCATION, AFTER THE JD: FIRST RESULTS FROM A *NATIONAL STUDY* OF LEGAL CAREERS (2004) [hereinafter *After the JD, First Results*].

[229] KELLEY, STARS AT WORK, *supra* note 134 at 230–31.

[230] *Id.* at 221.

[231] *Id.*

[232] *Id.*

[233] *Id.* at 222.

[234] *Id.* at 235.

[235] *Id.* at 34.

[236] *Id.* at 238.

[237] *Id.* at 239.

[238] *Id.* at 236–237.

[239] *Id.* at 237.

[240] *Id.*

[241] *Id.* at 240.

[242] *Id.* at 242.

[243] SUSSKIND, THE END OF LAWYERS, *supra* note 54 at 145 *quoting* William Gibson, author of *A Science Fiction Winter*.

INDEX

References are to Pages